TAKING
CARE

TAKING CARE

Ethical Caregiving
in Our Aging Society

The President's Council on Bioethics
Washington, D.C.
www.bioethics.gov

September 2005

Contents

LETTER OF TRANSMITTAL TO

THE PRESIDENT OF THE UNITED STATES

The President's Council on Bioethics
1801 Pennsylvania Avenue, N.W., Suite 700
Washington, D.C. 20006
September 28, 2005

The President
The White House
Washington, D.C.

Dear Mr. President:

I am pleased to present to you *Taking Care: Ethical Caregiving in Our Aging Society,* a report of the President's Council on Bioethics. It seeks to gain attention for a burgeoning social problem and to offer ethical guidance regarding the care of our elders who can no longer care for themselves.

American society is aging—dramatically, rapidly, and largely well. More and more people are living healthily into their seventies and eighties, many well into their nineties. With birth rates down, with the baby boomers approaching retirement, we are on the threshold of the first-ever "mass geriatric society." The fastest growing segment of our population is already the group over 85. Historically speaking, it is the best of times to be old.

Yet the blessings of greater longevity are bringing new social challenges. Although people are living healthier longer, many are also living long enough to suffer serious age-related chronic illnesses, including dementia. Alzheimer's disease now afflicts more than four million Americans, and the number is expected to triple before mid-century. Already by far the most common trajectory toward death is a lengthy period of debility, frailty, and dementia lasting not months but years. Already millions of American families are struggling nobly to provide steady and demanding long-term care for their incapacitated loved ones, often with little respite or communal support, usually for many years. Yet precisely as the need for caregiving rises greatly, the number of available caregivers—both professional and volunteer—is dwindling. We appear to be on the threshold of a crisis in long-term care.

As a society, we have not yet faced up to this difficulty, especially in its human dimensions. And the popular legal instruments that we are being encouraged to employ to avoid the problem will fall short of what we need as individuals. As this report points out in great detail, living wills, drafted years in advance, are not the answer. They simply cannot substitute for reliable and responsible caregivers on the spot, devoted to the welfare of the incapacitated person here and now. Even worse is the deadly "solution" of legalizing assisted suicide and euthanasia, advocates for which are again active in several state legislatures. Caring wholeheartedly for a frail patient or a disabled loved one is incompatible with thinking that engineering their death is an acceptable "therapeutic option." Betrayal and abandonment of the elderly can never be part of a decent and compassionate society, one devoted to the equal worth and dignity of every human life, from start to finish, regardless of personal strengths, weaknesses, or disabilities.

In addition to calling attention to the larger social issues of long-term care, this report therefore also tries to articulate the goals and principles of ethical caregiving for persons no longer able to care for themselves. We emphasize both the singular importance of seeking to serve the life the patient still has and the moral necessity of never seeking a person's death as a means of relieving his suffering. At the same time, we emphasize also that serving the life the patient still has does not oblige us always to elect life-sustaining treatments, when those interventions impose undue additional burdens on that life or interfere with the comfortable death of a person irretrievably dying. Even when the doctor's black bag of remedies is empty, comfort and care remain inviolable duties.

If our elderly are to be well cared for and if family caregivers are to be able to care well, caregiving needs to be supported by our civic and faith-based communities but also with the help and encouragement of government. Yet as we bend our efforts in support of the elderly, we can ill afford to neglect the needs of the young, who, unlike the old, have no organized voice to speak up for their needs. We must at all costs avoid a conflict between the generations over scarce resources.

To help us think through these very complex issues, we need sustained research, hard thinking, and a creative search for modest reforms that could make a big difference. And we need leadership at the highest level. Therefore, among our recommendations, we call for a Presidential Commission on Aging, Dementia, and Long-Term Care, to focus the nation's attention and to carry forward this work. Any approach our society takes must attend to the ethical and humanistic dimensions of our situation, not only the economic and institutional ones. For we will be judged as a people by our willingness to stand by one another, even as the flame of life flickers and fades in those who have brought us here and to whom we owe so much.

Mr. President, allow me once again to thank you, on behalf of my Council colleagues and our fine staff, for this opportunity to offer you and the American people our assistance in promoting a future in which human well-being will be served by science and medicine, human beings will be respected at every stage of life, and human dignity will always be upheld and preserved.

Sincerely,

Leon R. Kass, M.D.
Chairman

MEMBERS OF
THE PRESIDENT'S COUNCIL ON BIOETHICS

LEON R. KASS, M.D., PH.D., Chairman.
> Addie Clark Harding Professor, The College and the Committee on Social Thought, University of Chicago. Hertog Fellow, American Enterprise Institute.

BENJAMIN S. CARSON, SR., M.D.
> Professor and Director of Pediatric Neurosurgery, Johns Hopkins Medical Institutions.

REBECCA S. DRESSER, J.D., M.S.
> Daniel Noyes Kirby Professor of Law and Professor of Ethics in Medicine, Washington University, St. Louis.

DANIEL W. FOSTER, M.D.
> Professor of Internal Medicine, John Denis McGarry, Ph.D. Distinguished Chair in Diabetes and Metabolic Research, University of Texas Southwestern Medical School.

FRANCIS FUKUYAMA, PH.D.
> Bernard L. Schwartz Professor of International Political Economy, Paul H. Nitze School of Advanced International Studies, Johns Hopkins University.

MICHAEL S. GAZZANIGA, PH.D.
> David T. McLaughlin Distinguished University Professor, Professor of Psychological and Brain Sciences, Director of the Center for Cognitive Neuroscience, Dartmouth College.

ROBERT P. GEORGE, J.D., D.PHIL.
> McCormick Professor of Jurisprudence, Director of the James Madison Program in American Ideals and Institutions, Princeton University.

MARY ANN GLENDON, J.D., M. COMP. L.
> Learned Hand Professor of Law, Harvard University.

ALFONSO GÓMEZ-LOBO, DR. PHIL.
> Ryan Family Professor of Metaphysics and Moral Philosophy, Georgetown University.

WILLIAM B. HURLBUT, M.D.
  Consulting Professor in Human Biology, Stanford University.

CHARLES KRAUTHAMMER, M.D.
  Syndicated Columnist.

PETER A. LAWLER, PH.D.
  Chairman of the Department of Government and International Studies,
  Dana Professor of Government, Berry College.

PAUL McHUGH, M.D.
  University Distinguished Service Professor of Psychiatry, Johns
  Hopkins School of Medicine. Professor, Department of Mental Health,
  Bloomberg School of Public Health, Johns Hopkins University.

GILBERT C. MEILAENDER, PH.D.
  Phyllis & Richard Duesenberg Chair in Christian Ethics, Valparaiso
  University.

JANET D. ROWLEY, M.D.
  Blum-Riese Distinguished Service Professor of Medicine, Molecular
  Genetics and Cell Biology, and Human Genetics, Pritzker School of
  Medicine, University of Chicago.

MICHAEL J. SANDEL, D.PHIL.
  Anne T. and Robert M. Bass Professor of Government,
  Harvard University.

DIANA J. SCHAUB, PH.D.
  Professor and Chairman of the Department of Political Science, Loyola
  College in Maryland.

COUNCIL STAFF AND CONSULTANTS

Richard Roblin, Ph.D.
Acting Executive Director

Tonia Busse
Staff Assistant

Rita Koganzon
Intern

Eric Cohen
Senior Research Consultant

Yuval Levin
former
Acting Executive Director

Judith E. Crawford
Administrative Director

Michael Murray
Intern

Michael Fragoso
Intern

Adam Schulman, Ph.D.
Senior Research Consultant

Diane M. Gianelli
Director of Communications

O. Carter Snead, Esq.
Consultant and former
General Counsel

Ginger Gruters
Staff Assistant

Audrea R. Vann
Information Technology
Specialist

Laura Harmon, Esq.
Senior Aide to the Chairman

Bethany Warner
Receptionist/Staff Assistant

Emily Jones
Executive Administrator

Lee L. Zwanziger, Ph.D.
Senior Research Analyst

Preface

Taking Care: Ethical Caregiving in Our Aging Society is a report of the President's Council on Bioethics, which was created by President George W. Bush on November 28, 2001 by means of Executive Order 13237 and renewed on September 23, 2003 by means of Executive Order 13316.

The Council's purpose is to advise the President on bioethical issues related to advances in biomedical science and technology. In connection with its advisory role, the mission of the Council includes the following functions:

- To undertake fundamental inquiry into the human and moral significance of developments in biomedical and behavioral science and technology.
- To explore specific ethical and policy questions related to these developments.
- To provide a forum for a national discussion of bioethical issues.
- To facilitate a greater understanding of bioethical issues.

Among the several topics mentioned in the executive order as deserving of possible Council attention are ethical issues surrounding the end of life. Several of those issues are the subject of this report.

Taking Care addresses the ethical challenges of caregiving in our rapidly aging society, with special attention to the care of people with dementia. Our purpose is to provide a humanly rich account of the caregiving dilemmas—social, familial, and personal—and to offer some important ethical guidelines for the care of persons who can no longer care for themselves.

There is no question that we are on the threshold of a "mass geriatric society," a society of more long-lived individuals than ever before in human history. For this great gift of longer and healthier life for ourselves and our loved ones we are, and should be, enormously grateful. No sensible person would wish to return us to a time—not that long ago—in which the diagnosis of uncontrolled diabetes meant certain death within a month or two, in which women commonly died giving birth, children often died of smallpox and polio, and nothing could be done for tuberculosis, syphilis, and other deadly infectious diseases. Old age today is—for the most part and for most people—much better than it used to be: millions of Americans are staying healthy and active well into their seventies and eighties, and some deep into their nineties. By historical standards, it is a wonderful time to be old.

At the same time, however, there are good reasons to be concerned about the human and moral shape that a mass geriatric society will take, especially if the "price" many people pay for the gift of added years of healthier life is a period of protracted debility, dementia, and dependence stacked up at the end before they eventually die. Such a reshaping of the lifecycle will create enormous challenges for nearly every family and for the entire society. The economic challenges facing Social Security, Medicare, and Medicaid are more or less well known. A looming crisis of long-term care for the incapacitated has received less attention, partly because we prefer to avert our gaze, largely because we lack an adequate human and ethical understanding of this issue.

Socially, we have preferred to place our hopes in programs that promote healthy aging and in scientific research seeking remedies for incapacitating diseases like Alzheimer's. Insofar as we do approach the topic of long-term care, we worry mainly about numbers and logistics: How many will need it? Who will provide it? How will we pay for it? The ethical questions of what the young owe the old, what the old owe the young, and what we all owe each other do not get mentioned. Neither do the questions of social support for the caregivers or a good end of life for us all.

In the meantime, millions of American families, more each decade, already face the difficult task of caring for frail and incapacitated elders, often entirely on their own with very little social support. And millions more, "the worried well," live anxiously, dreading the prospect that the curse of untreatable dementia and disability will descend on them before a cure arrives, to ruin their final years, deplete their savings, and burden their loved ones with the obligation to care for them. Their generalized anxiety often focuses on end-of-life decision-making, commonly expressed in a fear that others will impose life-sustaining treatments on them when they are too demented to choose for themselves or too diminished to benefit from the intervention.

Largely in response to these anxieties of the worried well, our society has embraced the idea of advance directives, especially living wills, in which individuals try to determine in advance how they wish to be treated should they become incapacitated. This approach to the dilemmas of caregiving gives major ethical weight to personal autonomy and choice and personal pride in self-sufficiency. But in so doing, it deliberately ignores the truth of human interdependence and of our unavoidable need for human presence and care, *especially when we can no longer take care of ourselves.* The moral emphasis on choosing in advance needs to be replaced with a moral emphasis on caring in the present. The moral emphasis on independence needs to be supplemented with a moral commitment to serve the lives of those we love, regardless of their disabilities. A culture of caregiving requires moral support from an ethics of care.

In the first chapter of this report ("Dilemmas of an Aging Society"), we offer a sociological overview of aging in America and inquire into the special challenges of aging well in modern times. We pay special attention to the growing prevalence of Alzheimer's disease and other forms of dementia, and the implications this has for caregivers and the larger society. Although this chapter offers no proposed ethical guidelines, it presents a human picture that should inform policymakers in their efforts to encourage, support, and sustain dignified long-term care for the American people, and in settings that preserve the humanity of those who receive care and those who give it.

In the second chapter ("The Limited Wisdom of Advance Directives"), moving from the social picture to the personal one, we offer a practical and ethical critique of relying on living wills as the best and most human approach to dealing with the problems of incapacitated persons. At the same time, we endorse both the appointment of surrogate decisionmakers and the practice of advance care planning that encourages families to discuss and plan together how best to care for their loved ones.

In the third and fourth chapters, moving from critique to positive analysis and guidelines, we offer a constructive inquiry into ethical caregiving. In the former ("The Ethics of Caregiving:

General Principles"), we explore the general ethical principles and moral boundaries involved, emphasizing the importance of seeking the present welfare of the patient and of serving the life that the person still has, regardless of disability and frailty. In the latter ("Ethical Caregiving: Principle and Prudence in Hard Cases"), we show—through analyses of a series of very difficult clinical cases—how principle and prudence can collaborate in finding the best care possible for persons entrusted to our care. In both chapters we acknowledge how hard it can be to provide constant care for those who can no longer speak for or stand by themselves; and we recognize how painful it can be to see loved ones lose their most treasured human capacities, including the capacity to recognize the people with whom they have long shared a life. Yet before such loss and in the face of such difficulty, loving care and principled prudence are all the more required, if we are to answer the call never to betray or abandon, always to serve as best we can.

Our conclusions and recommendations are presented in a final chapter.

Taken as a whole, our report aims to enrich public discussions about aging, dementia, and caregiving, to encourage policymakers to take up these complicated yet urgent issues, and to offer ethical guidance for caregivers—professional and familial—who struggle to provide for those entrusted to their care. We also hope to encourage policymakers in this area to take into account the humanistic and ethical aspects of aging and caregiving, not only the economic and institutional ones. Staying human in our aging society depends on it.

* * * * *

The Council has been at work on this report since April 2004. All told, twenty-one sessions, of ninety minutes each, were devoted to this topic at public meetings. Transcripts are available online at www.bioethics.gov. The present report draws directly on those transcripts, as well as on writings of Council members, staff, and invited consultants. It is also informed by much previously published literature on this topic (see Thematic Bibliography, in the Appendix). The Council has benefited greatly from presentations by Robert Binstock, Robert Burt, Daniel Callahan, Thomas Cole, Charles Fahey, Robert Friedland, Geri Hall, Herbert Hendin,

Joanne Lynn, Peter Rabins, Greg Sachs, Carl Schneider, Dennis Selkoe, David Shenk, and John Wennberg, and from the wise advice of our former colleague, William F. May. We are grateful also to Drs. Callahan, Cole, Lynn, and May for their critical reviews of earlier drafts of the report, to Adam Wolfson for his careful editorial review of the penultimate draft, and to Laura Harmon for her outstanding work in preparing the report for publication. The Council also expresses its special gratitude to our senior consultant, Eric Cohen, for his extraordinary vision, thoughtful analysis, and literate drafting.

LEON R. KASS, M.D.
Chairman

1

Dilemmas of an Aging Society

Modern medical science has been an unrivaled benefactor of humankind—providing cures for terrible diseases, palliative care for the sick and suffering, and longer and healthier lives for the vast majority of us. Most citizens in developed countries can now expect to live into their seventies and eighties, with many living into their nineties and beyond. Not only are people living longer, but they are staying healthier longer, with a real chance to enjoy their "golden years." Even some of the chronic disabilities of old age are in decline,[1] as medical science and improved risk management continue to succeed in extending the disability-free stage of the natural life span. An ever-growing cohort of people enjoys today a period of true retirement, when the obligations of work and raising children are past, when body and mind remain in health, and when there's still time to pursue or renew the avocations of life.

Yet these great accomplishments have also brought new challenges. No one, of course, would want to "turn the clock back," but the problems accompanying medical progress are real as well as perplexing. Consider that around the world—and especially in the United States and other advanced industrial democracies—there is increasing concern about the "graying of the population," the "aging of society," and the "retirement of the baby boomers." This concern takes many forms—economic, ethical, social, and civic—and it promises to loom large in our private lives and public debates. Many of the questions center around caregiving: Who will need it? Who will do it? Who will pay for it? And perhaps most importantly, what kind of *care* is owed to those at the end of life?

When thinking about caregiving, we have concerns about pension insecurity, rising costs of health care, shortages of available caregivers, and the insufficient number of good nursing homes. We have concerns about the potential neglect or abandonment of the elderly, and the possibility of welcoming euthanasia or assisted suicide as ways to "solve the problem" of lingering old age. Many of us face decisions about forgoing careers in order to act as caregivers, or spending less time with young children in order to care for aged parents, or using funds set aside for a daughter's college tuition in order to pay for a father's nursing home. In short, we worry about whether we can afford to care, whether we will be willing and able to care, and what we must sacrifice in order to care for the elderly. And many of us in the middle of life, thinking about growing older ourselves, fear the loss of our powers, the deprivations and loneliness that often accompany old age, and the prospect of being a burden on those we love most.

Thus, while people are living healthier into old age and doing so on a mass scale, there remain many difficulties, both psychic and physical, that eventually come with growing old. Precisely because people are living longer, many are living long enough to suffer age-related degenerative diseases like Alzheimer's and Parkinson's—diseases that involve long-term decline and thus the need for long-term care. And precisely because many individuals have taken advantage of modern freedom's opportunities for education, careers, and geographic mobility, many elderly persons will live in greater isolation from loved ones, separated from children and grandchildren who have settled elsewhere or whose lives are defined primarily by work and school. Smaller and less stable families will likely compound these problems, as the burdens of caregiving fall on one or two adult children, who, in many cases, are called upon to care for parents who did not always care well for them. And many among the growing population of childless elderly will have no relatives at all to look after them. Taken together, the need for family caregivers will almost certainly increase while the availability of family caregivers may only decline. And the same difficult choices and trade-offs faced by individuals and families will confront society as a whole: the needs and plight of the elderly will only seem more urgent; the costs of medical and long-term care will only increase; and the need to balance the obligations of caregiving with other civic and human goods will only seem more difficult, even as America becomes wealthier.

Before these difficulties we are hardly resourceless. With our science and medicine, we are working to combat the ailments and limitations that aging brings, seeking to reduce or remove the disabilities that longevity has until now brought with it. We also look to insurance plans and public policies to make aging affordable and secure, whether by increasing Medicare benefits or creating retirement savings accounts or providing private long-term care insurance. And we use civil rights law to battle against "age discrimination," to ensure that old people are not treated as second-class citizens in employment. All of these approaches and efforts are necessary and welcome.

But they are also limited, and limited in principle. For senescence is best understood not as a problem but as an inescapable *condition*—as part of what it means to be human and to live in a human society. Absent awareness of this fact, we will be tempted to believe that medicine, social policy, economics, or law can solve the problems of aging, or that technological and social progress can make the dilemmas of growing old and approaching death less serious than they always were and always will be. Or else, preferring denial, we will be tempted to live as if we will be young forever, or as if the elderly among us will take care of themselves, or as if the seeming "pointlessness" of the end of life means that neglecting the elderly is nothing to worry about.

In the end, however, aging and dying—even with the progress we can still reasonably expect from medicine and social change—will not yield to either the genius of the manager or the utopian hopes of those who pretend that, by change of attitude, old age is somehow avoidable. Good public policy matters profoundly in this area, but even the best policies will never make aging, caregiving, and dying easy. As individuals and as a society, we will need deeper wisdom and resources of character if we are going to age well in the years ahead. We will need greater ethical reflection on what the young owe the old, what the old owe the young, and what we all owe one another. And we will need prudence in designing effective public policies and in making loving decisions at the bedside, so that we accept the limits of modern medicine and economic resources while never abandoning conscientious and compassionate human care.

The aim of this chapter is to contribute, in a concrete if necessarily limited way, to our understanding of the social question of what the "graying of the population" means for our society and the human question of what aging and dementia tell us about ourselves, as finite creatures in need of care.

The chapter has three major parts: Starting from a social perspective, we first present an overview of our aging society, looking at certain demographic, medical, and sociological trends; we try to understand what is novel about our current situation, and why we might be facing a "crisis" in long-term care. Second, we look at individual aging, to understand what it means to age well, what it means today to grow up and grow old within the cycle of the generations. Finally, we look at the special challenges and lived experiences of age-related dementia, a debility that in the coming decades will only become more common as people live regularly into their eighties and beyond. Our purpose here is to diagnose the dilemmas now before us, so that policymakers and civic leaders can seek to ameliorate some of the problems ahead and avoid the worst kinds of miseries and abuses. But by reflecting on the character of aging itself, including those aspects that cannot be "solved" but simply confronted and endured, we also want to insist that there is an inescapable need for care and caregiving, to be offered with as much equanimity, virtue, and mutual support as individuals, families, and communities can muster.

I. AGING AND CONTEMPORARY SOCIETY

How we care for the dependent elderly will test whether modern life has not only made things better for us but also made us better human beings, more willing to accept the obligations to care and more able to cope with the burdens of caregiving. Put simply: Can a society that values self-reliance, personal freedom, and careerism reconcile itself to the realities of dependence, diminished autonomy, and responsibility for others? To consider this broad question, we must first examine some sociological and demographic facts.

A. The Aging Society

In the years ahead, the age structure of most advanced industrial societies will be unlike anything previously seen in human history, with both the average age of the population and the absolute number of old people increasing dramatically. To think responsibly about the social and ethical challenges of aging and caregiving, we need some sense of this new demographic picture and what it will mean for crucial social institutions and ordinary families. Although our focus is on the United States, these same trends are visible—and often even more dramatic—in Europe and Japan.

Because demography employs a series of classifications, we need first to examine how we tend to classify people as "old." In America, we still look to age 65 as the cut-off between middle age and old age, between work and retirement, between income and pensions, between private health insurance and public health care. The place of 65 in the public imagination and in public policy is, however, largely a social construct. The designation of 65 as the age of retirement deserving of social support traces back to a decision by the 19th-century Prussian statesman Otto von Bismarck, who thought it unlikely that many people would live beyond this age to become burdens on the state. Our own national system of social security, put in place in 1935, adopted the same age, also with little expectation of many people living much beyond this point.

Today, as we are all well aware, the situation is quite different, and our understanding of what it means to be "old" has become more nuanced. There are the "young old," who despite having reached the official retirement age of 65 continue to live vigorous and productive lives. Then there are the "old old," who have perhaps begun to slow down but still lead lives of relative health and activity. And, finally, we now speak also of the "oldest old," or those who are 85 years and over, a group that tends to be mainly or wholly dependent for their care on others. These new labels and terms are, moreover, less about chronological age per se than about a person's bodily and psychological condition. A 65-year-old might be either among the "young old" in his well being and activity levels or, because of the afflictions of disease, already in experiential terms among the "oldest old."

Whatever its limitations, however, the magic number of 65 still provides a window of understanding into what's new about our condition. Life at 65 today is often different from what it was a century or half-century ago. For one thing, living to 65 and beyond is now commonplace, when in the past it was a rare occurrence. During the last century, the average American life expectancy at birth rose from 47 years in 1900 to 77 years and climbing in 2000.[2] According to a study published in 2000, 78 percent of Americans live past their 65th birthday;[3] and this figure is rising, from 69 percent for those born in 1925 to an estimated 80 percent for those born in 1955.[4] Moreover, living at 65 and beyond is usually a much different experience than it used to be. There is a much greater likelihood of being relatively healthy, with major and potentially deadly diseases (like heart disease or kidney disease) under better control and chronic ailments (like arthritis or orthopedic problems) better managed through pain-relieving medication or joint-replacement surgery. We know much more about what it takes to stay healthier longer, and many people have the good fortune and good sense to take advantage of this knowledge.

But if the "young-old" are younger than their predecessors, the "old-old" and the "oldest old" often pay the delayed price of healthier longevity. A very significant and growing number of people suffer (or will suffer) years of enfeeblement, disability, and dementia, eventually incapable of caring for their own elementary needs. As we take stock of the changing demography of American society, therefore, we need to keep both these dimensions of aging in mind: the unchanging and unavoidable decline that comes with old age and the fact that being old today usually does not mean utter debility. *The defining characteristic of our time seems to be that we are both younger longer and older longer*; we are more vigorous at ages that once seemed very old and we are far more likely to suffer protracted periods of age-related disability and dependence because we live to ages that few people reached in the past.*

However one defines "old age," there is no question that the age structure of American society is changing, the result of increasing longevity, lower birthrates, and the special anomaly known as the "baby boom"—the great increase in the birth rate between 1946 and 1964 that has produced an unusually large cohort of Americans now between the ages of 40 and 60. These factors guarantee that the dramatic shifts in age structure seen in the twentieth century will continue through at least the middle of the twenty-first century. In the year 1900, there were 3.1 million Americans over the age of 65 (or 4.1 percent of the population). By mid-century, there were 12.3 million people over 65 (or 8.1 percent of the population). In 2000, 35.0 million people were over 65 (or 12.4 percent of the population), a number that is projected to rise to 71.5 million by 2030 (or 19.6 percent of the population) when the youngest baby-boomers have passed age 65.[5] The rising average and median ages in the population are due also to fewer births. Not only are the baby boomers aging, but they had fewer children than their parents, and at present the American birthrate remains low by historic standards (though it is significantly higher than most of Europe and Japan and modestly higher than it was in America in the 1970s and 1980s.)

Moreover, and perhaps more significant for the subject of long-term caregiving, the oldest of the old (people age 85 or older) are currently the fastest growing segment of the population. In 2004, according to estimates by the U.S. Census Bureau, an estimated 4.9 million Americans were age 85 or older.[6] That number is expected to increase to 6.1 million by 2010 and to 9.6 million by 2030.[7] Over a somewhat longer term, the trends are even more startling: Between 2000 and 2050, the U. S. Census Bureau expects the population of Americans age 45 to 54 to grow moderately from 37 million to 43 million; but, in the same period, the population age 55 to 64 will grow from 24 million to

---

* It is, of course, a leading goal of current medical research to identify risk factors for our remaining chronic illnesses and to reduce the disability that afflicts the "old-old," with the ultimate objective of producing a pattern of life that is healthy almost to the end.

42 million; the population age 65 to 74 will nearly *double*, from 18 million to 35 million; the population age 75 to 84 will more than double, from 12 million to 26 million; and the population age 85 and above will *more than quadruple*, from 4 million to 18 million.[8]

Projected Population Age 45+, by Age: 2000-2050

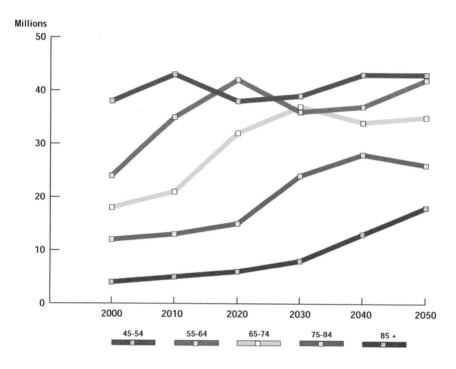

(Graphic used by permission of AARP Public Policy Institute. ©)

At present, roughly one third of Americans will live to age 85 and beyond, and that fraction is likely only to increase. Yet this greater longevity comes with many greater burdens. After age 85, only one person in twenty is still fully mobile; and roughly half the people over 85 will suffer major cognitive impairment or dementia as part of their final phase of life. At present, according to the Alzheimer's Association, an estimated 4.5 million Americans have Alzheimer's disease; by 2050, the number of Americans with Alzheimer's disease is estimated to range between 11 million and 16 million[9]—unless a cure or prevention can be found soon enough to change this grim forecast. (We will be discussing such medical efforts, which are not without hope of success, below.)*

This changing age structure will obviously have significant economic, social, and political effects—though what they are cannot be fully predicted in advance. The mass geriatric society will test the adequacy of our caregiving institutions (such as nursing homes) and the solvency of our caregiving programs (such as Medicare). We can hardly do justice to this complicated set of social and policy questions here, but a few salient facts seem worth noting, just to paint a picture of some of the changes and developments that we can expect in the years ahead:

- In 2000, only one state (Florida) had a population with at least 17 percent of the population aged 65 and older. By 2030, 44 states will have populations with at least 17 percent of the population aged 65 or older.[10]

- According to a recent estimate, 35 percent of the annual federal budget goes to programs benefiting older persons. If these programs continue unchanged, this percentage will only increase.[11]

- By the year 2020, it is estimated that nearly 157 million Americans will have some form of chronic illness, up from 125 million in 2000.[12]

- The estimated cost of Alzheimer's disease to Medicare and Medicaid totaled $50 billion in 2000 and is projected to be $72 billion in 2010.[13]

---

* It bears emphasizing that much could happen to alter these trends. For example, increasing obesity and its consequences, widespread industrial pollution, or greater vulnerability to global epidemics (avian flu or antibiotic-resistant bacteria) might markedly alter all the predictions, giving rise to a different set of medical and social challenges than those anticipated in this report. Still, it makes great sense to take our bearings from what we know and what seems likely to occur if present trends continue.

In a society with more elderly citizens and fewer younger workers, these changes will put ever-greater strain on programs like Medicare, Medicaid, and Social Security. When Medicare was introduced in the 1960s, only 9 percent (seventeen million) of the population was 65 or older, and only 0.5 percent (one million) was older than age 85. By the time the baby-boom generation starts turning 85 in about 2030, Medicare—as it is now constituted—would be paying for the care of an estimated 80 million Americans (22 percent of the population), including 9 million people who are 85 and older, nearly all of them with expensive health care needs. According to projections assuming a "middle costs" scenario, Medicare will grow from 2.4 percent of GDP today to 8.3 percent in 2050; and Medicare, Medicaid, and Social Security will nearly double as a share of the nation's economy by 2035. Moreover, the desire to expand these programs and to add new benefits will only become more powerful just as the capacity to pay for them is tested.

One of the greatest economic and social challenges will be funding long-term care—the provision of daily medical and personal assistance to individuals incapable of looking after themselves, ranging from in-home nurses to adult day-care services to full-time nursing homes. These services will grow more necessary in the years ahead and probably more costly, but they are not at present covered under Medicare. Medicaid pays a large percentage of the costs of long-term care for the poor; arguably, it has become in large measure a de facto long-term care program, as many middle-class people spend down their assets or shift them to relatives in order to become eligible for Medicaid. As a result, the strains on the system are already great, and getting worse. As physician and long-term care specialist Joanne Lynn points out: "The services needed during the last few years of life are expensive. In fiscal year 2000, Medicaid paid for 45 percent of the $137 billion annual cost of institutional long-term care. The Congressional Budget Office forecasts that the cost of long-term care, roughly $123 billion in 2000, will reach $207 billion in 2020 and $346 billion in 2040. These extraordinary costs risk bankrupting state budgets, which currently devote 20 percent of expenditures to Medicaid."[14] One likely response to these rising Medicaid costs will be demands to include long-term care coverage as part of Medicare, especially as middle-class persons are squeezed between providing for their parents and their children and forced either to forgo work to care for their elders at home or to pay the rising costs of professional or institutional care. This creation of a long-term care benefit would likely make Medicare's existing solvency problems far worse.

The effects of America's changing age structure are not limited to the pension or health care systems, important as these are. The coming of the mass geriatric society will affect every dimension of human and social life: the culture of the workplace, the consumer market, the housing market, and, most deeply, the rhythm and character of family life. We will live differently, work differently, and perhaps even think differently in a society in which the needs of the old become ever more dominant. Our politics might change as well, especially if older people increasingly vote their class interests as elderly; in the extreme, there is the unwholesome possibility of a "war between the generations," as people insist on securing their own advantage with little regard for the intergenerational common good and with no organized voice to speak up for the rising generations.

These broad social changes in how we live will be accompanied by radically new patterns in the end of life. New trajectories of illness and death will likely predominate in the coming decades, and new questions will arise about who will care for those suffering from chronic disabilities. If we are to understand what it means to live in an aging society, we must take up these two crucial issues—namely, *how we die* and *who will care*.

B. The Trajectory of Chronic Illness and Death

In addition to radical changes in the overall age structure of society, a growing percentage of the elderly are living through longer periods of dependence and disability, including, and especially, long periods of dementia. This rise in long-term disability and dependence is, as already noted, the unintended consequence of our success in preventing, curing, or managing the earlier and more acute causes of death that once predominated. But there is more. These advances have also changed the trajectory of chronic illness and—most important—altered the leading causes of death. Because we live longer, we die differently; and because medicine can better confront the illnesses that would kill us quickly, we are far more likely to die after a period of protracted physical disability and cognitive impairment.

In 1900, the usual place of death was at home; in 2000, it was the hospital. In 1900, most people died from accidents or infections without suffering a long period of disability. In 2000, people suffered, on average, two years of severe disability on the way to death. Acute causes of death (such as pneumonia, influenza, and septicemia) are in decline; prolonged causes of death from age-related degenerative diseases (such as Alzheimer's, Parkinson's, and emphysema) are on the rise. Already today, as Joanne Lynn points out, "Most Americans die with failure of a major organ (heart, lungs, kidneys, or liver), dementia, stroke, or general frailty of old age. . . . [T]hese conditions lead to long periods of diminished function and involve multiple unpredictable and serious exacerbations of symptoms."[15] Living longer also means suffering numerous chronic but not deadly conditions— such as arthritis, hearing and vision loss, dental decay, bowel problems, and urinary difficulties. Frailty becomes both more extended and more commonplace, which means that "the body's systems have little reserve and small upsets cause cascading health problems."[16]

A 2003 study by researchers at the Rand Corporation sought to explain, organize, and quantify the various "trajectories of chronic illness," in an effort to describe how the character of aging and dying has changed dramatically over the last many decades and to show how unequipped we are for the caregiving challenges ahead. To envision the caregiving needs of elderly people who are sick enough to die, the study classified them into the three most common groups, using the trajectory of decline over time that is characteristic of the major type of disease or disability.

The first group dies after a *short period of evident decline*; this is the typical course of death from cancer. Many malignancies are, of course, curable by surgery, radiation, and chemotherapy. And even many people who will die of cancer may be comfortable and function well for a substantial period, until the illness becomes overwhelming. Thereafter, the patient's status deteriorates rapidly, especially in the final weeks and days before death. Death usually occurs within a year. *Roughly 20 percent of all deaths are now of this type.*

The second group dies following *several years of increasing physical limitations*, punctuated by intermittent acute life-threatening episodes requiring hospitalization and vigorous intervention; this is the typical course of death from chronic cardiac or respiratory failure (for example, coronary artery disease or emphysema). Many of these patients are at first little handicapped in daily life. But as the disease progresses, "from time to time, some physiological stress overwhelms the body's reserves and leads to a worsening of serious symptoms. Patients survive a few such episodes but then die from a complication or exacerbation, often rather suddenly."[17] *Roughly 20 percent of all deaths are now of this type.*

The third—and already the largest—group dies only after *prolonged dwindling, usually lasting many years*; this is the typical course of death from dementia (including Alzheimer's disease or disabling stroke) or generalized frailty of multiple body systems. This trajectory toward death is gradual but unrelenting, with steady decline, enfeeblement, and growing dependency, often lasting a decade or longer. In the end, an overwhelming infection, a stroke, or some other insult that a severely weakened body cannot handle becomes the proximate cause of death. *Roughly 40 percent of all deaths are now of this type.**

---

* The study also points out how the different trajectories toward death require different strategies and instruments of care: hospice for the first; ongoing disease management, advance-care planning, and mobilizing service to the home for the second; Meals on Wheels and home health aides, then institutional long-term care facilities for the third. According to the study, the remaining 20 percent of all deaths "are split between those who die suddenly and others we have not yet learned how to classify."

Typical Chronic Illness Trajectories

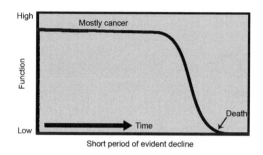

Short period of evident decline

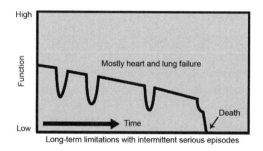

Long-term limitations with intermittent serious episodes

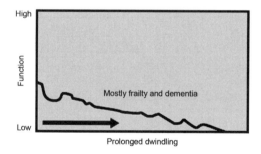

Prolonged dwindling

The Rand study highlights the single most dramatic and socially significant change in how we Americans die: four in ten of us die only after an extended period of worsening debility, dementia, and dependence. To be sure, most people over 65 at any given time are still healthy. But as the cohort ages further, hundreds of thousands slip into protracted dotage and feebleness, needing protracted long-term care. And virtually every American family will be affected—indeed, is already affected.

Consider this implication. Every married couple, each with two still living parents, may expect to be involved with or even fully responsible for the care of at least one and, more likely, two of these four parents who will live out their last five to ten years in an increasingly enfeebled or demented condition, incapable of looking after themselves.* And, because there is no reversing the disability, the better they are cared for, the longer they will be in need of yet more expansive (and often expensive) care. Later in life, close to half of these caregiving children will themselves be in need of similar long-term care.

C. The Availability of Caregivers

Dependence means being dependent on others—on family members, professional caregivers, and caregiving institutions. One's level of debility shapes one's level of dependence: Some people require assistance with only the most physically or mentally demanding tasks—like cleaning the house or managing investments. Others require help with daily activities—like preparing meals and paying bills. But those with advanced dementia and grave physical illness require assistance with the most basic activities of daily life—bathing, toileting, dressing, and staying safe. Of course, those who suffer "prolonged dwindling" progress through these stages of increasing dependence. And this raises a major social question: As the incidence of dementia and debility increase in the years ahead, who will provide such caregiving for those who need it? And what burdens—economic and personal—will such caregiving impose on caregiving individuals and on society as a whole?

---

* Based on the RAND finding that 40 percent of people will die only after a prolonged period of frailty and dwindling, elementary statistics suggest that a married couple with four living parents should have the following rough expectations: an 87 percent chance that one or more of their parents will die in this way; a 52 percent chance that two or more will; an 18 percent chance that three or more will, and a 2.5 percent chance that all four parents will.

*1. The Present Realities of Caregiving.**

Until now, unpaid family caregivers have supplied the bulk of long-term care. In a national survey conducted in 2000, more than a quarter of adult Americans reported that they had provided care for disabled family members during the past year; that translates into more than 50 million volunteer caregivers.[18] The federal Administration on Aging estimated that over 22 million Americans are providing such care at any one time.[19]

Within families, the practice of caregiving varies, but the responsibility falls mainly on women:

> For married elders, the first one to develop an eventually fatal chronic illness can usually rely on the spouse for most of the direct care needed. In a study of all caregivers assisting people age sixty-five and older, spouses accounted for 24 percent, daughters for 20 percent, and sons for 6 percent, meaning that immediate family members are 50 percent of all caregivers. The onset of illness in the caregiving spouse or in a widowed or unmarried elder often precipitates a crisis for the rest of the family, especially for daughters and daughters-in-law, who most often assume the role of caregiver.[20]

According to a 1999 study, the average length of time spent on family caregiving was eight years, with a third of respondents providing care for ten years or more.[21] Most family caregivers serve out of love and loyalty, and most of them find caregiving meaningful and rewarding.

But the challenges for family caregiving are increasingly weighty, and the availability of unpaid family caregivers is diminishing, in part because greater opportunities for women in the work force leave fewer people free for volunteer caregiving, and in part because of smaller family size and higher divorce rates. Single elderly individuals often have to rely on paid care, and

---

* In this section and the next we rely heavily on the work of Dr. Joanne Lynn, a practicing physician long active in hospice care, long-term care, and end of life issues, whose recent book, *Sick to Death and Not Going to Take it Anymore!* (University of California Press, 2004) offers a succinct summary and portrait of caregiving today and an analysis of what may be a looming caregiving crisis. Much of the following account of the present and future realities of caregiving is based on the first chapter of her book.

even when children can provide some care, they often find they need additional paid help. The average caregiving load is eighteen hours of direct services per week; for those who care for persons needing assistance with two or more activities of daily living (moving around, toileting, feeding and dressing), the average rises to forty hours per week. Yet most family caregivers also hold paying jobs, and the demands of caregiving compel most of them to rearrange their schedules, work fewer hours, or take unpaid leaves of absence. In addition, caregiving work can and does cause health problems for the caregivers.[22] The average unpaid family caregiver is 60 years old, and many already have chronic illnesses of their own.

2. The Future Availability of Caregivers.

In her recent book, Lynn cites a number of reasons why caregiving for the elderly is so much more challenging today than it was in the past, and why those challenges are likely to grow even more daunting in the future.

First, medical advances have enabled elderly and frail patients to survive much longer with serious chronic illness and disability than they could in the past. The patient's frailty, and the presence of multiple illnesses and disabilities, may necessitate many different kinds of care, including medication, cleaning, feeding, doctor's visits, trips to the hospital, physical therapy, etc. The caregiver's responsibility to provide some of these services and to supervise others may last for years. Future medical advances are likely to enable elderly patients to live even longer with an even greater variety of chronic illnesses and disabilities.

Second, families are smaller now, so that elderly patients on average have fewer descendants to rely on for care. In the past, there were few surviving grandparents, and they lived in large extended families with many potential caregivers. Now the ratios are changing, and an increasing percentage of the disabled elderly find themselves without any living relatives: it is estimated that, by 2020, 1.2 million people aged 65 or older will have no living children, siblings, or spouse.[23] The Institute for Health and Aging reports that, in 1990, for each person over 85 years old, there were 21 people between the ages of 50 and 64, the prime years for family caregiving; in 2030, for each person over 85 years old, there will only be 6 people between 50 and 64.[24]

Third, in the past, the typical family caregiver was a woman who did not work outside the home, young enough to be able to care for a sick parent alongside her own children; and the typical elderly patient did not live very long with serious disability. Today's—and tomorrow's—caregivers will typically have jobs outside the home, unless they are ill or disabled themselves. Such working family caregivers often have to give up years of income, or accept less pay or advancement, in order to care for their elderly family members for extended periods. Caring for elderly relatives will often come into competition with raising a family of one's own; already, women spend as long in caregiving for adult family members as in caring for children.[25] In addition, because the elderly infirm are living longer, the potential caregivers among their next of kin (especially spouses and children) are likely to be older themselves, and hence more prone to illness and less capable of the hard work required by care of the elderly. All these factors make family care of the elderly more costly, more challenging, and more burdensome to those providing the care.

Fourth, it does not seem likely that an increase in *paid* caregiving will be able to alleviate the growing strains on family caregivers. To begin with, there is an ever-shrinking pool of workers available for paid home health care. Home-care nursing used to be an important opportunity for steady employment among women who lacked advanced education and other skills, and especially among immigrants. But several factors have combined to reduce the availability of home-care aides and nurses, including the strenuousness of the work involved, compensation barely above minimum wage, difficult relationships with patients, language barriers, the lack of health insurance and other benefits, and hindrances to immigration. To reverse this trend, concerted efforts will be required to improve the working conditions, wages, and advancement opportunities of paid home-care providers. Without such costly improvements, we are likely to see a serious shortage of paid care workers even as the supply of unpaid family care-providers shrinks (for the reasons we have cited). Penny Hollander Feldman estimates that by 2010, when the baby boomers begin to reach old age, the pool of middle-aged women able and willing to provide basic elder care services, whether in nursing homes or at home, will be substantially smaller than it is now.[26] In addition, an ongoing shortage of trained nurses is likely to be exacerbated in the future; the number of U.S.-educated nursing school graduates who took the licensing examination for registered nurses fell by 25 percent between 1995 and 2002,[27] and 75 percent of all hospitals already have vacancies for nurses.[28] It would be a tragic irony if our greater opportunities for individualistic success have produced a world more in need of caregivers than ever, but one that has lost its way of generating them.

3. A Caregiving Crisis?

There is always a danger of declaring a social crisis prematurely, especially in the face of many unknowns. Indeed, as we think about the socio-economic dimensions of the challenge of caregiving, we cannot ignore the fact that we are, as a society, much wealthier than previous generations, with some reason to believe that the generations that follow will be wealthier still. It may be that changed patterns of saving and investment, new instruments such as long-term care insurance, higher birthrates, increased immigration of younger workers, and medical advances to prevent or treat these chronic illnesses will make some of our current worries overwrought. Just as it is foolish to ignore foreseeable problems, it is foolish to assume that we can foresee everything. Free societies are also creative societies, with a capacity to adapt to, as well as overcome, hard and novel circumstances.

But all that said, there *is* reason to think that a genuine caregiving crisis may be looming, not only for the least well off members of society but for those in the middle and upper classes as well. Three unprecedented trends are about to converge, potentially creating great stress on our systems of care. First, the age structure in America is shifting, such that both in absolute and percentage terms we are becoming a population of senior citizens. Second, although many of us stay healthier longer, and this is a great blessing, it is also the case that many of us will experience a lengthening twilight of disability and dwindling. Today, as never seen before, a vast majority of us will suffer a long period, as much as a decade, of chronic illness and dependency before death comes. And finally, just as these two trends create an increasing demand for good health care providers, the actual supply of available caregivers appears to be shrinking rapidly. Taken together these trends suggest an impending public policy or socio-economic crisis in providing long-term care for an expanding population of increasingly incapacitated seniors.*

Confronting this grave social challenge will test us not only as citizens and policymakers, but as individuals and families. It will challenge us not only economically, but humanly and morally. It will test our character and self-understanding, requiring us to set aside self-interest in order to care for those who can no longer provide for themselves.

But if we are to confront well the challenges of long-term care, we need also to attend to the human and ethical significance of aging itself. To begin with, we should resist all notions of "solving" the "problem of aging" and avoid acting as if aging is simply a problem to be solved. Aging is part of human life, and aging well requires the search for wisdom about what it means to ripen and die. It requires the cultivation of the character necessary to endure one's own decline. It requires a richer understanding of the lifecycle—seeing oneself, as one ages, in relation to the young, and seeing death in relation to the renewal of human possibility from generation to generation.

To think about the aging society, therefore, we must also think about what it means to be an *aging person*: What shapes the individual experience of growing old, and how does this experience change from person to person, culture to culture, society to society? For only by having some idea of what it means to age well and to stay human in time do we have a compass to guide us as we face our own potential crisis, as well as some way to measure whether we have indeed averted the worst possible outcomes of aging badly.

---

* Making matters worse is a concurrent *ethical* crisis: we are unclear about the moral significance of our new situation and especially about what is owed, humanly speaking, to those unable to care for themselves. We treat this subject in Chapters 2, 3, and 4.

II. INDIVIDUAL AGING AND THE LIFECYCLE

Aging is at once a biological, psychological, and social phenomenon. It is a universal feature of human life. We grow, we grow up, we grow older, and—if we are lucky—we grow old. In the broadest sense, we are aging from the moment of birth until the moment of death. In the *beginning* of life, to age means to develop—our bodies grow larger, our mental capacities expand, our physical powers develop. We learn to crawl, walk, run, speak, and write. In the long *middle* of life, aging means developing and declining all at once—developing new faculties and new perspectives but also gradually losing some abilities that once came easily. For many, growth amid decline is possible until the very end; the aging individual is still gaining in wisdom and experience even as the body enters its final senescence. But for others, at the *end* of life, biological aging eventually means almost entirely loss and decline; it means the gradual or swift eradication of one's physical and mental powers. In some cases, the body declines in advance of the mind; in other cases, the mind deteriorates in advance of the body. But in the end, for everyone, aging leads to death and, with it, the loss of the whole person as body-and-mind. This fact of being human and thus mortal is unavoidable for everyone.

Biological aging is not unique to human beings. All animals grow and die, and the capacity for growth seems intertwined with the reality of death. But for human beings, aging is not only a biological experience but a psychological, existential, social, and religious one: it involves seeing oneself in a new light as one's life progresses and one's body changes; it involves looking back on one's past experiences and looking ahead to one's shortening future; it involves treasuring life and independence as long as possible and accepting dependence and death when they can no longer be resisted. It involves changes of familial and social roles, changes of responsibility at work and at home, and differing forms of participation in civic and communal life.

Today, we have many images of being old—some perennial and some unique to our time. There is the revered matriarch who commands the respect of her entire family; the immobile and lonely resident of a nursing home; the old man who gives young-sters a run for their money on the tennis court; the doting grandmother who gives her grandchildren sweets when their par-ents aren't looking; the senior executive given "early retirement" by his younger and more ambitious colleagues; the elder states-man who advises those who now stand where she once stood; the demented elder statesman who no longer knows his own name. Old age comes with many faces, and our image of old age varies almost as much as the elderly persons we know most inti-mately. Sometimes we revere the old and sometimes we pity them. Sometimes we admire the timeless lessons they have to teach us and sometimes we belittle them for not adapting to the times.

The two most prominent images of aging today stand in deep opposition to one another: there is the idealized image of *healthy old age*, with vigor and vitality until the end, and there is the sorrowful image of *extended decline and dependence*, with the ravages of long-term dementia and physical deterioration. Ours is the age of both extended youth and extended degeneration—and often, for many individuals, a life trajectory that is marked by one after the other. *We are younger longer and we are aged longer. Living well with this paradox of modern aging is perhaps the special challenge of our time.*

Aging well is thus a deeply ethical activity. It does not simply mean having the good fortune of staying healthy and vigorous until the end, but requires exhibiting certain virtues for as long as one has the capacity to do so. As William F. May reflects in his seminal essay on the ethical life of the elderly:

> Such virtues do not come automatically with growing old. Even limited dealings with the elderly disabuse us of that sentimentality. Rather, the virtues grow only through resolu-tion, struggle, perhaps prayer, and perseverance. Further, these virtues hardly appear only in the elderly. Some com-mon human virtues—which men and women of all ages might do well to cultivate—simply take special form in the later years. When they do appear in the elderly, however, they can instruct and sometimes even inspire. Their example can encourage particularly the fainthearted among the young who believe that full human existence is possible only under

the accidental circumstances of their own temporary flourishing.[29]

May reminds us that the virtues required to age well are the universal virtues needed by human beings of every age; the old are not a separate species but human beings living human lives who should be held to human standards. These virtues do not develop and manifest themselves simply by living a long time; they require active cultivation throughout life, culminating but rarely beginning in old age.

Yet these virtues do take a special form among the elderly; old age is a particular time of life with particular ethical and existential demands, a time when vigor and ambition begin to wane and when the very meaning of one's existence presents itself with looming finality. May also reminds us that the old live (or should live) among the generations, not separate from them. He reminds us that the young often benefit from the moral example of the old, and that the old are more likely to age well when the rising generations stand with them—as caregivers, to be sure, but also as recipients of the gifts that the old alone are equipped to give. Even in their days of total dependence, the old can still be a gift to the young.

There is great human variation in how people age—variation dictated by the particularities of each person's circumstances and by the culture in which the aging person lives. But certain traits of character, as May suggests, are always necessary to age well: *courage*, including the capacity to keep one's fears in check even as one's prospects worsen; *simplicity*, including the capacity to "travel light" on one's final journey; *wisdom*, including the avoidance of excessive nostalgia and excessive remorse; and *humor*, including the wit that sometimes flourishes when the carefulness of middle age is no longer required.[30] These virtues of the elderly—to which could be added gratitude and acceptance, among others—*draw strength* from a society that honors the old even when they can no longer produce at the high levels they once did, and these virtues *give strength* to a society where the old always seek to benefit those who must replace them in the cycle of generations. The need to face aging and death—our own and that of our loved ones—with clear minds, caring hearts, and human solidarity reminds us that virtue has not become obsolete in our high-tech world.

The personal experience of aging is, of course, more than a matter of virtue. The particularities of that experience are shaped by many factors—biological, psychological, and sociological—that we might review in turn.

A. Biological Nature and Environment

Gerontologists define "normal aging" as follows: "A time-dependent series of cumulative, progressive, intrinsic, and harmful changes that begin to manifest themselves at reproductive maturity and eventually end in death. Primary aging would describe those changes that occur over time independent of any specific disease or trauma to the body, whereas secondary aging would describe disabilities resulting from forces such as disease."[31] While aging is a shared biological fact for human beings as a species, the trajectory of biological aging differs dramatically from person to person, due both to one's unique genetic inheritance and to variable environmental influences that shape each person differently throughout life. For some, nature tragically prevents even the possibility of old age, death arriving before the person can grow old or grow up; for others, genetic predilections toward longevity are inherited from long-lived ancestors. For those fortunate enough to live a long life, the process of aging and decline takes many different shapes: some live vigorously until the end, then die a swift or sudden death; some suffer a gradual period of bodily decline, with sufficient time and self-awareness to see aging as the final chapter of a complete life; some suffer dementia and live through long years of diminished awareness and total dependence.

This biological trajectory is influenced significantly in our time by the possibilities and limits of modern medicine. Medicine can prevent, reverse, or slow down some ailments; before other diseases and disabilities, medicine stands—at least for now—relatively helpless. Sudden and premature deaths are far less common than in the past; extended decline and disability are far more common. But the process of growing old always moves toward decline and death, even if the route is very different from person to person. The vital trajectory varies; the post-vital outcome does not.

B. The Presence or Absence of Loved Ones

In crucial respects, everyone ages alone: for it is the self's body alone that changes, the self's faculties alone that decline, and the self's death alone that looms; these personal realities cannot be shared fully by others. But at best, individuals do not age and die by themselves (even if they must age and die *as* themselves alone), but with family, friends, and caregivers who stand with them. The rhythm and happiness of old age are shaped greatly by the presence or absence of loved ones: by living with or outliving one's longtime spouse; by having one's adult children and grandchildren live nearby or far away; by living at home with family or in a nursing home; by having or not having family altogether. It is precisely because we must age and die alone that we need the presence of others to help us age purposefully; to remind us that life does not end with us but carries forward beyond us; and to show us that we are valued for what we have to offer and even when we can offer little in return.

Perhaps no friendship in life is deeper than that between husband and wife. As spouses think together about aging and dying, the meaning of being alone presents itself sharply: what loving spouse would not give his or her life to save a husband or a wife, and yet what spouse wants to leave his or her beloved to age and die alone. As with spouses, so it is with lifelong friends: It is a great blessing to live a long life, but also a burden to outlive all one's closest friends, and to face death without the camaraderie that they alone might offer. The weight of loneliness is also felt in the relation between an aging father or mother and his or her adult children and grandchildren: the noble desire not to disrupt the children's lives with one's own neediness co-exists with the desire to be needed by them even in one's days of dependence, and cherished by them when one's usefulness has passed. In the face of aging, our devotion to others is both most tested and most required. There is sometimes a powerful temptation to believe that elderly persons' lives are so limited that fellowship is insignificant, a temptation to regard being with them as little more than sitting awkwardly in a small room in a smelly nursing home. If, because they remind us of our own inevitable decline, we shun their company, we isolate them even more. But often, it is precisely because the elderly have nothing else that they need our fellowship most of all.

C. Wealth and Poverty

As the body ages, health problems proliferate and worsen. The capacity to face these problems—not only medically, but existentially—is affected significantly, often decisively, by one's economic condition. Money alone hardly ensures that wealthy individuals can age well; the absence of money alone hardly means that poor individuals will age poorly. Many wealthy persons suffer terribly in old age despite the best medicine that money can buy, and many lack the character to live well as their powers diminish. At the same time, many poor persons demonstrate heroic virtue despite the lack of economic means, and they still savor the gift of life despite its many hardships. But it is quite obvious that having reliable health care, good nursing, and the wherewithal to make life decisions free from severe economic pressures often makes it significantly easier to age well. Being wealthy ensures that one's bodily needs are attended to as well as possible, and it allows the elderly person (for as long as nature cooperates) to enjoy his or her final phase of life without living in a constant state of economic anxiety.

Of course, there will always be large disparities in the economic condition of the elderly; this fact is unavoidable in any free society (not to mention un-free societies, where the disparities between the wealthy and the poor are usually much starker). But as a society, we should aspire to provide every aging person some basic level of economic security and medical care—including long-term care—while always recognizing that providing support for the elderly is but one great civic good among many, and while always remembering that wealth alone is never a sufficient answer to the human dilemmas of aging.* Economic security does not translate simply into existential security. Money does not give life meaning in the face of death. But as one faces great physical trials and ultimate human questions in one's final days, it is surely a great blessing to do so without the constant fear or present reality of economic disaster, or the constant worry that good care for oneself means years of hardship for one's spouse, children, or grandchildren.

D. Vocation and Avocation

Since old age is a distinguishable phase of human life, it makes sense to consider the distinct purposes and obligations that define it and the connection of these purposes and obligations to the other phases of one's life. The answer is hardly the same for everyone, and it obviously shifts from one period of old age to the next. For some, old age is a time for novel pursuits—a time to explore interests that have been put off year after year in order to meet the demands of full-time parenting and full-time work. For others, it is a time to return to old passions or to renew the existing bonds of family and friendship. For some, aging is a time to continue one's life work. For others—and eventually for everyone—aging means learning to "let go" of the things one has done throughout life; it means "retirement" in the true sense—no more fixing cars, taking hikes, sailing boats, or attending concerts. To age is to experience intermittent finitudes on the way to the ultimate finitude that is death. And for some, the central work of growing old is learning how to die—how to let go, how to say goodbye, how to ask forgiveness, and how to put one's existence and one's memory in the hands of others.

At best, the vocations and avocations of old age are not mere distractions to pass the time, or simple amusements that temporarily blur the realities of finitude. Amusement is not to be disparaged; it is as essential to old age as to other phases of life, and being amused is sometimes an achievement of character in

---

* Of course, to the extent that this economic security is provided through public funds, it will come at the expense of other public goods and other segments of society, for example, politically powerless needy young children.

circumstances where there are many reasons to be miserable. But constant amusement—cruises, bingo, television, and so on—may not be the best way to confront the seriousness of being old. Aging rightly forces reflection on the character of one's life as a whole. It often involves living with opposites: cultivating new interests, new sensibilities, or new understandings of the world, while letting go of old loves, old jobs, and old pursuits that once loomed large in one's identity. Pursuing the ideal of aging well is never work for the weak-spirited. It invites us to see our final years as the culmination of a human whole, with a deepening sense that one's life is not simply an arbitrary sequence of events but a coherent narrative with a beginning, a middle, and a meaningful end. Not everyone, alas, is so fortunate as to be able to do so.

E. Male or Female

While aging is a common human experience, it would be a mistake to ignore some differences between men and women during this time of life. As a sociological and demographic fact, women tend to outlive men, and thus more often face the burdens of living as widows than do men the burdens of living as widowers. This means that women are more likely than men to sleep in beds that now feel empty, having spent months or years caring for the person who once slept alongside them. This comparatively longer life also means that women are more likely than men to become impoverished in their golden years, spending down their final assets on long-term care, including the kind of care they may once have provided to their husbands free of charge.

There may also be certain inherent differences between men and women when it comes to aging, both biological and psychological. As William May suggests:

> [W]omen receive an earlier and clearer biological preview of aging—if not of mortality; menopause gives them a clear signal that the wheel of existence turns downward toward the ground, while men find ways to obscure in themselves whatever signals they receive. Women tend more often than men to associate aging and death with the corruption of bodily form; men, with a flagging vitality. The corruption of

the body shows up relentlessly in the morning mirror; the failure of vitality overtakes in more elusive ways and is suppressed more easily in men.[32]*

Other existential realities—such as the transition from work to retirement or from a full nest to an empty nest—once affected men and women in profoundly different ways. But as the familial and social roles of men and women have become less clearly demarcated, the differential effect of these experiences on men and women is perhaps less significant, even as the experiences themselves are no less profound. Yet despite the fluidity of male and female roles, it still remains the case that women serve much more extensively than men as caregivers for the dependent, including and especially for the dependent elderly. And it may be that this experience of caregiving makes women more attuned to the realities of aging, and thus more prepared existentially and ethically when they age and decline themselves.

F. Mind and Body

Although aging proceeds in one direction—toward the gradual breakdown of the whole body, ending in natural death—senescence is not a unified process that affects equally all systems of the body and mind. Different people age in different ways, in part because they lose different capacities at different times, and in part because they lose some capacities and not others before they die. Some individuals suffer long-term physical disability with their mental capacities and self-awareness firmly intact until the very end of their lives. For others, cognitive disability or dementia sets in and grows severe even as the body remains relatively healthy, with the total breakdown of the body's systems coming only much later, often years later. The experience of aging is thus shaped profoundly by the health of the body in relation to the health of the mind, and the health of the mind in relation to the health of the body. It is also shaped by the specific manner in which the body fails or the mind deteriorates—as well

---

* How much of any such differences between men and women is natural and how much is cultural is, of course, a long and (for now, at least) unanswerable question.

as by how well the individual is able to adapt to and compensate for any diminution of function.

The combination of physical debility and cognitive health can bring a host of personal frustrations: the powerful desire to do something for oneself or another, even the simplest thing, but not being able to do it; the inability to control one's bowels, with enough awareness to be embarrassed by it; the heartache of watching loved ones sacrifice so much on one's behalf, when all one wants is for them to flourish themselves. Yet the gift of self-awareness until the end is also great. The aging individual with a healthy mind and sick body can still savor some of life's greatest joys—experiential, interpersonal, and intellectual. He might still be able to read his favorite books, listen to his favorite music, see a grandchild off to the prom, and thank a devoted family care-giver. But the grave imbalance of physical and mental powers also often brings its own special misery—including the feeling of being trapped inside a body that does not respond to one's desires, needs, and efforts at control.

The gradual and extended loss of one's mental powers brings different dilemmas, frustrations, and miseries, both for the suffering person and for his or her caregivers. With a disease like Alzheimer's, as we will explore more fully below, some people suffer at first by knowing what is coming—by seeing one's mental powers decline, one's memory erode, one's grasp of one's surroundings becoming hazy. Eventually, this self-awareness of decline fades into the loss of self-awareness entirely—including the inability to understand how to behave appropriately, the incapacity to recognize loved ones, and the confusion that comes with not remembering life from one minute to the next or the paranoia that comes from not understanding what others are doing and why. Eventually, with Alzheimer's and other senile dementias, this cognitive disability becomes so severe that it leads to physical disability—the inability to speak, to control one's bowels, to eat and drink. Eventually, as the mind shuts down completely, so too does the body.

As we contemplate the imbalances of physical and mental health that often shape how we age, we confront the puzzling unity and disunity that is the human person. We come to see that we are an indivisible unity of the mind-and-body, but that often our will wants what our bodies cannot do and cannot be. The individual both has a body and is a body, even when he resents all the things the body cannot do or all the pain the body causes, experiences, and endures. And eventually, in death, this experience of imbalance leads to a unified ending: the death of the whole self, mind-and-body together.

G. A Person's View of Death

Our views on death obviously shape how we age, though these views often take firmer shape only as we age. Aging leads to death—the final limit on earthly life and a fact of our humanity that cannot be disputed or avoided. But there is deep disagreement about what the end of embodied life means for the human person who once lived. Many of us live with great uncertainty about the meaning of death. We live between faith and doubt, fear and serenity, obsession and blindness. Many others have firmer ideas about what death is—whether a supreme faith in redemption and resurrection after death, or a firm belief that life here-and-now provides no evidence for life hereafter, or a belief that an obsession with personal death only blurs the perfect nothingness (or nirvana) that is being itself.

Moreover, there is no simple formula for judging how one's views on death will shape one's approach to aging. Some of those who believe that the self disappears entirely after death will resist death at all costs, struggling to preserve bodily life against the prospect of total oblivion. Others with the same belief conclude that the self is the final judge of its own existence, including the arbiter of its own exit. In this view, the ravages of aging might be justifiably preempted by choosing or embracing death, on the grounds that happiness here-and-now is the only measure of life's worth and that some kinds of old age are too miserable or undignified to endure. For still others, a belief in the utter finality of personal death might lead to a kind of stoic virtue, enduring aging and death as an example of uprightness for those who will one day die themselves.

The widespread belief that life does not end here—that salvation, resurrection, or reincarnation is possible after death—can also influence how one views one's own aging. For some, this means that aging is both a burden that must be endured and a sacred passageway to divine salvation. Such an emphasis on the hereafter might make death seem less horrible because it is less final; or it might make death seem more frightening because one fears eternal judgment. To believe in heaven often means believing in hell; the comforts of faith often coexist with terrible anxiety about the fate of one's immortal soul.

In the modern age, as suggested above, many people live somewhere between certainty and doubt about the meaning of death: they hope for salvation, but cannot be sure; they see little reason to believe in life hereafter, but know that the origin and destiny of life is a mystery they cannot finally solve. But whatever one's views on these ultimate questions, death is both an *evil* and a *necessity* for all bodily beings: Death is an evil, because it can strike at any moment, because it robs us of those we love, and because the overwhelming fear of death can deform how we live. And death is a necessity, because as biological beings we are not made to live forever, and because much that is good in human life depends on accepting and living out our roles as self-conscious mortals. In death, one generation stands aside for the next. The ripeness of age gives way to the freshness of youth. In some ways, aging appears as a series of small dyings on the way to death, but also the drama of taking one's place in the ongoing chain of generations, ideally with more gratitude than bitterness for the life one has lived.

H. Conclusion: Modernity and the Lifecycle

This drama of growing old, passing down, and passing on is hardly new. It has always been at the heart of the human lifecycle, recognized by the wise men and women of every age (even before old age as we know it today became so commonplace). In *De Senectute*, Cicero gave voice to this human reality of ascent and decline: "The course of life is fixed, and nature admits of its being run but in one way, and only once; and to each part of our life there is something specially seasonable."[33] The question we now face, however, is whether the idea of a "cycle of life," with its several and differently meaningful stages, still makes sense to us—both as a lived experience and as a guiding belief. Do we still regard each phase of life as possessing its own "seasonable" quality, where the trajectory of one's own life interlocks with the trajectory of the generations? Or do we live, in some sense, "after the lifecycle," with the expectation of extended youth or extended decline, and with a confused sense of how life's many phases fit together or how the self's demise relates to the ascent of those who will stand in our place?*

Already, we seem to be extending youthful vitality into what once seemed like old age, and at the very least, we now *expect* healthy living and medical progress to keep us "feeling young" at ages that were once considered old. In the future, we may not see 70 or 80 as part of old age but rather as part of the long middle of life. At the same time, however, we may be entering an age in which extended decline and dependence also become widespread, and when a long period of being unable to care for oneself becomes the normal pathway to death. These changes in how we age are taking shape alongside myriad changes in the rhythm of the earlier phases of life—including when people marry, when they have children, how many children they have, and the kind of work they perform. The old increasingly care for the very old, and the young increasingly see the old at a distance—both geographically and pedagogically, shaped by a culture that often prizes mobility and novelty over stability and tradition.

To say that we live "after the lifecycle" is surely an exaggeration: the outlines of growth and decline still hold in our lives, as does the sense that life has a shape, with different phases, each with different qualities. But we also seem to be living in a new moment, both sociologically and psychologically: The age structure of society has changed and is changing; the decades of life are starting to hold new meaning; and the expectations we impose on old age are evolving both positively and negatively, with high hopes and great fears. These changes have been brought about in part by modern medicine's transformation of the trajectory of life, illness, and death and by modern culture's emphasis

---

* Prof. Thomas Cole presented an extremely illuminating discussion of these questions at the June 24, 2004 meeting of the Council. For the transcript, see http://www.bioethics.gov.

on independence, individual self-rule, and career as the major sources of self-esteem.

The rising prevalence of Alzheimer's disease and other dementias in old age only makes these questions about the trajectory of life more acute. Besides the normal fear of senescence and death, many people are horrified at the thought of ending their lives only after a long period not just of physical frailty and disability but also of mental incapacitation, impaired memory, diminished awareness, loss of modesty and self-control, distortion of personality and temperament, inability to recognize friends and loved ones, and general dullness and enfeeblement of inner life. It seems a cruel irony that the very medical advances that have kept many of us reasonably healthy into a ripe old age have, by the same token, exposed us to the ravages of incurable and progressive dementia, and to the prospect that our life's drama may well end with an extended final act marked by a gradual descent into mindlessness. In the next section we set the stage for a deeper discussion of this dilemma by giving an overview of the clinical and experiential facts about dementia and specifically Alzheimer's disease—an illness that terrifies many and requires years of constant care.

III. DEMENTIA AND THE HUMAN PERSON

Dementia is not a specific disease but a condition of disordered and diminished intellectual functioning, usually involving disorientation, impaired memory, confused thinking, disturbed speech, defective judgment, emotional instability and (later) apathy, and erosion of self-awareness. These deficiencies, most often progressive, can result from a wide variety of underlying diseases and disorders of the brain, having a wide variety of causes— traumatic, toxic, metabolic, vascular, degenerative. The dementias of old age are largely of two types, though with possible overlap: the dementia caused by vascular disease (so-called multi-infarct dementia, the result of multiple small strokes) and the dementia caused by Alzheimer's disease. Because its incidence is rising rapidly as our society ages, and because it generates the most personal anxiety and public disquiet, we shall concentrate on Alzheimer's disease. But many of the implications for caregiving apply equally well for persons suffering from the other dementias and, indeed, from other forms of frailty that afflict the elderly.

The assault on a person's mental faculties brought on by Alzheimer's disease is insidious in onset and slowly but implacably progressive in character. It usually runs a course from onset to death of about 6 to 10 years, though it may last up to twice as long. In its early phase, the symptoms are mild and only modestly impairing. But as it advances, slowly and with no particularly defined signposts of its progress, essentially all aspects of human mental capacity are first disordered and then destroyed, with the patient at the end bedfast, helpless, and mute. It is a distressing condition to witness and a frightening one in prospect.*

Alzheimer's disease is one of the most common mental disorders, making up some 20 percent of patients in psychiatric hospitals and a far higher percentage of patients in nursing homes and assisted living facilities. Because the diagnosis cannot be definitively established save by autopsy, it is difficult to get accurate numbers for incidence (rate of new cases per year) and prevalence (total number of cases at a given time) of the disease. Still, almost all estimates indicate that both incidence and prevalence are increasing, and rapidly, in parallel with the rapid growth in the numbers of people living into their seventies, eighties, and nineties. Although the personal risk of developing Alzheimer's disease in the United States has not changed since Alois Alzheimer first described the illness in 1907, clinicians are seeing more new cases each year because Americans are living long enough to develop the disease.

---

* Very few other dementia illnesses are exactly like Alzheimer's disease. There is as yet no "biologic marker" identifiable during life, and only evidence from brain tissue can confirm a clinical diagnosis. However, in the 1980s a working group from the National Institutes of Health developed clinical criteria with which the diagnosis can be made with 85 to 90 percent accuracy (McKhann, G., et al., "Clinical Diagnosis of Alzheimer's Disease," *Neurology* 34(7): 939-944, 1984 and Tierney, M. C., et al., "The NINCDS-ADRDA Work Group Criteria for the Clincial Diagnosis of Probable Alzheimer's Disease," *Neurology* 38(3): 359-364, 1988). This achievement has been invaluable for epidemiologic studies (documenting the prevalence of Alzheimer's disease in the population) and for research purposes (identifying with confidence patients with Alzheimer's disease for closer analysis and clinical research).

Estimates vary as to the number of individuals affected by Alzheimer's disease, but all studies concur that risk increases with age. Estimates of the prevalence of Alzheimer's disease in the United States for the year 2000 range from 2.17 to 4.78 million cases;[34] [35] 4.5 million is the figure cited by the Alzheimer's Association.[36] Among persons 85 and over (4.86 million in 2004[37]), almost 40 percent (1.8 million) may be affected.[38] Assuming no major breakthroughs in treatment that would delay incidence or retard disease progression, estimates of future prevalence (in 2050) are about fourfold the 2000 rate. And even with new treatment modalities that might slow the onset of the disease, none of the projections expects less than a three-fold rise in prevalence in 2050.[39]

A. The Phases of Alzheimer's Disease

The typical course of Alzheimer's disease can be roughly divided into three phases of increasing severity and disability. Patients begin with barely noticeable lapses in "recent memory" (the memory of immediate events). This memory deficit—first recognized perhaps only by a tendency to repeat comments or questions—increases over time to disorientation and confusion. This confusion may provoke occasional but very distressing emotional reactions of bewilderment and anger, dubbed "catastrophic reactions," that frighten both patient and family. Many mental capacities, however, are retained in this first phase, which usually lasts two to four years. The basic personalities of the individuals remain intact and they can enjoy many of life's experiences. Even as their friends and family look with fear for the future, they also notice how engaged the afflicted individuals can often be in daily events.

As the cognitive decline worsens, the disorder enters a second phase of another two or three years, marked by a progressive collapse of language functions (word finding, reading, and writing) and difficulties in manual skills (dressing, eating, and personal care). The patients now tend to wander, becoming lost even in familiar neighborhoods as their disorientation and confusion worsens. They often become preoccupied with suspicions aroused usually by mistakes of comprehension and attribution, but also by hallucinations and delusions. These suspicions lead to more severe emotional outbursts and, sometimes, physical aggression. A depression can emerge and become a crippling and persisting state of mind. And as the disruptions of affect, thought, language, and manual skills alter all their relationships with others, patients begin to fail at recognizing friends and family and seem to be fading out of contact with others.

In the third and final stage, the disorder takes the form of loss of control of bodily functions and motor powers. Walking becomes impossible, soon followed by generalized paralysis, confinement to bed, and incontinence of bladder and bowel function. Within a year or two, the patients sink into a state of relative mutism and unresponsiveness, neglecting all external stimuli or inner needs and their continuing existence depends entirely on nursing care. They eventually die from inanition or some intercurrent infection such as aspiration pneumonia.*

This basic description of the clinical course emphasizes the growing losses of mental capacity that lead inexorably to the fading away of the self—a phenomenon distressing to witness and, for many patients early in their disease, distressing to experience. But the sense of "curse" now evoked by the very name, "Alzheimer's," overlooks the fact that patients—especially in the first phase—often have much to enjoy in life, even as much is lost. And these pleasures ("smelling the roses" is a useful shorthand)—perhaps becoming more momentary and transient over time—extend even into later stages, as patients wander in and

---

* Several clinical features help differentiate the Alzheimer's course from other forms of dementia and cognitive disablement. First, there are no abrupt neurological events such as occur with cerebrovascular strokes that can produce multi-infarct dementia. Alzheimer's disease advances slowly and smoothly, problems with memory and other psychological capacities dominate much of its course, and motor and sensory symptoms such as paralysis do not appear until the terminal phase. Second, the psychological impairments are global rather than specific to memory or language alone. Detailed psychological testing will often show this global feature even in the early stage when only the memory seems disturbed. Third, consciousness in the sense of awareness and wakefulness is also unaffected for most of the course. Indeed, many observers of a patient note how he or she retains much of their usual personality and interpersonal "style" even as the analytic reasoning power is lost. This feature is quite different from the states of mind associated with the intoxications from kidney or liver failure.

out of relative lucidity. Many doctors and nurses find great reward in caring for these patients and their families. Clinical efforts to treat symptoms of depression and delusion, to offer friendly social and occupational therapy, and to simplify and regularize daily routines produce much comfort and reassuring support for patients while they are still able to appreciate many of life's simple pleasures. Yet the truth remains that Alzheimer's disease is a most distressing human affliction in which almost all that is vital to human character and dignity is gradually lost, but for which certain forms of care, discussed below, can bring great benefits to both patient and families.

B. Cause and Remedy

The symptoms of Alzheimer's are caused by a generalized disease of the brain, characterized by loss of neurons and resulting atrophy of the cerebral hemispheres, especially in the frontal, temporal, and parietal lobes. Extreme atrophy of the hippocampus is uniformly characteristic, accounting for the early and severe memory loss typical of all patients. Eventually, though, the atrophy becomes generalized; at time of death, the brain has shrunken by more than 20 percent of its original volume. On microscopic examination, three identifiable pathologic changes are characteristic: (1) "amyloid plaques," extra-cellular deposits of accumulated beta-amyloid, an amorphous, insoluble, protein substance, surrounded by bits of degenerated nerve fibers; (2) "neurofibrillary tangles," diffusely distributed, shrunken neurons that are filled with thickened tangled fibers; and (3) "granulovacuolar" degeneration, which affects other neurons, particularly within the hippocampus. These pathologic changes in the brain advance steadily and correlate with the progressing severity of the patient's dementia.

The underlying causes of Alzheimer's disease are complex, with both genetic and environmental factors playing a role. But recent biochemical studies on the plaques and neurofibrillary tangles have led to a reasonably detailed hypothesis regarding the sequence of pathogenetic steps that lead ultimately to neuronal death, atrophy, and clinical dementia.* And this hypothesis is now directing intense scientific investigation in search of measures that could prevent, interrupt, or retard the pathological process that produces the plaques and tangles. For the first time, scientists are hopeful of finding interventions that could interfere with the pathogenic processes in ways that might make radical correction and even prevention possible.

At this time, therapeutic approaches are of three types: treatment of symptoms, replacement therapies, and experimental efforts aimed at interrupting the pathogenic process. Symptomatic treatments seek to help patients and families with the growing disability brought by the disease. They begin with aids to memory and orientation that regularly remind the patient of the present time and place and ultimately extend to protective services to help patients who wander or get lost, to nursing services for dilapidating self-care, and to the management (with medications) of some of the symptomatic depressions, hallucinations, seizures and the like that come with the progress of the condition.†

---

* Here is the hypothesis and its biochemical foundation. The plaques consist largely of beta-amyloid protein (containing 40 or 42 amino acids), produced by the normal turnover of a structural transmembrane protein in brain cells (APP, for "beta-amyloid precursor protein") that may have receptor functions. The neurofibrillary tangles are masses of helically wound filaments, which are tangled and thickened because they represent the aggregation of an insoluble pathologic form of a normally highly soluble, cytoskeletal protein called "tau." The "cascade" hypothesis for the pathogenesis of Alzheimer's disease draws these biochemical observations into a powerful explanatory idea. This hypothesis holds that the very gradual extra-cellular accumulation (either through over-production or slower clearance) of the beta-amyloid protein—particularly the 42-amino acid form—is in theory toxic to cerebral neurons and their synaptic connections. Accordingly, the beta-amyloid protein could generate (by several mechanisms still under study) a response in the neurons that leads (among other things) to the intra-cellular (intra-neuronal) appearance of the pathologic form of "tau" and gradual development of the destructive neurofibrillary tangles that disrupt neuronal functioning and lead to neuronal death. (See Dr. Dennis Selkoe's presentation to the Council, June 24, 2004, available online at http://www.bioethics.gov. See also Selkoe, D. J., "Alzheimer Disease: Mechanistic Understanding Predicts Novel Therapies," *Annals of Internal Medicine*, 140(8): 627-638, 2004.)

† Five particular psychic deficits call for symptomatic attention. Amnesia, particularly difficulty retaining immediate happenings, requires repetition and mnemonic

Replacement therapies seek to supply chemical deficiencies caused by the degeneration of neurons, for example, acetyl choline, a stimulating neurotransmitter whose reduced activity in the cerebral cortex correlates roughly with the degree of cognitive impairment in Alzheimer's patients. Medications that slow the breakdown of acetyl choline (by inhibiting acetyl-cholinesterase, the enzyme responsible for its turnover) and thus leave higher levels of this neurotransmitter in synapses have been demonstrated to slow the progress of the disease in some patients in the early first phase often by as much as a year or more.

Still unproven but extremely exciting are experimental trials aimed directly at the pathological process itself, and particularly at the presumptively toxic role of the accumulating beta-amyloid protein. These include measures that could decrease the production of the protein, block its agglutination, or protect the neurons from the toxic effects of its accumulation. Perhaps the most exciting experimental approach is the use of immunization to yield antibodies to beta-amyloid protein, so as to reduce its amount in the brain or to clear it after it has accumulated.*

---

aids. Aphasia or dysphasia, with breakdown in word choice, requires patience and acceptance of circumlocutions. Apraxia, particularly in managing simple manual tasks such as dressing and toileting, requires close management and assistance. Visual and spatial disorientation, including getting lost in familiar places, requires regular support and guidance. And affective disruptions, including episodic outbursts of anger and fright produced by the sense of loss of control or change of routine, are avoided more than treated by maintaining a daily routine and by the reassuring presence of regular caregivers. In addition, depression in the form of demoralized anxiety over the implications of learning the diagnosis afflicts many patients in the earliest phase; here, the reassurance of a committed physician promising continuing care and assistance for the duration of the disease is invaluable and essential. This "demoralization" must be differentiated from a depressive disorder resting on the brain pathology itself, quite frequent in Alzheimer's patients, which typically responds to anti-depressant medications.

* Such "vaccination" against beta-amyloid protein led to an antibody response and the clearing of the beta-amyloid in mutant mice that otherwise accumulated beta-amyloid in their brains. But the early trials in humans ran into difficulties. "Active" immunization of the antigen-antibody variety produced complications of an allergic kind in some patients, so investigators have turned to "passive" immunization by delivering exogenous anti-beta-amyloid antibodies to patients with the disease. This "passive" immunization effort is now undergoing clinical trial in human patients and the results are eagerly awaited.

All of these experimental approaches offer the promise of becoming disease-modifying treatments that could prevent the onset or greatly slow the progress of Alzheimer's disease. If it were possible by one of these means to postpone the onset of the disease beyond the normal lifespan or even for five to ten years, there would be a great reduction in the incidence of the disease and many of those who would get it later than they now do would die first of other causes. This might be especially true if subjects genetically vulnerable to Alzheimer's disease could be recognized before symptoms appear and could be treated with measures to forestall the pathogenetic "cascade." Optimism— long at a premium—is now growing in the research community, where the view is held that within the coming decades apt preventative and rational therapeutics will be found for Alzheimer's disease. Yet at least for the present elderly and the baby boomer generation, there is every reason to believe that Alzheimer's will remain a major public health problem that will persist for decades. Hope for a remedy is fitting; planning ahead based on its rapid arrival is not.

C. Alzheimer's Disease and Human Experience

Humanly speaking, Alzheimer's disease is not just a medical condition, with a biological cause and sociological implications. It is also a lived experience, for the ones who suffer it, for their family and friends, and even for thousands of people who live in fear of getting it. Not long ago, when dementia was less common and its causes were unknown, a case of senile dementia was regarded by family members as part of natural old age ("Dear grandpa has grown old and forgetful") and of no direct concern to their own future. Today, everyone is aware of this now-common disease that sometimes runs in families, lacks effective treatment, and carries a dreaded name; as a consequence, a case of Alzheimer's in the family is often experienced as a terrifying or stigmatizing curse. People feel themselves at risk of following the dreadful path they witnessed in parents or grandparents, and many of them notice fearfully every clumsy mental process they display after age 50, thinking it a harbinger of their fate. The differentiation of Alzheimer's disease by name has successfully launched effective and focused research enterprises, but it has done so at the price of human disquiet and even terror, often inducing depression in the "worried well," and sometimes even leading them to suicide.

The actual human experience of the disease itself varies greatly, depending in part on the person's character and temperament, in part on the progress of the disease. Many patients develop symptoms so imperceptibly and gradually that, by the time someone brings them for evaluation and the diagnosis is made, they are already sufficiently impaired that they worry little about their future. They are bothered rather by their present handicaps and especially by the restrictions imposed on them, such as loss of independence or revoking of driving privileges. But many people who come to doctors seeking an explanation of their new mental impairments are already worried about the import of their symptoms and are quite able to appreciate the prognostically grim diagnosis. Individuals typically respond according to their habitual ways of confronting bad situations. Those with broad horizons and calm demeanors might look similarly at this problem and seek to reassure their loved ones and themselves that they are equipped to manage what comes. Those fortunate enough to have a trusted physician who promises to stay with them all the way through the illness might gain some comfort and reassurance. Such support is, alas, unavailable to very many people, who lack either a caring family or a trusted physician, or both.

But for many, the uncertainty of their future is the most distressing feature. Those who have habitually fought uncertainty by seeking always to be in control will likely attempt a similar mastering stance against this situation. But as they confront their loss of control and their impotence to correct it, they can become the most distressed of patients. They are particularly susceptible to the urgings of those who advocate euthanasia and assisted suicide. Many do in fact become despondent and dangerous to themselves, and some contemplate suicide and occasionally succeed in the effort. Men are more likely than women to take desperate action. Women are more likely to become apathetically depressed. A kind, thoughtful, and experienced physician can often bring a more detached sort of support to this kind of patient than worried family members can. Indeed, many of these desperate patients respond well to anti-depressant medications and throw off their depression and their suicidal thoughts; with the anti-depressant treatment their cognition can for a time improve considerably.*

With the advance of the disease, the patients' long-term worries about prognosis are replaced by distress associated with their confusion and occasional suspicions. They have trouble making themselves understood; they cannot communicate what is bothering them. Here, as mentioned, considerable comfort is brought when their daily schedule or rounds of activity are routinized to minimize surprises, and they are frequently reminded of the daily plan. Medications can help calm patients, but if not used sparingly they can also undermine efforts to engage patients in occupational therapy, daily exercise, or other stimulating activities. With new nursing practices that emphasize cheerful and responsive environments, patients often do better in skilled nursing facilities than they do at home, and certainly better than they once did under the restrain-and-restrict-them approach of the old nursing homes. Ultimately, with the loss of all mental functions, however, patients fall further away from human interaction, becoming quite apathetic and absolutely dependent on nursing care. Yet even in their largely apathetic state, they can often recognize and appreciate the kindness shown to them and the affection represented in the visits and responses of family.

While the fear of Alzheimer's disease afflicts mainly the worried well and some of those in the early stages of the disease, the psychic distress caused by the disease often falls more heavily on loving family members than on the patients themselves, especially as the disease progresses. Paradoxically but mercifully, a patient's subjective suffering frequently diminishes as his mental diminishment worsens. The reverse is generally the case with the

---

* A crucial matter of differential diagnosis with middle-aged and elderly patients is that severe depressive illness can slow cognition severely all by itself. All neuropsychiatrists have seen patients believed to have Alzheimer's disease turn out to be afflicted by a recurrence of a depressive illness that, in attacks, had been seen earlier in their life but that on this occasion was misidentified (and thus long untreated) as Alzheimer's. Suicide in these depressed and misdiagnosed patients is also not rare.

family. As the patient fades from meaningful contact, the family's sorrow over what is being lost increases; such distress is often held at bay only because time and effort needed for the increased demands of care do not allow for such reflective "indulgences."

Alzheimer's disease is not the worst human affliction, nor is it the only condition that oppresses the frail and feeble elderly. But its special character—attacking not only the capacities that are central to a flourishing human life but also the existence of a self-knowing consciousness—creates its own special difficulties, first for the patients, eventually for the onlookers. True, in the early stages of the disease, reflective patients will suffer from looking ahead to a future that is at once utterly uncertain and utterly determined, a future before which those who like to be in control will feel enormously discomfited. They will feel the frustrations of failing to find the right words, of misremembering, of getting lost. But the more the disease progresses, the more the sadness resides with the family. The depression, the outbursts, the loss of self-command, the disappearance of civilizing inhibitions, the incontinence, and the inability to recognize or interact with loved ones tear at the heart of spouses, children, and friends. It is not easy to love in the same way a person who both is and is not really there.

Even those who believe in the redemptive power of suffering have a hard time saying anything good about a condition that renders the sufferer impervious to gaining any insight or improvement from his troubles and burdens. And at the end, there is no possibility for farewells, for reconciliations, for anything more than the harsh reality of death modified by a relief that the ordeal is finally over. Despite these hardships, many loving families continue to care for those who have been given to them to love—loyally, steadfastly, often heroically and without much outside support—continuing to benefit as best they can the life that the person they love still has. It is no wonder that this activity takes its toll, both mental and physical, on the family caregivers, many of whom are often quite elderly and infirm themselves and many of whom become depressed or sick in other ways during what can be up to a decade of giving care.

Generalizations, of course, are always risky. As with the patients, so different families will cope differently with their calling to care, depending on temperaments and character, previous patterns of family closeness and mutual assistance, and available economic resources and social support. Families that have ever felt close and supportive will be ready to do their utmost to care. Not only devoted spouses, but also adult children of an affected parent often take on the task of long-term care. Here the sense of loss can be partially offset by a sense of satisfaction derived from the giving of needed care, as well as from honoring the commitment to maintain the dignity and modesty of the patient as much as possible through the illness and its depredations.

Occasionally, however, this sense of commitment can develop into a guilt-ridden urge to do and give more than is reasonable or to protect the patient against all change. Guilt and stress afflict even the most devoted, strong, and resourceful families, who today frequently find themselves in a bind, especially when adult women try to care for their enfeebled parents or in-laws while holding down jobs and caring for their own small children. The decision to move Mom from her home into an assisted living facility, or Dad from the spare room in our house to the nursing home is, for such families, a wrenching decision, and the sense of betrayal that devoted spouses and offspring feel on such occasions is often much to their credit. But when home caregiving threatens the basic well-being of the rest of the family, institutional care often becomes the wisest choice under bad circumstances. Attentive physicians and social service providers can help the family weather all stages of the decline by advice, encouragement, medical interventions, and the recruitment of support services for the patient and respite-care for the caregivers.

Finally, there are the decisions that must be made, ranging from simple matters such as the use of ancillary medications to weighty choices such as the use of "heroic measures" or life-sustaining remedies. Choices that were simple and obvious early in the course become more problematic as the disease worsens, and ultimately heart-wrenching in their implications in the terminal phase. Close contacts between a devoted physician, other professional caregivers, and the caregiving family can help family members make their decisions conscientiously and thoughtfully, with due regard for the life reaching the end of this grim illness.

But no one should pretend that this is anything but anguishing for almost everyone involved.

IV. AGING AND THE COMMON GOOD

Looking broadly, we seem to be on the cusp of an historically unprecedented situation, both in the degree of care that elderly individuals will need and in the proportion of society's resources that will have to be devoted to such care. Medicine's success in combating many acute illnesses has enabled us to live long enough to suffer from various age-related chronic illnesses. For many, longer, healthier life is enjoyed at the price of longer, later periods of enfeeblement and disability. At the same time, our preoccupation with individual self-fulfillment has weakened many intergenerational attachments, and the privileged place of gainful employment and career advancement in our notions of self-worth has diminished the time available for and the value we place on caregiving.

It was one thing to say that families should be responsible for care of their aged relatives in an historical period when life expectancy was 60 or 70 years of age and the period of dependency was limited. But it is quite another when a period of dementia could stretch out ten years, the last five of which require nonstop nursing care. Moreover, the old social system that took care of aged family members was dependent largely on the uncompensated labor of women; there are extremely few families today that could provide this level of support (by modern standards) without help from other social institutions or social programs. And, as we have seen, many families are struggling, especially women, who continue to bear the greatest burden of care for the elderly, while also in many cases providing for growing children and working outside the home in order to help make ends meet.

We cannot pretend that either families or society as a whole will have unlimited resources, particularly as the age structure of our population continues to change, with more elderly persons and fewer young workers. We will have to make hard choices between competing goods, both as families and as a nation. For example: Should Medicare continue to cover every expensive new medical technology, and if not, on what basis should the public set limits? Should families accept inferior professional care for treasured elders to ensure adequate resources to buy a home or send children to college? Should we mandate that individuals with an annual income above a certain threshold purchase long-term care insurance in order to socialize the risk of dependence? These are not questions that we can address in substantive detail in this inquiry. But they are the kinds of questions that we must keep in mind as we think about the ethics of caregiving for those elders who need it, including the ethical dilemmas of deciding when to continue and when to forgo medical treatment for persons with dementia (the main subject of the analysis that follows). As we think about the meaning of aging and the moral dilemmas that arise at the bedside, we cannot ignore the practical realities that arise for society as a whole or the need to articulate and pursue some shared vision of the common good.

Of course, it is always best to state one's aspirations in the positive, in terms of what we hope to achieve—such as a society where aging has meaning, where death seems like the fitting conclusion to a life well-lived, and where we help one another from generation to generation. But there is also a wisdom in seeing clearly what we hope to avoid, especially in situations where perfection is impossible and where some hardship is inevitable. And here three points seem worth stressing in relation to aging and the common good.

First, we must avoid two errors or extremes: On the one hand, we must erect firm and permanent safeguards against certain inhuman "solutions" to the challenges of caring for the dependent elderly—such as active euthanasia or the promotion of assisted suicide, solutions that define a category of persons as "life unworthy of life" or as persons deserving of abandonment and beyond the scope of our care. On the other hand, we must avoid allowing long-term care for the elderly and medical care in general to crowd out every other civic good—such as educating the young, promoting human excellence in the arts and beyond, and providing for our common defense. We must never betray our elders, but we must also recognize that we cannot (and should not) always do everything conceivable on their behalf.

Second, we must avoid two crises of caregiving: The first is the danger that some old people will be abandoned or impoverished, with no one to care for them, no advocate to stand with them, and inadequate resources to provide for themselves. The second danger is the complete transformation of caregiving into labor, creating a situation where people's basic physical needs are efficiently provided for by "workers," but their deeper human and spiritual needs are largely ignored, because those with the closest ties are unable or unwilling to be with them.

Finally, we must avoid (or to some degree reverse) the full-scale medicalization of old age, both in our outlook and in our institutions. We increasingly see old age as both a bundle of needs and problems demanding solution and as a time of life whose meaning is largely given in terms of being and staying healthy and fit. This outlook has created discontent with the life-cycle itself, produced an insatiable desire for more and more medical miracles, created the illusion that we can transcend our limitations and that death itself may be pushed back indefinitely. More deeply, this outlook has engendered, at least in some individuals, the illusion that independence is in fact the whole truth about our lives, without giving full regard to those attachments and obligations that bind and complete us. We do not beget or rear ourselves, and neither do our children. At every stage of life, we belong together, in sickness as in health. Forgetfulness of these truths quickly converts independence into loneliness, especially for the old.

In the end, there is no "solution" to the problem of aging, at least no solution that a civilized society could ever tolerate. Rather, our task is to do the best we can with the world as it is, improving what we can but especially avoiding as much as possible the greatest evils and miseries of living with old age: namely, the temptation of betrayal, the illusion of perpetual youth, the despair of frailty, and the loneliness of aging and dying alone. In the chapters that follow we will attempt to begin this task, first, by outlining shortcomings in the current approach and then by sketching an ethics of best care for the patient now here.

ENDNOTES

[1] Manton, K. G. and Gu, X. L., "Changes in the Prevalence of Chronic Disability in the United States Black and Nonblack Population Above Age 65 from 1982 to 1999," *Proceedings of the National Academy of Sciences of the United States of America* 98: 6354-6359, 2001.

[2] *Health, United States, 2004*, Center for Disease Control/National Center for Health Statistics, table 27.

[3] Hogan, C., et al., *A Statistical Profile of Decedents in the Medicare Program*, Washington, DC: Medicare Payment Advisory Commission, 2000. Available online at http://www.cdc.gov/nchs/hus.html.

[4] "Getting Older, Staying Healthier: The Demographics of Health Care," Testimony of James Lubitz, Acting Chief, Aging and Chronic Diseases, Statistics Branch, National Center for Health Statistics, Centers for Disease Control and Prevention, before the Joint Economic Committee, U.S. Senate, July 22, 2004. Available online at http://jec.senate.gov/_files/Lubitztestimony.pdf.

[5] *Older Americans 2004: Key Indicators of Well-Being*, Federal Interagency Forum on Aging-Related Statistics. Available online at http://www.agingstats.gov.

[6] U. S. Census Bureau, 2005, *Estimates of the Resident Population by Selected Age Groups for the United States and States and for Puerto Rico: July 1, 2004*. Available online at http://www.census.gov/popest/states/asrh/SC-est2004-01.html.

[7] U.S. Census Bureau, 2004, *U.S. Interim Projections by Age, Sex, Race, and Hispanic Origin*, Table 2a, "Projected Population of the United States, by Age and Sex: 2000 to 2050." Available online at http://www.census.gov/ipc/www/usinterimproj.

[8] U.S. Bureau of the Census, *Census Population Reports*, P25-1130 (Middle Series of Projections), as quoted in Enid Kassner and Robert W. Bectel, *Midlife and Older Americans with Disabilities: Who Gets Help? A Chartbook*, AARP Public Policy Institute, 1998, p. 7.

[9] Alzheimer's Association, "Statistics about Alzheimer's Disease," http://www.alz.org/AboutAD/statistics.asp (accessed August 24, 2005).

[10] U.S. Census Bureau, 2005, *State Interim Population Projections by Age and Sex: 2004–2030*, Table 3, "Ranking of States by Projected Percent of Population Age 65 and Over: 2000, 2010, and 2030." Available online at http://www.census.gov/population/www/projections/projectionsagesex.html.

[11] Steuerle, C. E., and Van de Water, P., "Long-Run Budget Projections and Their Implications for Funding Elderly Entitlements," in Altman, S., and Shactman, D., eds., *Policies for an Aging Society*, Baltimore, MD: Johns Hopkins University Press, 2002, p. 82.

[12] "Chronic Conditions: Making the Case for Ongoing Care," September 2004 update, Johns Hopkins University Partnership for Solutions, http://www.rwjf.org/files/research/ChronicConditionsChartbook 9-2004.ppt (accessed August 24, 2005).

13 Binstock, R., Case Western Reserve University, presentation to the President's Council on Bioethics, Washington, D.C., June 24, 2004, available online at http://www.bioethics.gov.
14 Lynn, J., *Sick to Death And Not Going to Take It Anymore!* Berkeley, CA: University of California Press, 2004, p. 13.
15 Ibid., p. 21.
16 Lynn, J. and Adamson, D. M., "Living Well at the End of Life: Adapting Health Care to Chronic Illness in Old Age," Rand Corporation White Paper, 2003, p. 5.
17 Ibid., p. 9.
18 National Family Caregivers Association. 2000 "How Many Caregivers Are in the U.S.?" Available online at http://www.thefamilycaregiver.org/who/comp_survey.cfm (accessed August 24, 2005).
19 Administration On Aging. 2003. "Family Caregiving." Available online at http://www.aoa.gov (accessed August 24, 2005).
20 Lynn, *Sick to Death*, p. 15, citing Kassner and Bectel, *Midlife and Older Americans with Disabilities.* (For the latter, see endnote 8.)
21 National Family Caregivers Association, "Caregiving Statistics," http://www.thefamilycaregiver.org/who/stats.cfm (accessed August 24, 2005).
22 Schulz, R., and Beach, S. R., "Caregiving as a Risk Factor for Mortality: The Caregiver Health Effects Study," *Journal of the American Medical Association* 282: 2215-2219 (1999); Kiecolt-Glaser, J. K., et al., "Chronic Stress Alters the Immune Response to Influenza Virus Vaccine in Older Adults," *Proceedings of the National Academy of Sciences of the United States of America* 93: 3043-3047 (1996).
23 National Aging Information Center, *Aging In The Twenty-first Century*, U.S. Administration on Aging. Washington, DC: Government Printing Office, 1996.
24 Institute for Health and Aging, University of California, San Francisco, *Chronic Care in America: A Twenty-First Century Challenge*. Princeton, NJ: Robert Wood Johnson Foundation, 1996.
25 Hooyman, N. R. and Kiyak, H. A., *Social Gerontology*, Boston, MA: Allyn and Bacon, 1996.
26 Feldman, P. H., "Labor Market Issues in Home Care" in Fox, D. M. and Raphael, C. eds., *Home-Based Care for a New Century*, Malden, MA: Blackwell Publishers, 1997.
27 National Council of State Boards of Nursing (2002) National Council Licensure Examination-Registered Nurse/Practical Nurse (NCLEX-RN and NCLEX-PN) examination statistics. Statistics from years 1995-2002.
28 American Hospital Association. June 2001. "TrendWatch." Available online at http://www.hospitalconnect.com/ahapolicyforum/trendwatch/twjune2001.html (accessed August 22, 2005).
29 May, W. F., "The Virtues and Vices of the Elderly" in Cole, T.R. and Gadow, S., eds, *What Does It Mean To Grow Old?: Reflections from the Humanities*, Durham, N.C.: Duke University Press, 1950, p. 50.
30 Ibid., pp. 51-61.
31 Moody, H. R., *Aging: Concepts and Controversies*, Thousand Oaks, CA: Pine Forge Press, 2002, p. 4.
32 May, "The Virtues and Vices of the Elderly," pp. 56-57.

[33] Cicero, *De Senectute* [On Old Age], Harvard Classics, Paragraph 8. http://www.bartleby.com/9/2/1.html (accessed August 24, 2005).

[34] Grant, W. B. "Year 2000 Prevalence of Alzheimer Disease in the United States" *Archives of Neurology*, 61: 802-803, 2004; author reply 803.

[35] Hebert, L. E., et al., "Alzheimer Disease in the US Population: Prevalence Estimates Using the 2000 Census" *Archives of Neurology* 60: 1119-1122, 2003.

[36] Alzheimer's Association website.

[37] US Census Bureau, July 1, 2004 estimates.

[38] See Hebert et al., 2003, *op. cit.*

[39] Sloane, P. D., et al., "The Public Health Impact of Alzheimer's Disease, 2000-2050: Potential Implication of Treatment Advances," *Annual Reviews of Public Health* 23: 213-231, 2002.

2

The Limited Wisdom of Advance Directives

As the American population ages, the dilemmas and obligations of making caregiving decisions for incapacitated patients—including decisions about when to initiate, forgo, or cease potentially life-sustaining treatments—will only become more widespread and more acute. As we described in the previous chapter, more people will experience longer periods of dependence, including years of mental incapacitation. Deciding the best course of medical care during this extended period of debility will typically fall to surrogates—including family members and friends, health care professionals and social workers, and sometimes state guardians called upon to speak for those without proxies or courts called upon to adjudicate cases in which surrogates disagree. If we fail to think ahead about what we want done and what we owe to those who can no longer speak for themselves, we are more likely to make the necessary decisions in a state of excessive confusion and crisis. But if we plan ahead thoughtlessly or unwisely, we may in fact hamper efforts, when the time arrives, to provide the kind of care that we will then need and deserve.

In the United States, our effort to think ahead about caregiving for incapacitated persons has taken shape mainly around the legal instrument of advance directives—both "instruction directives" that aim to dictate how one should be cared for and "proxy directives" that appoint others to make or execute caregiving decisions.* Advance directives came into existence at a particular time in our recent history, when people began to worry that the healer's art on which we all rely to make life better could also be used in ways that seemed ambiguous or even harmful.

---

* "Living wills," about which we will speak at length, are a formal kind of advance instruction directive in which treatment preferences and instructions are put in writing.

People worried especially that life-sustaining medical technologies might keep them alive for too long in what they perceived to be an undignified state, unrewarding to themselves and excessively burdensome to their loved ones. More generally, people worried that decisions might be made without sufficient regard to their own wishes and welfare. Advance directives were created as a way to alleviate these concerns.

A series of high-profile court cases, from the *Quinlan* case of 1976 to the *Cruzan* case of 1990, gave further credence to the value of leaving explicit instructions in advance about future treatment preferences, to be followed should one become incapacitated, and of formally designating a trusted surrogate to make medical decisions on one's behalf should one no longer be able to decide for oneself. A consensus seemed to emerge, formally ratified in the federal Patient Self-Determination Act of 1990, that widespread completion of advance directives is the best way to ensure that medical care of the incapacitated near the end of life will conform to the wishes and protect the interests of the patient. More recently, the Schiavo case has led to renewed calls for living wills: If only she had made her treatment preferences clear in advance, some argued, everyone might have been spared the wrenching decisions, bitter court battles, and national drama that ensued.

Of course, the Schiavo case—involving sudden injury to a young person, leading to a persistent vegetative state—is hardly paradigmatic of the social and ethical challenge facing our society. Vastly more typical is the patient suffering the gradual, degenerative decline toward incompetence and physical vulnerability associated with Alzheimer's disease and other dementias. It is primarily for such persons that the value of advance directives has been especially urged. And yet, studies indicate that only a small percentage of Americans actually have formal advance directives, and those that exist are often vague or limited. Thus, in most cases, the burden of decision-making for incapacitated elderly patients still falls on caregivers making contemporaneous decisions. This should not be surprising. Indeed, as we will indicate, in most cases, it will be inevitable.

Our goal in this chapter is to evaluate the wisdom and limits of advance directives—both instruction directives and proxy directives—building on the extensive work of numerous social scientists, legal scholars, medical experts, and bioethicists who have studied the subject in recent years.* We seek not only to gauge the effectiveness of advance directives in practice, but also to reflect on the broader significance of this approach to aging and caregiving.

We state the conclusion in advance: The need to make decisions on behalf of others will only become more complicated as the American population ages; and it is misleading to think that, through wider use of living wills, competent persons will be able to direct their own care simply by leaving detailed instructions in advance. In fact, the evidence suggests that this "solution" to the problem of caregiving in an aging society is not only unrealistic but in several respects undesirable. Despite years of urging, most Americans do not have living wills, either because they would rather not think about their own dependence and death, or because they are wise enough to know that aging and dying sometimes mean placing oneself in the care of others. Not only are living wills unlikely to achieve their own stated goals, but those goals themselves are open to question. Living wills make autonomy and self-determination the primary values at a time of life when one is no longer autonomous or self-determining, and when what one needs is loyal and loving care. This paradox is at the heart of the trouble with this approach to caregiving.

This does not mean that advance directives or advance care planning are useless or unnecessary. Proxy directives serve the wise and helpful purpose of putting one's trust explicitly in the hands of loved ones who rightly bear the burden of providing care and making decisions. And advance care planning—not only

---

* A list of these works appears in the Thematic Bibliography in the Appendix. We rely especially on two essays: one by Angela Fagerlin and Carl Schneider, "Enough: The Failure of the Living Will," *Hastings Center Report* 34(2), March-April 2004, pp. 30-42, the other by Council Member Rebecca Dresser, "Precommitment: A Misguided Strategy for Securing Death with Dignity," 81 *Texas Law Review* 1823, June 2003. We rely also on Prof. Schneider's presentation to the Council on this topic, December 2, 2004 (transcript available online at http://www.bioethics.gov).

about treatment preferences but also about housing arrangements and long-term care options—is a wise way to come to terms with the possibility of one's own future dependence, at a stage of life when one can still participate in such planning. But in the end, no legal instrument can substitute for wise and loving choices, made on the spot, when the precise treatment dilemma is clear and care decisions are needed. Proxy directives can appoint decisionmakers, but only ethical reflection and prudent judgment can guide them at the bedside. And advance care planning can help prevent future decisions from being made in ignorance or in crisis. But such planning should always aim at providing the best care possible for the patient as he or she might be in the future, which means providing care for a person whose precise needs can never *fully* be known at the time such advance planning occurs.

We acknowledge at the outset that even the most passionate advocates for living wills, the major focus of the analysis that follows, do not see these legal instruments as sufficient in themselves to address the needs of long-term care for those who suffer from age-related debility and dementia. But living wills serve as an example—perhaps a defining example—of how our society tends to approach the question of caregiving for the incapacitated, including and especially those with dementia. Seeing the limits of this legal approach clarifies the need for the kind of ethical approach that we offer in Chapters 3 and 4. Our critical analysis of advance directives is thus a prelude to the positive ethical guidelines that follow, focused not simply on discerning or executing an incompetent person's prior wishes but on providing the best care possible for the person now placed in our care.

I. DEFINING KEY TERMS

In order to understand and evaluate advance directives more fully, we first need to define some key terms more precisely:

THE LIMITED WISDOM OF ADVANCE DIRECTIVES | 57

Advance treatment directives are written or oral declarations by individuals capable of making informed and voluntary medical decisions. These declarations aim at shaping future care decisions if and when the individual loses the capacity for independent choice. Advance treatment directive (or just "advance directive") is an umbrella term that encompasses both "instruction directives" and "proxy directives."

Instruction directives are written or oral statements expressing a person's actual treatment preferences. Instruction directives can be quite specific, offering detailed descriptions of the medical interventions a person would want administered or withheld in different health situations. More often, they contain general statements, reflecting the person's basic values, about the considerations that should guide those at the bedside.

Living wills are *written* instruction directives. The earliest living wills typically expressed the person's wish not to receive "heroic" or "extraordinary" measures if death was "imminent." Later versions moved away from these vague terms and gave people the opportunity to refuse specific medical interventions, such as resuscitation, respirator care, antibiotics, or medical nutrition and hydration. Later versions were also designed to allow individuals to *request*, as well as refuse, particular types of treatment. Many living wills use standard legal forms that individuals can easily fill out at the direction of an attorney; others involve extensive narrative statements about one's personal values and treatment preferences.

Because relatively few people go through the formalities of completing a written advance directive, oral statements are the most common instruction directives available to caregivers. Relatives and clinicians sometimes consider a person's past remarks about the kind of treatments or quality of life that would be acceptable as relevant information in making medical decisions on that person's behalf. Like written instruction directives, oral directives vary in specificity and precision. They can also be more difficult to evaluate because the seriousness of the speaker's intent is not always obvious. For example, statements made in response to watching a film or visiting an ailing relative may or may not be well considered, and their significance for future caregiving decisions is often hard to judge.

Proxy directives, frequently called "health care powers of attorney," may also be written or oral. People making a proxy directive designate someone they trust to make medical decisions on their behalf and to act as their representative if they become incapacitated. People who would prefer one relative over another or a friend over a family member as their representative can use proxy directives to give effect to their preferences. Appointing a formal proxy can be especially valuable if a patient has no close family members, if the patient's relatives are dispersed, or if relatives disagree among themselves.

The two types of directives may be combined in a form that both sets forth the individual's instructions about future care and designates a proxy to cope with the actual treatment situations that later arise.*

II. THE EMERGENCE OF ADVANCE DIRECTIVES IN POLICY AND LAW

Advance directives cannot be understood in the abstract, separate from the specific context in which they emerged or the legal and public policy environment in which they now operate. Viewed historically, advance directives originated largely as a response to novel clinical circumstances, in which more and more people whose basic mental and physical capacities had been permanently lost due to illness or injury could be kept alive for extended periods by medical intervention. Many people feared living indefinitely on machines in a profoundly diminished condition. They worried about burdening loved ones, existing as mere

---

* Other terms that have been used in court cases regarding end-of-life decisions for incompetent persons, "substituted judgment" and "best interests" standards, will be defined and discussed in the next section.

shells of their former selves, or bankrupting their family with the costs of long-term care. In response, people sought means to restrict the kinds of medical interventions they would accept should they become incapacitated, or to appoint trusted surrogates to make medical decisions armed with the necessary legal authority to forgo or stop unwanted interventions.

Legal thinkers had a major role in promoting advance directives. A lawyer, Luis Kutner, described an early version of the living will in 1969. Expressing concern about medicine's increasing ability to prolong life in what he called "a state of indefinite vegetated animation," he suggested a written document for people seeking to avoid this fate.[1] By preparing such a document, individuals could register in advance their consent to or refusal of proposed future treatments if and when they were unable to engage in independent decision-making. Kutner offered the living will as a device that would allow people to express religious or other beliefs relevant to medical care and would protect clinicians from potential liability for withholding or withdrawing life-sustaining interventions.

During the 1970s, state legislatures and courts began to extend formal legal recognition to advance treatment decision-making. In 1976, California became the first of many states to enact a law designed to allow "natural death" or "death with dignity." The California Natural Death Act declared that adult patients had the right to decide about life-sustaining medical procedures, including the right "to make a written directive instructing [their] physician to withhold or withdraw life-sustaining procedures in the event of a terminal condition."[2] The directive would take effect if patients became unable to communicate their contemporaneous views on life-sustaining interventions.

The first judicial support for basing such clinical decisions on a patient's past wishes also came in 1976. Like Theresa Marie Schiavo, Karen Ann Quinlan was a young woman who had suffered severe brain damage and been diagnosed in a persistent vegetative state. Her family sought removal of the respirator that was believed to be sustaining her life. Worried about possible legal implications, physicians and hospital officials asked for a court ruling on the matter.

In its opinion resolving the case, the New Jersey Supreme Court first noted that a competent patient would be free to refuse the respirator. It then engaged in the following thought experiment:

> We have no doubt, in these unhappy circumstances, that if Karen were herself miraculously lucid for an interval (not altering the existing prognosis of the condition to which she would soon return) and perceptive of her irreversible condition, she could effectively decide upon discontinuance of the life-support apparatus, even if it meant the prospect of natural death.[3]

The court then determined that the onset of incapacity failed to eliminate the patient's right to refuse treatment. Although she could then no longer assert the right for herself, her father-guardian could do so on her behalf. And though there was no clear evidence indicating how Quinlan would choose, the court said physicians could forgo treatment if this was her family's "best judgment" as to how she would exercise her right to decide.*

Legal authorities in other states soon joined California and New Jersey in recognizing the competent individual's right to control future treatment. Today, all states have laws authorizing some form of advance directive.[4] These laws vary in scope and coverage. For example, some state laws authorize directives for patients with any irreversible, incurable condition expected to cause death in the near future if treatment is forgone; other state laws adopt a narrower definition of eligible patients. Some state laws require an explicit statement from individuals seeking to refuse medical nutrition and hydration, while others include these measures in the general category of life-sustaining interventions that may be refused. Despite these differences, all of the existing statutes endorse the concept of advance treatment decision-making and protect from liability clinicians who act according to the terms of a properly made directive. The laws do not require

---

* As it turned out and as some experts predicted in advance, Karen Ann Quinlan lived another 10 years after the "life-sustaining" respirator was removed, breathing on her own.

individuals to make directives, however; nor do they represent the sole legally acceptable basis for forgoing life-sustaining treatment.

Federal officials, too, have offered support for advance directives. In 1990, Congress enacted the Patient Self Determination Act (PSDA).[5] The law requires hospitals, nursing facilities, and other health care organizations receiving Medicare and Medicaid funds to give adults under their care information about their rights under state law to make advance directives. If someone has an advance directive, the information must be noted in that person's medical record.

Finally, the United States Supreme Court has indicated that decisions about future care may be part of the individual's constitutionally protected liberty interest. In *Cruzan v. Director, Missouri Department of Health*,[6] the Court considered the case of another young woman diagnosed in a persistent vegetative state. Nancy Cruzan had no living will or other advance directive, and Missouri state officials, as well as the state courts, blocked her family's request to remove the feeding tube that was sustaining her life. The U.S. Supreme Court held that Missouri could prohibit cessation of treatment in the absence of Cruzan's explicit and precise wish to refuse nutrition and hydration in her current circumstances.

Writing for the majority, Chief Justice Rehnquist said that the Constitution permits (but does not require) states to demand clear and convincing evidence of an incapacitated patient's wish to refuse life-sustaining treatment. This evidentiary demand was justified, he asserted, as "a procedural safeguard to assure that the action of the surrogate [decision-maker] conforms as best it may to the wishes expressed by the patient when competent."[7] The Court's decision thus affirmed state policies that granted a privileged place to a patient's prior wishes in making current treatment decisions, but also affirmed the right of individual states to establish their own criteria for deciding if and when those prior wishes are clear and thus operative in particular cases.* Many commentators believe that *Cruzan* imposes an *obliga-*

---

* At a later probate court hearing, witnesses offered more evidence on Cruzan's previous statements and the judge ordered the feeding tube removed.

tion on states to respect patients' explicit advance treatment decisions, but since the case did not involve or address this question directly, the specific contours of any putative constitutional right are as yet unclear.

The widespread embrace of advance treatment decision-making by many legal officials is traceable to the law governing medical decisions by competent patients. When courts began to encounter cases involving adult patients refusing life-sustaining interventions, they proceeded to examine the strength of the individual's interest in controlling medical care and to balance that interest against competing considerations, such as the state's interests in protecting life and the ethical integrity of the health professionals caring for the patient. Courts assigned significant weight to the patient's interest in controlling care, on grounds that the patient must bear the physical and other burdens associated with life-prolonging measures. They also observed that in a pluralistic nation such as the United States, individuals have different views on the relative importance of survival and quality of life. Accordingly, very strong justification would be required to impose treatment against the competent individual's wishes.[8]

When patients could no longer choose their preferred treatment alternative, judges thought that the next best option would be to consult any previous instructions offered by the patient about life-sustaining measures. By giving priority to the individual's former wishes, legal authorities could seemingly continue to respect the individual's interest in controlling medical care. The courts also maintained that this approach would protect vulnerable patients from the risks of having their care determined by relatives and clinicians with their own concerns and agendas.[9]

Nearly three decades after *Quinlan* and the first Natural Death Act, advance decision-making remains popular among legal officials, at least in the abstract. Courts regard the patient's prior instructions as the preferred basis for treatment decisions, and both state and federal lawmakers have promoted this approach in legislation. Nevertheless, courts and legislatures also recognize the limits of advance treatment decision-making. The dearth of explicit directives, as well as the implementation problems discussed below, have compelled officials to develop and use other approaches to resolving questions about treatment for incapacitated patients.

Besides legislation authorizing health care proxies to make decisions at the bedside, many states now have statutes recognizing family members as appropriate surrogates for incompetent patients lacking formal directives. Moreover, when advance directives are absent or fail to offer clear guidance to surrogates, two other approaches to clinical decision-making may come into play. These two approaches are based on traditional legal standards governing financial and personal decisions for legally incompetent persons (that is, minors and adults judicially determined to lack decisional capacity). Courts, policymakers, and medical ethicists sometimes apply these approaches in the medical setting as well.

The "substituted judgment" standard combines information about a patient's past with an evaluation of that patient's current situation. As with advance directives, the goal is to determine the treatment alternative most consistent with the patient's earlier values and preferences. But the substituted judgment standard is applied when the patient failed to issue a formal advance directive. The aim is to guess, here and now, what kind of treatment the patient would choose, were he (miraculously) to become competent just long enough to say what he would want done. To reach the substituted judgment in practice, caregivers must rely on more general information, such as the patient's religious affiliation, cultural background, or attitudes toward medical care.

Several difficulties can arise in applying the substituted judgment standard. Relatives and friends may report remarks and behavior that point in different directions or that support a range of treatment options. Questions may arise about whether a patient's statement or action was meant as a deliberate and thoughtful indication of personal beliefs and values. Clinicians may wonder whether evidence about the patient's past is being accurately reported. For these reasons, many believe that the substituted judgment standard should also include a close examination of the incapacitated patient's existing condition and an evaluation of the benefits and burdens that would accompany a decision to administer or forgo treatment.[10]

The "best interests" standard applies when information about the patient's previous views fails to point to a particular treatment choice. Instead of focusing on evidence about the patient's personal, subjective views, the standard adopts "the perspective of a 'reasonable person,' choosing as most people would choose for themselves."[11]

Relatives and clinicians applying the best interests standard focus on the patient's present circumstances and consider the positive and negative effects of different treatment decisions. They examine matters such as pain, distress, and probability of treatment success. The best interests standard requires others to weigh and balance different dimensions of the patient's situation, such as the burdens that administering or forgoing treatment would impose and the benefits of the extended life that treatment could provide. Because people value quality of life and survival differently, they may reach different conclusions about appropriate treatment under this standard.*

Nine years after its *Quinlan* decision, the New Jersey Supreme Court offered an extensive analysis of the dementia treatment situation, developing both the substituted judgment and best interests standards in its own specific directions. *In re Conroy*[12] involved an elderly nursing home resident with severe dementia and other health problems. She was conscious but significantly impaired and had a life expectancy of about a year. Her nephew, her only biological relative, asked the court to authorize removal of her feeding tube. There was no advance directive in this case, but the nephew maintained that she had rejected medical interventions throughout her life and would never have permitted the tube to be inserted.

---

* Different courts and experts have introduced their own variations and refinements on these terms—such as the "limited-objective standard" and the "pure-objective standard," used in the *Conroy* case discussed below. In the end, however, the crucial distinction is between trying to discern what the person would want if the competent self of the past could speak and trying to do what is best for the incapacitated patient here-and-now. In some cases, these two standards of care lead to similar conclusions; in other cases, there is tension and ambiguity, resulting from different interpretations of a patient's real wishes in the past and different judgments about a patient's real interests in the present.

In its ruling, the court set forth three standards to apply in cases like Conroy's. First is the "subjective standard," which applies when there is "clear evidence" that the patient would have made a particular treatment choice in her current circumstances. This evidence could be in the form of a living will; it might also be testimony about the patient's verbal comments, conduct, or religious beliefs. The court found that the available information on Conroy's prior preferences was insufficient to satisfy the clear evidence required under the subjective standard.

Acknowledging that it will sometimes be impossible to know for certain what the patient would choose, the court described two standards (its own versions of substituted judgment and best interests) that would permit non-treatment when clear evidence of a patient's prior wishes and intent is lacking. One is the "limited-objective standard," which applies when, as in Conroy's case, there is "some trustworthy evidence that the patient would have refused the treatment." Under this standard, treatment may be forgone if "it is clear that the burdens of the patient's continued life with the treatment outweigh the benefits of that life for him."

Conroy's third alternative is called the "pure-objective standard." This standard applies when there is no trustworthy evidence that the patient would have opposed treatment. This standard allows treatment to be forgone if two conditions are met: first, if "the net burdens of the patient's life clearly and markedly outweigh the benefits that the patient derives from life," and second, if "the recurring, unavoidable and severe pain of the patient's life with the treatment [are] such that the effect of administering life-sustaining treatment would be inhumane."

In making its decision, the court recognized that the evidence of prior preferences might be more or less probative, depending on the specificity of the individual's statements and the "remoteness, consistency, and thoughtfulness of the prior statements or actions." Its version of substituted judgment, the limited-objective standard, restricts the effect that general evidence of the patient's previous preferences may have on later care. When the evidence is less than clear, the court required decisionmakers to focus on the patient's contemporaneous interests.

By now, several other state supreme courts have joined the New Jersey court in limiting the impact of general evidence about a patient's previous beliefs and values. When asked to resolve cases involving conscious dementia or brain-injured patients, these courts refused to authorize cessation of treatment based on evidence of a patient's informal statements about medical care and quality of life.[13] In the absence of a formal advance directive or relatively explicit verbal instructions, the courts based their decisions on the patient's current welfare.

Yet discerning a person's true welfare is a complicated and often controversial legal and ethical question. For some, a person's welfare is best served by always following the advance instructions given by the once-competent self, if such directions exist, even if doing so seems to harm the incapacitated person now here. For others, patient welfare hinges entirely on whether "the net burdens of the patient's life clearly and markedly outweigh the benefits that the patient derives from life," as the *Conroy* decision put it, suggesting that life with certain burdens is sometimes better not extended even if the life-sustaining treatment itself is not very burdensome. And for still others, serving a patient's welfare means always benefiting the life the person still has, however diminished or burdened by debility and disease.

So far, neither the courts nor policymakers have adequately investigated what patient welfare really means—a task that properly begins in ethical reflection, not legal decision-making. And indeed, the vast majority of cases regarding medical treatment of incompetent patients never come to court (or even to hospital-based ethics committees). Those that do reach the courts do so only because of serious disagreements among the caregivers, because no family member or proxy is available to make decisions, or because hospitals and medical professionals are worried about liability. But these cases remain the minority. Most difficult cases will be resolved not in courts by judges but at the bedside by family, friends, and clinicians struggling with the question: What do we owe the person now in our care? Thus, reflection on what it means to benefit (or burden) incompetent and incapacitated patients will remain a grave necessity. Our legal procedures and arrangements surely influence these ethical deliberations, but they can never replace them and in some cases they might even limit or deform them. We shall explore the ethical dimensions of caregiving in the chapters that follow. But first we must evaluate advance directives on their own terms—by looking at the ethical principles that guide this approach to caregiving and the evidence of this legal instrument's success or failure in practice. We focus first and primarily on advance instruction directives and living wills, the instrument that often gains the greatest enthusiasm but also presents the greatest problems.

III. THE PRINCIPLES AND AIMS OF ADVANCE INSTRUCTION DIRECTIVES

To its advocates, the instruction directive (or living will) seems to offer an effective way of resolving the dilemmas of end-of-life care by keeping the patient firmly in charge of his or her own medical treatment. Since decisions about continuing or withdrawing medical care near the end of life are always weighty, often agonizing, and sometimes highly contentious, the living will appeals to many people as a convenient *procedural* solution that can bypass the endless *substantive* debates about what would constitute "best care" for a particular incompetent patient. The living will is seen as a vehicle by which the patient, freely exercising his or her right to informed consent, can authorize the preferred course of treatment or non-treatment, thereby relieving other persons and institutions of the burden of deciding what to do in the hardest cases, where medical intervention or non-intervention is often the difference between living longer or dying sooner.

Here, in greater detail, are the various purposes that living wills are thought to serve, both ethical and practical, and the various arguments offered in their favor.

First, living wills serve and preserve self-determination. Since it is the patient who primarily receives the benefits and bears the burdens of any medical treatment (or non-treatment), most individuals wish if possible to remain active participants in important decisions regarding their own medical care. Facing the prospect of diminished mental competence in old age, many of us are understandably concerned that such medical decisions will increasingly be made for us by others without our participation. A proxy directive can help ensure that those decisions will always be made with input from or at the direction of those who care about us. But filling out a living will seems to provide a way whereby *we* can direct what happens to us. We can make choices now, while still in possession of our faculties, that would determine the kinds of medical care we receive later in life, when those faculties may have diminished. In this way, the benefits and burdens of end-of-life medical care will be, in some measure, freely chosen by us rather than simply imposed from without. Each individual would remain—by this "remote control"—a self-determining agent, even when he can no longer directly or contemporaneously determine his own fate.

Second, and continuing the theme of personal freedom, living wills provide an opportunity for people to express and give effect to their personal ideas about how they would like their lives to end. In his book *Life's Dominion*, Ronald Dworkin argues that all of us have certain "critical interests," that is, hopes and aims that lend coherence, integrity, and meaning to our lives. According to Dworkin, these critical interests rightly shape how we see the final chapter of our lives and the specific actions we take to ensure the personal ending we want. In particular, many of us hope to avoid dying in circumstances that are out of character with the rest of our lives or in ways we find unworthy or undignified. As Dworkin puts it, most people "want their deaths, if possible, to express and in that way vividly confirm the values they believe most important to their lives."[14] The choices inscribed in a living will can later safeguard these critical interests at a time when the patient is losing or has lost reflective control of his or her own life.

Third, and more practically, living wills offer protection against maltreatment. Many people are concerned about the possibility of over-treatment or under-treatment at the end of life, when they are no longer in a position personally to accept or decline such care. We may be worried that life-sustaining measures will be pursued too aggressively, or we may be worried that too little will be done on our behalf, once we are unable to speak up for ourselves. The living will would seem to be a way to protect ourselves prospectively against the imposition of unwanted interventions or the premature cessation of all interventions.

Fourth, living wills can relieve anxiety and facilitate choice. Decision-making about medical care near the end of life sometimes involves a painful dilemma: should the patient's ailments be treated aggressively, with a view to maximizing longevity, or should the main focus be on insuring physical comfort, personal dignity, or the possibility of dying peacefully at home with loved ones? Rather than letting such decisions be made haphazardly or under duress, when the patient is no longer able to make his wishes known, the living will offers a way to adjudicate such tensions calmly and rationally, well in advance of the extreme circumstances in which they are likely to become manifest.

Fifth, living wills can help our loved ones. Patients are often concerned that the painful burden of end-of-life medical decision-making will fall too heavily on the shoulders of their family members, friends, or other devoted caregivers. The living will recommends itself as a way for us, in advance, to give permission to our loved ones to continue treatment in some circumstances or to surrender in others, and thereby to ease their distress in the face of our decline and death. The concern addressed here is not that they might decide badly, but that the very responsibility to decide without explicit guidance would unnecessarily add to their anguish. Even if the course of treatment chosen is ultimately the same as what the family would have chosen uninstructed, the guidance provided by a living will can help the patient's family (as well as the physician) make the painful decisions with a degree of confidence and closure.

Sixth, living wills can protect financial resources. Many people approaching the end of life worry that, in the absence of written directives explicitly limiting medical treatments, a disproportionate share of their family's resources could be squandered on costly medical interventions of limited value. They hope to avoid such a gross misallocation of resources, in which nearly all of their assets are spent down in the final months of life, when they would rather see that wealth used on behalf of their spouse, children, or grandchildren. The living will offers a way to prevent (or at least limit) excessive spending in the patient's final phase of life, by instructing surrogates not to undertake certain costly treatments in circumstances where the benefits seem limited or where life itself has become so diminished, painful, or unrewarding that extending it seems undesirable.

Seventh, living wills can decrease the risk of litigation. Physicians tend to welcome them not only as a guide to treatment but as a hedge against legal liability, should things turn out badly or relatives later regret what was decided. And prospective patients sometimes also want to forfend possible legal battles among family members who, when the time for treatment decision arrives, might disagree strongly about the preferred course of action.

Finally—an indirect benefit—living wills can foster necessary communication. The process of preparing and executing a living will can be seen as a way to promote conversation among loved ones and with doctors about one's values and preferences regarding illness, medicine, and dying. Regardless of whether the explicit directives contained in the document eventually guide the patient's medical treatment, the mere exercise of preparing a living will can encourage greater thoughtfulness and communication between the patient, his family, and his doctor as to how he would like to be cared for. Preparing a living will might be, for many people, the first occasion to articulate for themselves and for those who might care for them just how they would like their lives to end or how they would like to be cared for until the end.

These aims and purposes invite two different kinds of questions: First, how successful are instruction directives and living wills in meeting their own goals? Second, are those goals and purposes adequate to the task of caring well for those who cannot care for themselves? In the two sections that follow, we address these questions in some detail—first empirically, then ethically and philosophically.

IV. LIVING WILLS IN PRACTICE: EVALUATING SUCCESS AND FAILURE

Enthusiasm for instruction directives and living wills, as we have noted, has been widespread in many professional quarters. The idea of the living will has been enthusiastically endorsed not only by Congress and the courts, but also by state legislatures, the Veteran's Administration, medical and legal associations, doctors, lawyers, ethicists, and patient advocacy organizations. A much cited 1991 article in the *New England Journal of Medicine*, for example, concluded that advance directives are desired by the great majority of patients and by the public in general, and that they can be easily completed in a 15 minute office visit with a physician.[15]

Advance instruction directives and living wills have been available now for some decades, and enough evidence has begun to emerge to permit a preliminary assessment of the success or failure of this particular form of advance decision-making. A number of serious problems have been documented that call into question whether living wills or other instruction directives will ever achieve the goals set out by their advocates, at least for the vast majority of patients.

1. Few people actually complete living wills.

Despite the widespread acclaim for the idea of living wills, and despite more than thirty years of encouragement, studies show that most Americans do not have one. While the rate of completion of living wills did rise in the years right after the *Cruzan* decision and the Patient Self-Determination Act (PSDA), there remains a large gap between the number of Americans who claim to believe that living wills are a good idea and the number of Americans who actually have them. By 2001, despite more than a decade of efforts under the PSDA to increase the number of people filling out advance directives, the completion rate nationwide remained under 25 percent.[16] Even the chronically or terminally ill do not seem to prepare living wills in substantially higher numbers; one recent study suggested that only about a third of dialysis patients had a living will, even though most of them thought living wills "a good idea."[17]

In their review of the literature, Angela Fagerlin and Carl Schneider point to a number of reasons why people fail to complete living wills: Some people say they don't know enough about them; others find them too difficult to execute; others simply procrastinate or hesitate to discuss living wills with their doctors. Some people doubt they need a living will; others think that living wills are appropriate only for the elderly or infirm; many suspect that living wills do not affect how patients are treated. Some people are content to delegate decisions to family members, and some see living wills as incompatible with their cultural traditions or ethical beliefs, by putting too much emphasis on self-determination rather than solidarity or by implying that disabled persons are better off untreated.[18]

The problem does not seem to be lack of information. Many studies suggest that programs designed to increase people's awareness of living wills do not appreciably increase the likelihood of their completing them.[19] Instead, people—including many who claim to believe that living wills are a good idea—seem to have substantial reasons for not completing a living will, and by and large they cannot be easily persuaded to change their minds. One recent study suggests, in particular, that most patients prefer not to put specific treatment preferences in writing; and even when individuals complete instruction directives, they typically prefer "to allow surrogate decision makers leeway in decision making."[20]

It should be acknowledged that, under certain favorable conditions, relatively close-knit communities have succeeded in considerably raising the rate of completion of advance directives. The "Respecting Your Choices" initiative established in La Crosse, Wisconsin in 1993 was a large-scale education and implementation effort throughout the community that featured training and education sessions, standardized materials, and coordination between local hospitals and clinics to ensure that directives would be available when needed and would play a role in treatment decisions.[21] A subsequent study reported that up to 85 percent of the targeted patients had completed advance directives at the time of their deaths, and of these, most were recent (the average date of completion was a little more than a year before death), and 95 percent were available to doctors when needed. Nearly all the patients involved felt they had benefited from the process. Several other small, locally based initiatives have shown similar success, but the possibility of generalizing these efforts remains unknown.[22] In 2004, Joan Teno and her colleagues reported on a 22-state survey of bereaved family members which estimated that 71 percent of the patients dying in these states had completed either a living will or durable power of attorney, many of them doing so soon before death. But the preponderance of evidence suggests that despite outreach and education efforts to increase the writing of living wills, the majority of Americans at present do not have them.[23]

2. People who complete living wills may not have clear treatment preferences and may not fully comprehend the clinical conditions they might face in the future.

Even when people are prepared to execute living wills, it is doubtful whether they have clear and definite ideas about the treatment they would want if and when they become incapacitated. There are, to begin with, simply too many possible future situations that the patient must try to imagine, each with its unique combination of burdens, benefits, and risks, making the notion of "informed consent" long in advance of treatment a highly questionable one. And those patients who are tempted to reject certain kinds of future medical intervention (on the ground that they "wouldn't want to live like that") may not understand how short-term use of some of the same interventions could restore them to basic or even normal function. In many cases, people end up contradicting themselves in the instructions they leave, or contradicting their instructions when asked concurrently or subsequently what their real preferences are. As Fagerlin and Schneider suggest, most people find it difficult to accurately predict their preferences "for an unspecifiable future confronted with unidentifiable maladies with unpredictable treatments."[24]

Indeed, most people contemplating filling out a living will know very little about the various illnesses and treatments that might one day affect them, and they often rely for that information on severely limited discussion with doctors. Moreover, studies suggest that the specific preferences recorded in living wills depend a great deal on how the questions are asked; people often change their minds about what treatment they would want in any given scenario when the illnesses and interventions are described

differently. Studies also suggest that patients' individual preferences are often not very stable over time, meaning that a snap-
shot of those preferences frozen in a living will may not accurately reflect a person's real past preferences when a future decision needs to be made on his behalf. A meta-analysis of several
studies suggested that, over periods as short as two years, almost
a third of preferences for life-sustaining treatment changed.[25]

Data from the Robert Wood Johnson SUPPORT study suggests that many patients filling out living wills are confused about
what they are being asked to decide, and vague or misinformed
about the purpose and effectiveness of the medical interventions
they are being asked to choose among.[26] More deeply, on such
difficult life-and-death questions, patients may simply not have
clear and delineable preferences that they can state authoritatively
in advance. The healthy may incautiously prefer death to disability, but then change their minds when they are actually sick and
find themselves on the precipice between life and death. There is
in fact an extensive body of research showing how poor we are
at predicting our own preferences and desires, especially in regard to choices far off in the future.[27] This inability is likely to be
acutely present here, since we have no experience deciding how
and when to die.

*3. The living wills people complete often fail to convey treatment preferences
clearly.*

Living wills range from short questionnaires that give room for
only the most general answers, to elaborate charts that allow the
individual to check off which particular interventions he would
or would not want in a variety of possible circumstances, to
lengthy "values histories" designed to elicit the patient's over-
arching beliefs and core values, from which others are supposed
to infer what medical treatment the patient would want if he ever
becomes incapacitated. The shorter living wills offer families and
clinicians very little specific guidance as to how to resolve actual
treatment dilemmas. It is not very helpful, for example, to be
told merely that the patient would prefer to forgo medical treatment "if the burdens of treatment outweigh the expected bene-

fits." The more elaborate documents contain considerably more information about how the patient would like to be treated in specific scenarios. But unless the patient actually finds himself in one of the covered scenarios, that information may not offer adequate guidance as to how he should be treated. And given the complexity and particularity of every real-life clinical case—often involving co-morbidities, chronic conditions, novel treatment options, and complicated personal narratives—it is unlikely that the imagined scenario fits perfectly with the real-life one.[28]

There is a further complication. Studies show that patients, having completed relatively precise living wills, are often ambivalent about whether their written instructions should be followed.[29] It is therefore questionable whether even the detailed living wills people fill out can be considered reliable or decisive guides to their actual treatment preferences.

Fagerlin and Schneider argue that the short questionnaires convey too little specific information to be very useful, the elaborate scenario-based charts overwhelm the patient with specifics that he cannot comprehend, and the values histories, even if a patient could be induced to complete one, would not provide much clear guidance for health care decisions in concrete situations. As they conclude: "The failure to devise workable forms is not a failure of effort or intelligence. It is a consequence of attempting the impossible."[30]

4. The living wills people complete often do not get transmitted to those making medical decisions.

Even if a person were to have his clear preferences inscribed in a living will, in many cases the document itself or the information contained therein will not actually reach the people responsible for the incapacitated patient's medical care. A living will signed years in advance may be misplaced or forgotten by the time it is needed. Most patients do not give their living will to their physician; and, even if they do, that physician may not be the one treating the patient by the time he has become incapacitated. One study found that, even when patients had completed living wills before being hospitalized, their medical charts contained accurate information about their directives only 26 percent of the time, and only 16 percent of the charts contained the actual form.[31]

One novel form of instruction directive has shown high rates of compliance and effectiveness: Physician Orders for Life-Sustaining Treatment (POLST). First developed a decade ago in Oregon and now in use in fifteen other states as well,[32] a POLST document (unlike a standard living will) takes the form of a signed doctor's order; it is not completed by the patient, but by a doctor or nurse-practitioner after consulting with the patient or his surrogate. The POLST is a concise form containing specific medical instructions that can be acted on immediately by nurses, doctors, or emergency personnel; it may include "do not resuscitate" and "comfort measures only" orders, and it may indicate whether to administer CPR (cardio-pulmonary resuscitation), antibiotics, intravenous fluids, feeding tubes, artificial respiration, and other medical interventions. Unlike the living will, the POLST governs medical issues that are considered very likely to arise in the near term. According to its developers, it is really only suitable for those expecting to die within the year.[33]*

---

* Inasmuch as the POLST form is focused on decisionmaking in the short term, it cannot be regarded (and is not presented by its sponsors) as a living will in the full sense, viz., a set of instructions that a competent patient can fill out well before the time when he might suffer mental incapacitation. Moreover, the animating idea of the POLST program does not seem an appropriate principle for the prudent use of living wills: the POLST document was designed in the belief that, to be most effective, an instruction directive should be conveyed with the patient everywhere he goes in a simple, standardized form, already signed by a doctor, and capable of being implemented at once by any clinician who encounters it. Yet a living will that is so "effective" in this sense might well be *too effective*, too easy to act on quickly, when the family might wish to make care decisions more deliberately, in light of changing circumstances and new information. See the exchange of letters between Susan E. Hickman, et al., and Angela Fagerlin and Carl Schneider, "A Viable Alternative to Traditional Living Wills: A Response to 'Enough: The Failure of the Living Will,'" *Hastings Center Report* (Letters to the Editor) 34(5): 4-6, 2004.

5. Even when they are transmitted to the medical decisionmakers, living wills often have little effect on surrogate decisionmaking and little impact on the care incompetent patients actually receive.

A recent study by Peter Ditto and colleagues set out to assess whether instruction directives or living wills are effective in improving the accuracy of surrogate decision-making.[34] An experiment was performed involving competent outpatients aged 65 or older and their preferred surrogate decisionmakers (mostly spouses or children). All the patients completed a questionnaire asking whether they would want any of four life-sustaining medical treatments in nine different illness scenarios. Subjects in two experimental groups filled out scenario-based instruction directives and subjects in two other experimental groups filled out values-based instruction directives. Subjects in the control group filled out no advance directive at all. The surrogates were then divided into five corresponding groups: In the control group, the surrogates were asked to predict the patient's preferences for the life-sustaining medical treatments in each of the illness scenarios without the benefit of an advance instruction directive. In the four experimental groups, surrogates made such predictions after reviewing the patient's scenario-based or value-based written directive. Surrogates in two of the experimental groups also discussed the contents of the directive with the patient. The researchers then measured the accuracy of surrogate judgment in the various groups, by comparing the predicted preference with the preference actually expressed by the patient.

Strikingly, what the researchers found in this study was that, compared to the control group, *none* of the interventions produced significant improvement in the accuracy of the surrogates' judgment in *any* illness scenario or for *any* medical treatment. When spouses or children of elderly patients made surrogate "decisions" about medical treatment based *only* on their familiarity with the patient, their judgments were *just* as accurate as that of spouses and children who had read or read and discussed a detailed living will drawn up by the patient. In all five groups, the accuracy of surrogate decision-making was found to be about 70 percent.

In a companion study, some of the same researchers examined the effectiveness of instruction directives in improving the accuracy with which *physicians* could predict the treatment preferences of their older patients.[35] What they found was that (a) family members generally predict patient preferences more accurately than physicians; (b) the accuracy of predictions by the patient's primary care physician (that is, a doctor who knows the patient) was not significantly improved by reading either a values-based or scenario-based living will; but (c) hospital-based physicians (that is, doctors unfamiliar with the patient) could make more accurate predictions in certain scenarios if they had read the patient's scenario-based living will.

These studies call into question whether living wills are likely to have a significant impact on the medical care received by an incompetent patient, at least in cases where surrogate decisions are made either by relatives of the patient or by physicians who know the patient. This conclusion is borne out by several studies cited by Fagerlin and Schneider, such as one completed in 1998 by Martin Goodman and colleagues,[36] which concluded both that "few critically ill seniors have advance directives" and that "the level of care delivered to elderly ICU [intensive care unit] patients is not affected by the presence or absence of advance directive statements." Another study suggests that, in roughly three out of four cases, "previously executed advance directives are not accessible when patients are admitted to hospitals for acute illness";[37] and yet another study gives evidence that incompetent patients frequently receive care that is inconsistent with their living will.[38]

In a recent study, Howard Degenholtz and colleagues found that completing a living will was in fact associated with a lower rate of in-hospital deaths, perhaps suggesting that living wills are effective at communicating patients' preferences regarding life-sustaining medical treatments.[39] But, as Joan Teno has pointed out, the mere correlation between having a living will and dying outside the hospital setting does not suffice to prove that the use of living wills *causes* a lower rate of hospitalization. It could simply mean that those who complete living wills have, on average, a stronger preference for dying at home than those who do not. Teno's own research suggests that, the increased prevalence of advance directives notwithstanding, bereaved family members report many problems with the end-of-life institutional care received by their loved ones.[40]

6. The side-benefits of preparing living wills are uncertain.

Over the years, responses to these general criticisms of living wills have yielded some alternative arguments in their defense. Supporters of living wills, conceding some of the limitations, argue that *in particular cases*, they remain appropriate and useful. For example, for competent people about to undergo risky medical procedures, living wills may serve as effective treatment guides. Or, for people who lack close friends or relations to whom they can entrust decision-making power, living wills offer an alternative to what might otherwise be impersonal and unsympathetic care. But advocates also argue that, even in cases in which the living will has no impact on treatment decisions, filling one out is a useful way to get people thinking and talking about end-of-life treatment preferences. Such conversations, they contend, may help doctors and proxy decisionmakers later on when they are asked to make decisions on the patient's behalf.

Living wills are also said to provide a measure of comfort to patients and their surrogates, whether or not their instructions are followed. Their existence can bolster the patient's confidence that his wishes will be followed and relieve some of the stress and misery that beset family members compelled to make decisions about withdrawing life-support from a loved one. Even if the living will does not actually ensure that the patient's preferences are accurately carried out, so advocates claim, its mere existence can help make the burdens of end-of-life care more bearable for all concerned.

Needless to say, some of these alleged benefits are hard to measure. We know of little empirical research that either supports or undermines those claims regarding dementia patients.[41] Besides, living wills might give much less comfort if people understood how ineffective they generally are in accomplishing their other stated purposes.

V. CONCEPTUAL AND MORAL LIMITS
OF CHOOSING IN ADVANCE

In the previous section we considered a growing body of empirical evidence suggesting that living wills are encumbered with a host of practical problems that severely limit their capacity to realize the goals they were designed to achieve. Some of the practical problems could perhaps be mitigated by improved procedures: for example, longer doctor-patient consultations could be mandated, living wills could be updated more frequently, and so forth. But, in light of the many obstacles, there is little evidence that improved procedures of this sort would measurably enhance the effectiveness of the living will program. The practical value of living wills for the general population would seem to remain highly doubtful, even if we accepted the general principle behind them: the notion that individuals can decide long in advance (as able-bodied and competent persons) what is best for them if and when they become disabled and incompetent. But that principle is itself open to question, even apart from the practical problems. There are more fundamental difficulties with living wills— conceptual and ethical—that cannot be overcome by merely procedural changes.

As we have seen, one of the central goals of the living will is to preserve for the incapacitated patient the same measure of autonomy, self-determination, and freedom of choice that he or she enjoyed while still competent. The living will is based on an attractive idea: that the right of privacy in one's own body—a right from which it follows that no patient should be subjected to medical treatment without his consent—ought to be respected even when the patient is no longer in a position to articulate his preferences. The living will aims to extend "informed consent" into the future by allowing the individual to articulate his values and wishes in the present. But there are serious reasons to doubt the wisdom of treating patient autonomy as the crucial guide for making end-of-life care decisions for patients who are, in fact, no longer autonomous but absolutely dependent on others for their care.

A. The Problem of "Informed Consent"

The living will, as distinguished from the durable power of attorney, binds a currently incompetent patient to limitations he imposed on himself in the past, when he was not able to take into account all the particular circumstances of his present situation. In the most detailed instruction directives, the person presumes to understand the personal and clinical details of an unforeseeable future, and in some cases the healthy self aims rather explicitly to decide whether life in a future diminished state is worth sustaining. But it is hard to see how prudent judgment and informed consent can operate so far removed from the real-life case in all its fine human detail and medical complexity.

This problem is especially clear in those cases in which a living will written long ago requests that particular treatments be withheld that could benefit the patient here-and-now. In such cases, to honor the patient's "autonomy" by carrying out his wishes as stated in his living will may actually be harmful rather than beneficial to the present patient. And since the incapacitated patient is unable to revise his preferences in light of vital new information, it is questionable whether carrying out his written instructions is really an exercise of *informed* consent at all. Informed consent usually means an agreement made in particular cases in light of *current knowledge and well-understood facts*. But for incompetent persons, informed consent is always impossible: the patient cannot understand the choices available or the knowledge needed to make them. To claim that the living will extends the right of free choice and self-determination to those who can no longer make informed choices seems like an illusory quest, since the written "choices" are imposed on individuals who are no longer free to change their minds.

It would seem reasonable, in such cases, that those making treatment decisions on behalf of the incapacitated patient should be able to revise or supersede the instructions recorded in the living will, in light of new information unavailable at the time the living will was executed. But then the question becomes: By what standard should the surrogate's judgment be governed when he departs from the patient's explicit instructions? Should the surrogate attempt to conjecture what the incapacitated patient would have wanted, had he known what new circumstances would arise? Or should the surrogate give up on such speculations and simply be guided by a sense of what would constitute the best possible care for the patient here-and-now?

These are surely hard questions, requiring *substantive* ethical judgments about what being a "benefit" to those entrusted in our care really means. The doctrine of "informed consent" is not a sufficient guide to the perplexities and obligations of ethical caregiving, and a person's prior wishes, even when clearly expressed, should not be the *only* relevant factor in making caregiving decisions. We need to think foremost about the patient's present welfare, and about our own role as moral agents making life-and-death decisions for others.

B. Prior Wishes and Present Welfare

A challenging illustration of the dilemmas involved in caring for incapacitated patients can be found in an account by Andrew Firlik of an Alzheimer's patient he called Margo, whom he described as "pleasantly demented."[42] Firlik, a medical student, visited Margo regularly, and she was cheerful and pleased to see him but never knew his name. Margo enjoyed reading but "her place in the book jumped randomly from day to day." She enjoyed music, seemingly unaware that she was listening to the same song over and over. She enjoyed painting, but always painted the same simple pastel shapes day after day. Firlik eventually concluded that, "despite her illness, or maybe somehow because of it, Margo is undeniably one of the happiest people I have ever known":

> There is something graceful about the degeneration her mind is undergoing, leaving her carefree, always cheerful. Do her problems, whatever she may perceive them to be, simply fail to make it to the worry centers of her brain? How does Margo maintain her sense of self? When a person can no longer accumulate new memories as the old rapidly fade, what remains? Who is Margo?[43]

Using this account of life with dementia, both Ronald Dworkin[44] and Rebecca Dresser[45] ask us to imagine the following scenario: Suppose that Margo executed a living will when she was first diagnosed with Alzheimer's, asking that no treatment be given to her if she contracted another serious life-threatening illness. Now Margo contracts pneumonia, which could probably be ameliorated with antibiotic treatment. Should her living will be honored and the antibiotics withheld? Or does her present contentment make her continued life worthwhile and override her past misgivings about living with dementia?

Cases like this raise the most profound questions about how much it is given to us to control or orchestrate the shape of our lives in advance, and whether we always possess the wisdom or authority to dictate what is best for a future self. Defenders of the principle of autonomy will argue that we have a right, if we wish, to escape dying under circumstances that are inconsistent with the character of the lives we chose to live. They argue, with Dworkin, that people "want their deaths, if possible, to express and in that way vividly to confirm the values most important to their lives." This means allowing individuals to decide, by means of living wills, whether life-sustaining medical interventions should be abandoned when one becomes mentally incapacitated. Dworkin suggests that it would be an "unacceptable form of moral paternalism" to disregard a patient's written instructions on the ground that he or she still derives some benefit from life in a diminished state. In Dworkin's terms, the patient's "critical interests" (her long-term desire to lead a life of "integrity" and "coherent narrative structure") outweigh her "experiential interests" (her apparent enjoyment of life with dementia).

Certainly many of us, contemplating the prospect of disability or dementia from the perspective of vigorous physical and mental health, are tempted to reject with horror the possibility of a lengthy period of mental and physical incapacity at the end of our lives. Yet, as we have seen, patients who complete living wills sometimes do so without full awareness of what life would be like in all the various circumstances that might arise. They do not and cannot know in advance whether the experience of old age with dementia will still seem valuable to a future self, even though it is not the life they would freely choose. Can individuals really know in advance that such a life would be worse than death? And, more fundamentally, do we possess a present right to discriminate against the very life of a future self, or—even more problematic—to order others to do so on our behalf?

Giving absolute priority to a patient's earlier choices in such cases may seem injurious to the patient in his or her current state; and the significant possibility that a living will was executed without full and necessary knowledge means it lacks the moral weight of an autonomous and contemporaneous choice. More-over, as Rebecca Dresser has put it, "A policy of absolute adher-ence to advance directives means that we deny people like Margo the freedom we enjoy as competent people to change our deci-sions that conflict with our subsequent experiential interests."[46]

A person's prior wishes and instructions surely count in any judgment about providing care. Simply ignoring the patient's written instructions would give too little regard to the person's former beliefs about the shape and character of a good life. But giving those wishes trumping power may force caregivers to forgo doing what is best for the person who is now entrusted to their care; as moral agents themselves, caregivers cannot simply do what they were told but must also try to do what is best. Margo's apparent happiness would seem to make the argument for overriding the living will morally compelling in this particular case.

But we also need to think about what to do for those pa-tients with dementia who are not quite so happy, whose lives seem filled with difficulty and distress. Does a person's claim on us for treatment, even if she has a living will requesting that treatment be forgone, depend entirely or primarily on the per-son's experiential well-being? Or are there also "interests" that are not critical or experiential but ontological—the interest of a living person in being alive, in being cared for as an equal mem-ber of the community, even in a profoundly diminished and of-ten unhappy condition? These larger considerations take us be-yond autonomy to consider the meaning of human dependence and, in our case, the meaning of being a caregiver (and care-receiver) for persons with grave disabilities and advanced demen-tia. It forces us to ask: Who is this person with dementia now before us, and what do we owe her even or especially when her life seems so diminished?

C. Personal Identity and the Obligations of Care

How we care for Margo—or any person with dementia, with or without a living will—will depend in great measure on how we see her identity: Is she the same person she was when competent, with the same rights and interests? Or is she a quite different person, with possibly different rights and interests? Philosophically puzzling as it is, we are probably inclined in different moments to answer "yes" to each of these questions.

One way to think of Margo as still the same person is to focus on the rational will—on the person as one who deliberates and chooses. If Margo is the same person she was, and if twenty years ago she chose to enact certain directives about her future care, then one might argue that those directives should now be honored, even if they no longer seem to further the care she most needs. Yet this way of picturing her as the same person over time seems, actually, to ignore the significance of time. Instead, it focuses on a single moment in Margo's existence—the moment her living will was enacted—and gives it governance over all future moments. As her capacity to choose diminishes, she can no longer change her instructions; she is stuck forever in that timeless point that is her earlier choice.

If we find this puzzling, as well we might, and if we doubt that Margo's instructions from twenty years ago are really the best guide to the care she now needs, we may be tempted to say that she is no longer the same person. It may seem that the only way to get out from under the tyranny of that timeless moment of choice is to say, however paradoxically, that she is now someone different—a new person with different needs, ways, and satisfactions. We can understand the attractiveness of such a position; for it does, at least, free us to care for Margo in a way that genuinely serves what are now her best interests. It takes seriously both the person she now is and the obligations we have to her.

Understandable as this perspective may be, perhaps it is possible to affirm her continuity of identity over time, yet to do so in a way that allows us to take seriously her previously expressed wishes without giving them trumping power. Margo is still the same person she once was because the body—the fact that human beings have and are bodies—is so important to our understanding of personal identity. Throughout life—both in times when our reason and will are fully developed and active, and in times when they are undeveloped or quiescent—we are physically present in embodied form as the unity of body and psyche. This is true even (as in the case of dementia) when our reason and will have been compromised by disease. It is this continuing bodily presence that is fundamental to being human and that is the locus of all personal presence. Those who embraced or held her hand years ago and who do so again today are sure that they are embracing Margo.

From this perspective, therefore, we want to affirm that Margo remains one and the same person, even as she slides ever deeper into dementia. That helps us understand why, of course, we would not want to ignore preferences she had expressed earlier in life*—or, more important, the character she had developed over time and the things she had cared about. We should respect these central aspects of her person and her story, even if they are not always decisive for the care we think best for her when she is afflicted with dementia.

But although she is still the same person, she is also greatly changed; for one of the truths about embodied beings is that they change over time. The body may reach an optimal moment when reason and will are at their height, but it is also characterized by beginnings and decline—by change, development, and decay. What Dworkin terms our "critical" interests, important as they are to all of us, are themselves only part of that story of the person's development. We would do less than justice to the person Margo is—an embodied person who grows, flourishes, and declines in time—were we to designate one moment as the deci-

---

* If, as some people speaking loosely allege, Margo is an altogether different person, then Margo's earlier living will should be regarded as irrelevant to the care of her "replacement." Worse, on this theory of altered identity, to refuse treatment for the "new person" solely because Margo so instructed us years ago would be culpable negligence.

sive moment for all decisions about her care, as if an instruction directive enacted twenty years earlier could be an adequate expression of her needs and desires here and now.

There is, of course, another way out of this identity conundrum. We could say that Margo was once a person but is no longer. This would not so much solve as dissolve the problem; for it would suggest that *no* "person" is present any longer in the bodies of those stricken by dementia, that Margo's living body is simply the corpse in which the real Margo once lived. To take this course, as some have done in recent years, would involve a radical transformation in our civilization's understanding of what it means to be human. It would sanctify reason and will (and qualities such as consciousness and self-awareness) as the qualities which, *alone*, give one membership in the community of care. It is far better, we think, to take seriously the truth that, whatever else they may be, human beings are embodied beings in time. Each person's life is a story marked at first largely by potential of what is yet to come, then by flourishing of the organism's most characteristic capacities, and finally by decline. But none of these moments in the story *is* the person. On the contrary, the person is simply the one whose story it is.

What began in this chapter as an attempt to trace our society's search for a largely procedural solution to the problem of caring for those who become incapacitated—a solution that respects patients' wishes and prevents mistreatment by others—has led us to realize that procedural solutions cannot free us from hard philosophical and ethical questions. Indeed, we need to cultivate in ourselves a deeper sense of our solidarity in body and in time—a richer sense of what it means to be dependent on others and to care for those who can no longer make choices for themselves.

The depiction of identity that we have given—of personal identity as continuous throughout the trajectory of the body's life, but of a continuity that incorporates countless changes—does not provide concrete answers to any of the difficult treatment decisions that caregivers must make when caring for dwindling patients. A great deal will always depend on the clinical and personal particulars of each case, and much of this cannot be fully anticipated in advance. But this understanding of the human person does suggest two insights that should guide the ethical reflections that follow. First, those who have lost some characteristically human cognitive capacities *are still human beings with identities and still worthy of our care.* Second, however much we understandably cling to our autonomy and dread our decline, dependency is very often part of the normal course of human life.

In the end, living wills can never relieve us of the responsibility we have to care for one another as best we can, even in difficult circumstances such as those dementia creates. Nor should we want such relief from responsibility; for our aim is not simply to execute instructions given us, but to develop a true ethic of caregiving. Writing a living will requires facing up to the possibility of decline, debility, and death, but it does so by seeking to exert more self-mastery than may be possible at a time of life when accepting limits and trusting others are often the virtues most needed. In the very effort to spare loved ones the excessive burdens of care, we may send a message that we do not trust them enough to put ourselves in their hands.

Of course, trusting others requires the presence of others who are trustworthy—surrogates who are willing to care, able to make wise decisions, and willing to let go when the time comes to do so. The comparative virtue of *proxy* directives is that they embody such trust, even if they do not, in themselves, provide ethical guidance about what to do in the face of those dilemmas that devoted proxies ultimately face. And the comparative virtue of *advance care planning,* as distinct from the more narrowly focused living will, is that it invites individuals and families to face up to the dependencies of the future without necessarily dictating every medical decision. At its best, such planning aims instead at being better prepared for the unknown dilemmas ahead. In our final section, we look beyond living wills to examine, briefly, these other ways of thinking in advance, so that we might understand their genuine virtues and inherent limits.

VI. BEYOND LIVING WILLS:
THE WISDOM AND LIMITS OF PROXY DIRECTIVES
AND ADVANCE CARE PLANNING

The proxy directive does not ignore the significance of our desire to participate (in advance) in shaping treatment decisions made for us at a time in the future when we can no longer participate concurrently. Precisely by naming someone to serve as our proxy, we take that desire seriously. At the same time, however, this approach emphasizes less the importance of self-determination and correspondingly more the importance of solidarity and interdependence. It invites us to move toward our final days and years not in a spirit that isolates our free decisions from the networks of those who love and care for us but, instead, in a spirit that entrusts our dying to those who have supported us in our living. It enlists them to stay by our side, to the very end.

In this way, the proxy directive is more in accord with our ideals of family and community life than is the instruction directive. Indeed, if we try too hard to solve all problems in advance by stipulating directions for our care, we may cut off the family discussion that is needed when difficult caregiving decisions must be made. It is precisely such discussion that forces us all to take seriously the continued presence of a loved one who is no longer able to participate in decision-making. The very activity of seeking the best possible care pushes us all toward deepened understanding and concern. This does mean, of course, that a proxy directive places greater burdens on family members than does an instruction directive (one of whose aims, as we have seen, is precisely to relieve family members of such stressful burdens). But to care about one's family is to accept such burdens, and we may well wonder whether families would really be better off without the trials of fidelity that aging and dying often present, or whether we would want to live in families if families did not need to care.

To be sure, there are some, especially the very elderly, who may have no family or who may outlive all their obvious proxy choices. And there may be others who, because their family has been a source of pain rather than support, may feel unable to entrust themselves to the care of a family member. In some of these cases a living will may seem the better course to take. But such cases should also spur us all to consider more seriously how to expand the boundaries of communal solidarity—recapturing, for instance, the deep significance of friendship, or finding in community or religious institutions others to whom we can entrust decisions about our care. We should not too readily acquiesce in a vision that isolates us in the time of our dependency, or a vision that rests on the false notion that individuals can precisely determine and manage every fact of their lives until the very end.

The limits of controlling one's own future does not mean that individuals and families should not plan for the future together. The shortcomings of living wills should not obscure the real advantages, both to the patient and to his family, of thinking ahead about some of the dilemmas that might arise as one's capacities diminish, through conversation and prudent planning before an illness like dementia takes its course. Such conversation might focus not so much on the specific medical treatments a patient would or would not want as on other aspects of aging and dying that might matter even more to the person: for example, being steadily cared for during the long period of illness, having the company of one's family and friends at the end, making peace with God, having a chance to say good-bye to a particular person, dying in a quiet and dignified setting, sparing one's family additional anguish, and other considerations not strictly medical. Is the patient concerned more about pain at the end of life or about loneliness? About mental deterioration or about physical dependency? What are his deepest fears, what are her fondest hopes? Knowing how the person feels about these matters, at a stage of life when true collaboration is still possible, can give both guidance and comfort to family members who must eventually make wrenching decisions for the patient, including in many cases the decision to stop treatment and accept death.

Such conversations do not make the decisions, of course, but enrich the perspective of the decisionmakers. For in the end, the best laid plans always require devoted and prudent caregivers, who know what it means to benefit the lives of those in their care, and who possess the character to care well even in the darkest times. Ethical caregiving, in all its aspects, is the order of the day. It is therefore also the subject of the remainder of this report.

ENDNOTES

[1] Kutner, L., "Due Process of Euthanasia: The Living Will, a Proposal," 44 *Indiana Law Journal* 539, 1969.

[2] California Health & Safety Code sec. 7186 (West 1976) (repealed 2000).

[3] *In re Quinlan*, 355 A. 2d 647 (N.J. 1976).

[4] For detailed information on state laws, see Meisel, A. and Cerminara, K., *The Right to Die: The Law of End-of-Life Decisionmaking.* (3d ed.) New York: Aspen Publishers, 2004 (Supp. 2005).

[5] 42 U.S. Code Service sections 1395i-3, 1395l, 1395cc, 1395bbb (2005).

[6] 497 U.S. 261 (1990).

[7] Ibid., p. 280.

[8] See, for example, *McKay v. Bergstedt*, 801 P.2d 617 (1990).

[9] Dresser, R. and Robertson, J., "Quality of Life and Nontreatment Decisions: A Critique of the Orthodox Approach," 17 *Law, Medicine and Health Care* 234, 1989.

[10] Buchanan, A., and Brock, D., *Deciding for Others: The Ethics of Surrogate Decision Making,* New York: Cambridge University Press, 1989.

[11] New York State Task Force on Life and the Law, *When Others Must Choose*, New York: New York State Task Force on Life and the Law, 1992, p. 33.

[12] 486 A. 2d 1209 (N.J. 1985).

[13] Dresser, R., " Schiavo's Legacy: The Need for an Objective Standard," *Hastings Center Report* 35(3): 20-22, 2005.

[14] Dworkin, R., *Life's Dominion: An Argument About Abortion, Euthanasia, and Individual Freedom,* New York: Knopf, 1993, p. 211.

[15] Emanuel, L. L., et al., "Advance Directives for Medical Care—A Case for Greater Use," *New England Journal of Medicine* 324: 889-895, 1991.

[16] Eiser, A. R., and Weiss, M. D., "The Underachieving Advance Directive: Recommendations for Increasing Advance Directive Completion," *American Journal of Bioethics* 1: W10, 2001.

[17] Holley, J. L., et al., "Factors Influencing Dialysis Patients' Completion of Advance Directives," *American Journal of Kidney Disease* 30: 356-360, 1997.

[18] Fagerlin, A., and Schneider, C. E., "Enough: The Failure of the Living Will," *Hastings Center Report* 34(2): 30-42, 2004.

[19] Eiser, A. R., and Weiss M. D., *op. cit.*

[20] Hawkins, N. A., et al., "Micromanaging Death: Process Preferences, Values, and Goals in End-of-Life Medical Decision Making," *Gerontologist* 45: 107-117, 2005.

[21] Hammes, B. J. and Rooney, B. L., "Death and End-of-Life Planning in One Midwestern Community," *Archives of Internal Medicine* 158: 383-390, 1998.

[22] Garas, N., et al., AHRQ Evidence Reports. Chapter 49. *Health Services Technology/Assessment Texts*. Available online at http://www.ncbi.nlm.nih.gov/books/bv.fcgi?rid=hstat1.section.62397 (accessed September 5, 2005).

[23] See Teno, J. "Advance Directives: Time to Move On," *Annals of Internal Medicine* 141: 159-160, 2004; Teno J. et al., "Family Perspectives on End of Life Care," *Journal of the American Medical Association* 291: 88-93, 2004.

[24] Fagerlin, A., and Schneider, C. E., "Enough," p. 33.

[25] Ibid., p. 34.

[26] Teno, J., et al., "Do Advance Directives Provide Instructions That Direct Care?" *Journal of the American Geriatric Society* 45: 508-512, 1997. These researchers found directives from 569 patients out of 4804; few of those contained any instructions and some of the ones with instructions showed clear lack of understanding.

[27] Fagerlin, A., and Schneider, C. E., "Enough," p. 34.

[28] Brett, A. S., "Limitations of Listing Specific Medical Interventions in Advance Directives," *Journal of the American Medical Association* 266: 825-828, 1991.

[29] Sehgal, A., "How Strictly Do Dialysis Patients Want Their Advance Directives Followed?" *Journal of the American Medical Association* 267(1): 59-63, 1992.

[30] Fagerlin, A., and Schneider, C. E., "Enough," p. 35.

[31] Morrison, R. S., et al., "The Inaccessibility of Advance Directives on Transfer from Ambulatory to Acute Care Settings," *Journal of the American Medical Association* 274: 501-503, 1995.

[32] For information about POLST, see http://www.polst.org, a website sponsored by the Oregon Health Sciences University's Center for Ethics in Healthcare.

[33] "Dr. Tolle helped design the POLST form. 'A POLST form is not for every adult. A POLST form is for someone who their doctor wouldn't be surprised if they died in the coming year.'" Quoted in "A Different Kind of Living Will," Ivanhoe Broadcast News, June 27, 2005. Available online at http://www.ivanhoe.com/channels/p_channelstory.cfm?storyid=11510 (accessed September 5, 2005).

[34] Ditto, P. H., et al., "Advance Directives as Acts of Communication: A Randomized Controlled Trial," *Archives of Internal Medicine* 161: 421-430, 2001.

[35] Coppola, K. M., et al., "Accuracy of Primary Care and Hospital-Based Physicians' Predictions of Elderly Outpatients' Treatment Preferences With and Without Advance Directives," *Archives of Internal Medicine* 161: 431-440, 2001.

[36] Goodman, M. D., et al., "Effect of Advance Directives on the Management of Elderly Critically Ill Patients," *Critical Care Medicine* 26: 701-704, 1998.

[37] Morrison, R. S., et al., *op. cit.*

[38] Danis, M., et al., "A Prospective Study of Advance Directives for Life-Sustaining Care," *New England Journal of Medicine* 324(13): 882-888, 1991.

[39] Degenholtz, H. B., et al., "Brief Communication: The Relationship Between Having a Living Will and Dying in Place," *Annals of Internal Medicine* 141: 113-117, 2004.

[40] Teno, J. et al., "Family Perspectives on End-of-Life-Care at the Last Place of Care" *Journal of the American Medical Association* 291: 88-93, 2004. The authors conclude that "many people dying in institutions have unmet needs for symptom amelioration, physician communication, emotional support, and being treated with respect."

[41] But see Martin, D. K., et al., "A New Model of Advance Care Planning: Observations from People with HIV," *Archives of Internal Medicine* 159: 86-92, 1999. This study presents some evidence that advance care planning helped people prepare for death.

[42] Firlik, A.D., "Margo's Logo" (letter), *Journal of the American Medical Association* 265: 201, 1991.

[43] Ibid.

[44] Dworkin, R., *Life's Dominion,* pp. 221-222.

[45] Dresser, R. "Dworkin on Dementia: Elegant Theory, Questionable Policy," *Hastings Center Report* 25(6): 32-38, 1995.

[46] Ibid., p. 35.

3

The Ethics of Caregiving: General Principles

In the years ahead, the challenges of caring well for elderly persons—including and especially those suffering from debility and dementia—will become more apparent and more urgent. As Chapter 1 suggested, we may face a genuine caregiving crisis—with more needy individuals and fewer available caregivers, with growing costs of long-term care and fewer workers to support social programs, with longer periods of diminished function and the ever-present temptation to neglect or abandon those in need of constant attention. Looking ahead, it is thus incumbent upon us to ask: What constitutes good care, what makes it possible, and how can we become or support good caregivers?

In a certain sense, the answer is obvious: good care is possible when there are people willing to care, able to care, and having resources to care. Good care is possible when family members and friends make the sacrifices necessary to be caregivers, when health care professionals and social workers tend to the real needs of their patients, and when society does not leave families to fend entirely for themselves. But the obligations of caregiving often confront us with some hard human questions: What does good care require in the face of worsening physical and mental deterioration? What is the relationship between good care and a good death? What should we do when the duties of caring for our father or mother with dementia make it much harder to care for our young children? What moral aims and ethical principles should guide caregivers-in-action?

The following analysis attempts to address these questions in some detail, in an effort to offer guidance to families, doctors, and policymakers striving to care well for vulnerable persons as they approach the end of life. In this chapter we take up general ethical considerations, looking for principles and guidelines; in the next chapter we consider concrete cases, looking to display ethical caregiving in action. We will pay primary attention to the ethical dilemmas of caring for persons with dementia, and especially to the wrenching decisions about life-sustaining treatment that arise at the bedside when persons with dementia get sick in other ways.

Before turning to the ethics of caregiving, we need to make sure that we understand *who* the caregivers are and that we recognize the many *social, economic, and institutional factors* that dictate whether good care is truly possible. Although the Council's special responsibility requires us to develop sound ethical analysis and evaluation, we recognize the limited value of such ethical reflection in the absence of adequate caregiving institutions and devoted caregivers with the character and resources to stay the course.

For many aging persons, and notwithstanding the many changes in the American family over the past few decades, family is still the primary home of care and caregiving. Most men and women who marry still take an oath of fidelity to care for one another "in sickness and in health, for better and for worse." Such fidelity—not only between spouses, but between parents and children—has surely been tested in the modern world: by divorce, geographical separation, smaller families, and a culture that often does not value caregiving as much as other pursuits and occupations. Often, in families, no one is willing, able, or available to care; and many people, by the time they reach old age, have no family at all. Moreover, even within the most devoted families, there are often disagreements about what best care requires for a person in need, or about who should shoulder which caregiving responsibilities. But despite all the challenges faced by and within families, the family remains the anchor of caregiving for most elderly persons, who age and die as members of families.

Family caregivers cannot care well in isolation, however. Without the support of community institutions and social programs, even the most devoted family caregivers often face burdens too great to be shouldered alone; they want to stand with their dependent loved ones, but they often cannot stand by themselves. Such community and social support can take many forms: government funded or faith-based "respite care" programs that give caregivers a needed rest; federal laws that protect caregivers who leave work temporarily to care for a dependent family member; state programs that support a flexible menu of long-term care options, including intermediate options like elder day-care and in-home nursing. Without the support of community and society, even the most devoted caregivers can break under the weight of their task, with all its physical, psychological, and economic demands. And even the most ethical caregivers can contemplate less-than-ethical actions, often out of understandable desperation.

Of course, every society is both imperfect and limited: it never treats everyone as well or as fairly as it should, and it must balance many civic goods and obligations. But in no small measure, the kind of society we are will be measured in the years ahead by how well (or how poorly) we care for those elderly persons who cannot care for themselves; by whether we support the caregivers who devote themselves to this noble task; and by whether we sustain a social world in which people age and die in humanly fitting ways—always cared for until the end, never abandoned in their days of greatest need.

This will require the creation and preservation of good caregiving institutions. We will need reliable and decent professional caregivers; humane design of long-term care institutions, preserving as much as possible some of the warmth and comfort of home; effective coordination of long-term care with hospitals, rehabilitation centers, and faith-based or spirit-sustaining communities. Building and preserving good institutions requires valuing those who make them good—not only the doctors who treat dementia patients, but also the nurses who provide daily care, the social workers who explain and coordinate services, and the nurse's aides who clean up after incontinent residents. Much caregiving involves hard physical work; it involves being sensitive to the needs of people who often cannot make themselves understood; it involves many tasks that individuals would not likely choose for themselves, even if they perform them with great equanimity. If we want good caregivers, we need to honor and reward caregiving, rather than seeing it as unskilled or undignified labor. This is a moral challenge as well as a social and economic one.

Good will and good character alone do not make willing caregivers into good caregivers, however. Competence also matters a great deal—not only for doctors, nurses, and other caregiving professionals, but also for volunteer family caregivers who must learn how to care well in matters small and large. It requires learning how to prevent bedsores; how to bathe frail and often resistant individuals without causing accidents; how to navigate the complicated and sometimes unsupportive health care bureaucracy; how to maintain important yet difficult daily routines.

Even in the best circumstances—with loving family members and competent doctors ready to care, with neighbors and community institutions ready to support caregivers, with ample resources in place to pay for needed care—we still face difficult decisions case-by-case, from individual to individual. And precisely because real-life situations often fall short of the ideal—with no intimates willing or able to care, with no money available to pay for care, and with overburdened professional caregivers incapable of attending to every patient's every need—we need ethical guidelines to protect those without advocates from being mistreated or forgotten.

Without question, the challenge of long-term care is social, economic, and medical: good caregiving is not possible without good social policies, adequate economic resources, and competent doctors and nurses who see caregiving as a vocation. But good care also—and perhaps first of all—requires seeing what the good for vulnerable patients really is, especially in the most difficult circumstances. Without some ethical compass to guide us, the effort to provide social and economic supports for caregiving will lack a clear foundation and guiding purpose. And unless we can learn to discern the humanly good or best possible in individual cases, we may lack the wisdom to develop the large-scale social programs and small-scale community supports that are surely necessary to sustain caregivers in their important work.

Of course, the best caregivers, both professionals and volunteers, do not "practice care" by engaging in the kind of searching ethical analysis that follows. They act largely on tacit moral beliefs and in light of experience, guided by love, or standards of professional practice, or great reservoirs of compassion and skill. Good caregivers often "muddle through" wisely, guided by the moral intuitions and moral compass that help them do the best they can for those entrusted to their care, often in circumstances of great difficulty. But it is also the case that such moral intuitions do not develop out of nowhere; they are shaped by the ethos of the society in which we live, by the general culture and specific guidelines that govern the practice of medicine, and by the role models who serve as our teachers and our guides.

It is precisely the novelty of our aging society and the gravity of the challenges it raises that may tempt us or force us to re-examine what we have long taken for granted about what we owe vulnerable patients—such as the fundamental belief that every person is "worthy of care." And although unearthing our foundational ethical principles for discussion is perhaps unnecessary and even dangerous in normal times, doing so becomes necessary when the norms themselves are called into question. It is precisely because caregivers are not saints that we need to ensure that certain moral boundaries are firmly in place and that the necessary freedom to act exists within a social world where certain kinds of actions are unthinkable because they are ethically out of bounds. And it is precisely because of the heartache that accompanies seeing those we love suffer the ravages of dementia that we need to guide compassion with ethical reason, so that our compassion does not unwittingly lead us astray.

One final, introductory note: In the discussion that follows, it is important to keep in mind the complicated relationship between the legal and the ethical. In many areas of life, we are legally free to do what we should not do, and we are not legally obligated to do what we should do. In a liberal society like ours, we tend to prohibit only the gravest evils and only those evils that directly compromise the rights of others; we aim to give individuals maximum possible freedom, under law, to make moral choices for themselves. This is as it should be, given the complexity and particularity of most moral choices and the grave evils that usually accompany excessive efforts by the state to dictate the personal lives of its citizens. But the wisdom of limited government does not mean that free choice is the only or highest moral aim of our society, or that public bodies, like this council, should remain silent or neutral on the most profound moral questions. As a society, our aim should be justice as well as freedom, and the pursuit of justice begins by trying to see clearly what we owe one another, including what we owe our most vulnerable members at the end of their lives. This is, to begin with, an *ethical* question—one seen most vividly as we contemplate what best care means in particular cases.

In seeing the limits of advance instruction directives, as we did in Chapter 2, we do not turn our backs on the partial usefulness of legal instruments or propose a legal revolution, though we can imagine small-scale changes in the law that might improve caregiving. But we do need to recognize that our existing procedures affect our moral sensibilities, by teaching us that self-determination is the primary value in need of defense, rather than instructing us in the solidarity necessary to make good decisions on behalf of those entrusted to our care. For this task, we need an ethics of caregiving, one that guides how we think about the law without offering any easy answers about what the best legal procedures might be or should be. Our focus in the next two chapters, therefore, is squarely on the ethical, and when we speak of aims, limits, and obligations, we do not speak directly to the issue of what should be promoted, limited, or required by law.

I. DEFINING THE SUBJECT

What in the broadest sense do we mean by "the ethics of caregiving"?

To think about *ethics* is to think about the goals we pursue for ourselves and others (the good); about the kind of actions we do (the right); and about the sort of people we hope to be (our character). Each of these aspects of ethics is important, and each makes its claim upon us.

In whatever we do, we should strive for worthy and estimable goods, evaluating our actions as better or worse means to achieve those goals. At the same time, we should assess our actions not only as means to desired ends, but also in terms of the character of the actions considered in themselves: their conformity to our moral duties that prescribe certain actions as obligatory, and their adherence to our moral norms that proscribe certain actions as wrong (even if performed in pursuit of true goods). In addition, we cannot discern rightly the goods we should seek or actions that are obligatory or forbidden unless we strive to become the sort of people who can see well and truly.

To think about growing old draws us into all three aspects of ethical thinking, especially when we consider the moral significance of dementia. We need to ponder the shape of a good life, and especially the relation between flourishing and decline within a good life. We need to think about right and wrong (or better and worse) ways to age, and especially our duties toward those who, even if they once cared for us, must now be almost entirely the recipients of our care. And we need to cultivate within ourselves and our society virtues such as courage, justice, and fidelity—courage as patients in facing the progressive loss of our powers, justice as caregivers in meeting the needs of those who can no longer reciprocate, fidelity in preserving the ties that bind us to one another, resisting the temptations of despair and abandonment.

To think about *care* is to think of how we care *about* others and care *for* others. We learn to care *about* others usually because others have cared about us—first in the family and then with friends and others among whom we live. We are marked by those near attachments and, therefore, we inevitably and properly care about some people more than others. Those special attachments are always limited, however, by our duty not to harm or do injustice even to strangers. Caring *for* others takes many forms, some quite simple and others very demanding. It surely includes medical care, but it is much broader than that. In particular, caring for those who suffer from dementia may mean helping in the activities of daily living, making treatment decisions on their behalf, or simply being humanly present in order to honor the dignity and meaning of the demented person's past and present life.

All caring for others, and certainly its most demanding forms, requires acts of *giving*. Most often in human life we both give and receive care—in ways too complicated ever to be perfectly reciprocal. Parents give care to their children in ways that can never be fully repaid; yet in most cases, they are happy to do so. Children "repay" the care they received only when they later give care to their own children. Yet increasingly in our world, adult children also are summoned to care for their aging parents. The cycle of giving and receiving from generation to generation comes full circle—not as the realization of a contract (which could never capture the complex reciprocities of family life) but in the mutuality and fidelity that are both goods we seek and virtues we hope to develop.

In certain respects the task of those who care for persons suffering from dementia is more demanding than that of parents raising children. For parental sacrifice is oriented toward developing and increasing the capacity of the child, a goal that brings meaning and fulfillment to the nurturing parents. But caring for those with dementia means selfless and uninterrupted giving in the face of irreversible decline. For many, this kind of sacrifice on behalf of needy persons at the end of their lives, however difficult, is also a source of great fulfillment. Providing long-term care sometimes yields concerted engagement among family members, improved recognition of priorities, genuine expressions of love, and in some cases a certain "completion" of the cycle of relationship and reconciliation. Such care is often, simply, good in itself, an expression of human beings at their best, standing with one another. But it is also true that in days of struggle, some caregivers may wonder whether sacrificing so much on behalf of such a diminished life is really "worth it," or even whether helping to sustain life in such a diminished state is really a benefit to the diminished person.

To think about this task is the ethical challenge facing our society, a responsibility which the Council hopes to help meet in offering this report. A first step, to which we now turn, is to think about the threefold human context of caregiving—about the worth of human lives, about the meaning of human deaths, and about the capacities and limits of modern medicine.

II. HUMAN CONTEXTS OF CAREGIVING: LIFE, DEATH, AND MODERN MEDICINE

Caregiving is an activity that invites reflection about who we are as human beings—about how we live, how we die, and how we use medical knowledge and technique to sustain life and resist death. We can hardly do justice to such momentous subjects in the present report. But without some attention to these deeper human matters, it will be difficult—for both policymakers and actual or prospective caregivers—to think clearly and well about both the nature and the limits of caregiving in the coming decades.

A. The Worth of Human Lives

The increasing incidence of dementia is forcing—or inviting—us to think in particular about the meaning of human worth. What makes a diminished life worthy of our care, or worthy of life at all, or worth the resources society expends to sustain it?

These are not congenial questions, especially for a society rooted in ideas of the equal dignity and incalculable value of every human individual. Such questions are also foreign to the ethical outlooks of physicians and health care professionals, who are taught to devote themselves to the well-being of their patients regardless of their infirmities and disabilities. Indeed, they regard each patient as worthy of their ministrations simply and precisely by virtue of being in need of them. Patients have "worth" in the eyes of the doctor because they are human beings who have presented themselves as patients. Ethical medicine serves health and life, it does not judge life's quality—and certainly not as a criterion for treatment eligibility.

Nevertheless, public discussions today of end-of-life issues frequently speak of "quality of life," implying that certain "poor" qualities of life might disqualify one from a claim to treatment or from further prolongation of life. Questions about the worthiness of expending time and resources treating the severely disabled or demented patient seem increasingly tied to tacit—or sometimes explicit—judgments about the worth of the life being cared for. Like it or not, alien or not, we must take up this topic, if only to be better equipped to deal with public arguments that traffic casually in these grave matters.

In common parlance, we speak of the worth or worthiness of a human life in many different ways and with many different meanings. One way invites assessments of comparative worth. In the economic sense ("How much is he worth?"), different people are worth very different amounts, and the same person is worth different amounts at different stages of life. In organizations, some people are worth significantly more than others: for example, the League MVP (most valuable player) is worth more to a baseball team than a backup infielder, and so protecting the health of the MVP is a much higher priority. At the same time, the promising rookie with many good years ahead may be worth more than the all-star nearing retirement. Beyond economic and utilitarian considerations, many of us believe that some people live lives that are more admirable than others: the hero or statesman who defends his country (a Washington or Lincoln), the great poet, painter, composer, thinker, scientist, or inventor (a Shakespeare, Raphael, Mozart, Plato, Newton, or Edison), the devoted humanitarian (a Jane Addams or Mother Teresa), and, on a less grand scale, people we know in everyday life whom we admire for their character, accomplishments, or contributions to the community.

In these respects, human worth can be both variable among persons and changeable over time. In happy times, one's life seems to be worth more. In terrible times, we might wonder whether being alive is really worth it.

And yet, even as we make such comparative judgments, we also affirm another, *non*-comparative, way of speaking about the worth of human lives, based on the recognition of what all human beings have in common. For if we make human worth depend entirely on those roles or capacities or accomplishments that some people find worthy, or on the changing feelings and perceptions of the moment, we risk ignoring or denying a more basic human worthiness to which we are committed. If we value *only* the great ones, we do an injustice to the dignity of ordinary human beings, ourselves included. If we value *only* those whose potential is still open to be fulfilled, we risk dishonoring those whose potential has largely already been fulfilled. If we value someone solely because of the powers he now has, we risk abandoning him when those powers are gone. In some areas of life—like professional sports—it makes perfect sense to put individuals "on waivers" when their talents dry up. But in other contexts—like basic human rights or decent medical care—valuing only the healthy, wealthy, or competent seems to deny the worth that all individuals possess equally, simply by virtue of our shared humanity.

When thinking about human worth in the caregiving context, we have at least four fundamental principles that might guide us: *autonomy*, where one's worth is manifested in one's power to choose and determined entirely by one's own judgment; *utility*, where one's worth depends entirely on one's usefulness to oneself or others; *quality*, where one's worth depends on possessing or exercising certain humanly fitting, admirable, or enjoyable traits and capacities; and *equality*, where every human being possesses an equal and intrinsic worth simply by being part of the human community.

Each of these perspectives may be useful for certain purposes and in certain circumstances. But in matters regarding life, death, and basic rights, the most basic commitment of our society is and has been to human equality. In a society "dedicated to the proposition that all men are created equal," we must ensure that we do not allow the genuine inequalities of human capacities and human character to blind us to the equal humanity of all human beings. In part, our equality arises out of our shared vulnerability. We are all vulnerable to the deprivations of illness or injury and to the limitation of mortality, and thus we all have a personal interest in ensuring that needy persons are treated equally and adequately.

But our commitment to equality is more than simply calculating; it is more than a future's contract in human care, purchased by the healthy to insure against the contingency of biological misfortune or the inevitability of decline. Rather, the commitment to equal human worth stands as the basis of a welcoming community—one that assures all living human beings, even those in a disabled or diminished state, that their lives still have meaning, worth, and value for all of us. It assures them that we would not prefer them dead even if we would like to see an end to the suffering that marks their present condition.

Those with advanced dementia test our commitment to human equality. They force us to ponder whether treating people equally is *always* the best way to treat them well or the most fitting way to give them their due. We wonder about those who cannot enjoy even the most basic physical pleasures; or those who lack even minimal consciousness; or those whose lives are marked by the permanent loss of self-control and the constant need of sedation, with death looming and no hope of recovery. Surely, no one, given alternatives, would choose such a life for himself. We may sometimes wonder whether such a life is "useful" to oneself or to others. We may be unable to find in such lives the "qualities" we most value. And we may suppose that any "autonomous" person should be able to decide ahead of time whether to continue living in such a state. Even if equality grounds our ultimate obligations to such persons, it does not always seem to accord with our experience of being with and caring for them, or replace the lived sense that human beings in such a diminished state have lost much that is humanly worthy.

In crucial respects, therefore, the "ethic of equality" (valuing all human beings in light of their common humanity) exists in deep tension with the "ethic of utility" (measuring lives by what they are worth to oneself or others), with the "ethic of quality" (valuing life when it embodies certain humanly fitting characteristics or enables certain humanly satisfying experiences), and with the "ethic of autonomy" (valuing each person's freedom to decide what sort of life has worth for us as individuals). If the worth of a human life depends entirely on a person's utility, then some lives are clearly more valuable than others: we need workers, soldiers, leaders, and doers, and we rightly admire people who achieve great things or produce the means of their own subsistence. If the worth of a human life depends upon the presence of certain uniquely human qualities (such as, for example, memory, understanding, and self-command), then we may judge that some lives never had such worth and others (such as those with advanced dementia) no longer do. If the worth of a human life depends on one's "autonomous" assessment of self-worth, then clearly some lives will be judged to have little worth, and other lives (such as those incapable of autonomous choice) may seem to lack human worth altogether.

Against these dangerous and erroneous temptations, the "ethic of equality" defends the floor of human dignity, ensuring that *even the most diminished among us is not denied the respect and care that all human beings are owed.* The Council embraces this teaching as the first principle of ethical caregiving. Yet, in some respects, equality will always stand in tension with what may seem to mark the *height* of human dignity: the qualities that distinguish our humanity, that make us useful to others, and that we freely choose and affirm for ourselves. That tension will always mark our thinking about the process of aging and the ravages of dementia.

In the face of these tensions, it may often be difficult to know how to honor properly the several strands and claims of human dignity and human worth. Consider, for example, a virtuoso violinist whose mother gets Alzheimer's disease, whose musical calling must now compete with long days of caregiving, her pursuit of human excellence in conflict with the demands of human neediness. How does she strike the right balance between her two callings? And how do we honor the virtuoso herself when she gets dementia and her treasured capacities disappear? We do not doubt for a moment that the virtuoso with dementia remains a full member of the human community, equally worthy of human care. But this hardly settles what it means to care for her well, or what it means to defend her dignity when her special qualities are fading or gone. For all people—and perhaps most vividly for those who once stood high above the ordinary—the regression to dementia and incompetence, with all its accompanying indignities and loss of self-command, may seem dehumanizing and humiliating; and extending life in such a condition may seem like a cruel mockery of the person's former stature.

In every human being, dementia erodes many estimable and beloved human qualities, gradually eliminating the things that make one's life truly lovable. It makes each human being less than what he or she once was, even if we rightly see that the diminished person still retains his fundamental and equal human worth and is still equally worthy of human care—and perhaps *more* worthy of care *because* his or her dependence is so complete. Yet even as we cling proudly to those powers that once defined us, we must also humbly remember that we possess those powers not simply because we merited them, and never in perpetuity. Although the desire to die with as much dignity as one has displayed while living is understandable and even admirable, it fails to appreciate the human surrender that death unavoidably brings to us all.

B. The Meaning of Human Deaths

In modern societies—and perhaps in every age—we are prone to two kinds of extremes in thinking about the meaning of death: The first is believing that death is the worst thing possible and the greatest evil, to be opposed by any means and at all costs. The second is holding that death is "no big deal," that it is *simply* a natural part of life.* To think of death as the greatest evil tempts us to do great harm in the cause of overcoming it and seduces us with the belief that human beings *ought* to conquer death by human will and oppose it always by human effort. But to think of human death as simply natural ignores the dreadful reality: the earthly extinction of a human soul, the erasure of a unique person with a never-to-be-repeated life. And it ignores how consciousness of mortality distinguishes human beings from the other animals for whom death cannot be more than "merely natural," and how this self-consciousness contributes to our being persons with interests, aspirations, and longings.

Perhaps the first thing we realize about death is its inevitability: everyone dies, and knows it. Death is the event that announces our ultimate limitations, our lack of mastery over embodied life, our final need to learn how to surrender ourselves or surrender with-and-for those entrusted to our care. To be sure, we can and do exert some control over the circumstances of our death: by the healthy or unhealthy choices we make throughout life; by our chosen vocations and avocations; by how we act in moments of danger or crisis; and by the choices we make about the use (or non-use) of medical interventions. But such decisions and actions rarely ensure a particular *moment of death*, even if they make a certain *type of death* more likely or more imminent. The only way to assert perfect control over the time and manner of one's death is by suicide—which embraces oblivion in the quest to assert one's mastery, often in the face of misery and anguish we cannot escape or control.

---

* Death is, of course, a natural part of life, or, more precisely, the natural termination of life, giving life its finite character. But *humanly* speaking, it is not *simply* or *merely* a "natural part of life."

Although death is never a "good" in itself—even if good things, such as the end of terrible suffering or (in the belief of many) a passage to heaven, may accompany its arrival—it is surely possible to speak of "better" and "worse" ways to die. Many types of death are undesirable; they are ways and times of dying we would all avoid for ourselves and never wish for our loved ones: The young child killed in a car crash or dying of leukemia (an untimely death); the person captured, tortured, and beheaded (a lonely, brutal, and humiliating death); death after a long period of excruciating physical suffering (a prolonged and painful death). Yet, there may be times when the only way to avoid such an undesirable death—say, by betraying one's comrades or taking one's own life—seems equally or even more horrible.

There are also ways of dying that are humanly ambiguous. Consider, for example, a very old man who dies swiftly and suddenly of a heart attack. We do not call his death untimely, even if it was unexpected. Perhaps he was ready to die, and perhaps he always hoped to avoid a long, painful decline into debility and dementia. Yet such a death might also deny a dying person the chance to say his final goodbyes, to reconcile himself to his own demise, to put his affairs in order, and to die in the company of those who love him and will remember him. And it might deny those loved ones the same last chances—to say goodbye, to reconcile, to be there at the very end. Such a death, while swift, is denied one final twilight.

Consider, as a second example, a young fireman who dies rescuing a child from a burning building. Such a death is surely untimely, in that the person may leave behind a young wife or young children, or perhaps never lived long enough to have children who will follow him. In every sense, to die so young is to be a life cut short. Yet such a death—and more importantly, such a life—is marked by nobility; it spurs the moral imagination of those who remember the person who died; it is, in every sense, an admirable and noble death, if not a death most people want for themselves.

Death at the end of long-term debility and dementia is an especially complicated case. Most people who die of Alzheimer's disease, for example, have been blessed with a full life; they have avoided untimely or sudden death; they have lived to see children and grandchildren born, or careers pursued, or wealth accumulated. But such a death also entails certain special burdens for the dying person—at first, the burdens of *looking ahead* to a period of lost self-awareness; throughout, the burdens of *living in* a condition of growing, and ultimately total, dependence. Looking ahead, one might foresee one's own children or spouse changing soiled garments; or fear hurting the grandchildren's feelings by not remembering shared experiences; or making inappropriate comments at inappropriate times; or causing long days of struggle for the people one loves most, without the privilege or possibility of sacrificing one's own good on their behalf. And one must eventually live through the burdens of dementia itself— from the terror of treatments one does not understand to the disorientation of being moved from one's home to the nursing home to the hospital. When death finally comes for those with advanced dementia, they are no longer fully aware of the self whose life is being surrendered. Perhaps they can no longer fear or hate death in the way a self-conscious person often does, and so they can die more peacefully. But this absence of awareness might also be seen as a deprivation, for it denies individuals the chance to face death frontally, with the dignity that requires an awareness of death's coming.

Appalled or terrified by such prospects, and refusing while still in self-command to submit themselves to what nature has in store for them, some people may be tempted to orchestrate the time and manner of their dying, by rejecting all medical care or even electing suicide here and now. In a discussion of the ethics of caregiving, ethical arguments about suicide—as opposed to ethical arguments about euthanasia—are largely beside the point,* and a full discussion here is neither necessary nor possi-

---

* Self-destruction is not an issue for caregivers dealing with dementia patients who have lost self-awareness and who can no longer care for themselves. True, as we pointed out in Chapter 1, suicidal thoughts do occur to some patients with *early* Alzheimer's disease, despairing of their future. But as we also pointed out, this is generally the result of an overlaid depression, and with the aid of a discerning physician and anti-depressant medications these desperate patients commonly throw off their depression and their suicidal thoughts. The failure to diagnose and treat depression—often the result of despair that afflicts the patient's family even

ble. But because both of these subjects—taking one's own life and caring for others—relate in some measure to judgments about human worth and our understanding of human mortality, we offer a few observations about the meaning of suicide that are especially germane to thinking about *caregiving* in relation to death.

In some cases, suicide is a deliberate choice against the need to be cared for by others; it is a self-conscious choice against becoming dependent. In other cases, suicide is a desperate act of loneliness or isolation, taken by those who fear that no one will be present to care for them; it is a self-conscious choice against being abandoned. Suicide can be motivated by the desire to live only if one can stand alone, or by the desire to die because one fears standing alone.

Yet to be human is, inevitably, to exist in community with others. None of us becomes a self on our own, and our lives are connected in countless rich and complicated ways with the lives of others; from birth to burial, we depend on and are attended to by others, and we touch others' lives in deep and often mysterious ways, even in our days of decline and dependence. Hence, to take one's life is to take part of others' as well—sometimes deliberately, sometimes knowingly, sometimes (paradoxically) out of fear that others will want no part of us. Yet there is no reason for loving caregivers to tolerate or embrace such a desperate act of rejection, only a greater reason to affirm the bonds of fidelity and care that give individuals the needed strength to face whatever life has in store for them.

However understandable the motive, to seek death by human self-destruction seems to misunderstand the *limits* of human will. Orchestrating the precise manner of our dying seems like one last attempt at control and mastery—at the very time when, paradoxically, aging and dying are announcing to us the limits of our control and mastery. It invites us to pretend that we can entirely transcend the uncertainties of nature and the limits of our finitude. It blinds us to the sad truth—but a truth with which a life humanly lived must come to terms—that aging announces

_____

more than it afflicts the patient—is a common and grave error in caring for patients with dementia.

what death means: the limits of the autonomous self, limits visible both in the corpse we become and in the pain of those who must bury it.

These humbling reminders notwithstanding, caregivers for persons with dementia will unavoidably exert some measure of control over the time, manner, and circumstances of the person's death, whether by action or inaction. With numerous life-and-death decisions now foisted upon us as caregivers, it is less and less possible just to live and care well, letting death "take care of itself." This grave responsibility for others is often wrenching, leaving caregivers to wonder what truly loving care requires: Do we benefit or harm the person by extending a life that is terribly painful? Do we benefit or harm a person by extending a life that the person himself might have found undignified? Do we benefit or harm a person by extending a life that burdens the very people the person loved most? On the one hand, we might believe that there is a better way for a person entrusted to our care to die, and fear that extending his life is only making a worse death more likely in the future. On the other hand, we should recognize that caring for another entails certain obligations, including (as we discuss more fully below) the obligation not to seize an occasion for the person's death, and the obligation never to allow our own desire for relief from caregiving to corrupt our sense of what it means to benefit the (even minimal) life the person still has.

In the age of modern medicine, how we die also depends on how we use medical interventions—both for ourselves and for others. The advance of medicine allows us to hold off death in more ways than ever before, and, in doing so, it makes certain kinds of death or patterns of dying more common. Of course, chance still has a large say in the manner of our "going hence"— both for better and for worse. Nature (or fate or chance) robs human beings of life with no rhyme or reason; it sometimes robs the young of a ripe old age or robs the old of the final chance to say goodbye. But human life also seems to have a natural shape: the ascent of the child, the maturity into adulthood, the raising of one's own young, and the coming of death in the cycle of the generations. One question we face is whether the technological powers that enable us to resist the inhospitalities of nature have also introduced new dilemmas or even deformations into the natural course of human life, especially regarding how we die.

A peaceful death in a ripe old age is widely regarded as the human ideal. "Gathered to his kin, old and sated with years," is the biblical description of the death of the patriarch Isaac. And Xenophon described the good death as follows:

> It may be . . . that God out of his great kindness is interven-ing in my behalf to suffer me to close my life in the ripeness of age, and by the gentlest of deaths. For if at this time sen-tence of death be passed upon me, it is plain I shall be al-lowed to meet an end which . . . is not only the easiest in it-self, but one which will cause the least trouble to one's friends, while engendering the deepest longing for the de-parted. For of necessity he will only be thought of with regret and longing who leaves nothing behind unseemly or discom-fortable to haunt the imagination of those beside him, but, sound of body, and his soul still capable of friendly repose, fades tranquilly away.[1]*

The question we face is whether modern medicine, by coming so readily and heroically to our aid, has made such a tranquil and timely death less likely, and, by intervening against the "gentlest of deaths," has increased the likelihood of an "unseemly or dis-comfortable" decline.

C. Modern Medicine

The benefits of modern medicine are obviously too varied and too significant to delineate fully here: the dramatic reduction of infant mortality; the near-eradication of infectious diseases such as polio and tuberculosis; new strategies for preventing early and

---

* Appealing as it might sound, Xenophon's description of the good death also raises many questions: If we are still sound of body and mind, can we ever really accept death with tranquility? And if we are still a source of happiness to our friends, would they let us "fade away" if they had the power to keep us going? Do human beings deserve the most tranquil death? Or is death, in some ways, the very opposite of tranquility—a nasty robbery of life, to which we can surrender gracefully but never happily? And what is the meaning of the fact that the peace-ful death here described (the death of Socrates) is brought about by deliberate—or deliberately imposed—human action (that is, by the drinking of hemlock)? Nevertheless, Xenophon is clearly on to something: a peaceful death, in the right season, is for most of us the best we can humanly hope for.

sudden causes of death such as heart disease; vast improvements in the management of pain; and, in general, a longer and better quality of life for many people into their sixties, seventies, eighties, and beyond. Thanks to modern medicine, old age has become the social norm, rather than the rare exception—and for this gift, among others, we should surely be grateful. Those of us fortunate enough to live in the age of modern medicine probably cannot fully imagine the miseries of life without it, and what it meant to be so fully at the mercy of errant nature, or what it meant to become sick without understanding the biological cause of one's symptoms.

But as we discussed in Chapter 1, new technologies also create new dilemmas, and some of the effects of modern medicine on the trajectory of life and death are more ambiguous in their human significance. Because earlier, swifter causes of death are more frequently held at bay—a great good in itself—more individuals live long enough to suffer long-term debility, decline, and dementia. Death from sudden illness is now the exception; death following lengthy chronic illness is now the rule. A vast menu of medical machines and novel therapies can keep individuals alive for longer stretches in old age, but not necessarily make them well again, either in body or in mind. In addition, because of our reliance on modern medicine—and the constant hope that nature's final blow can be averted—the vast majority of individuals now die not at home but in hospitals or other professionalized health care settings, institutions whose animating spirit is to resist death and delay its arrival rather than to teach people how to face death with as much serenity and courage as the dying individual and his loved ones can muster.

Looking ahead to an age in which dementia will likely become more prevalent, some wonder whether modern medicine has deformed the natural shape of life by preventing death in the proper season. Those causes of death that once might have been seen as merciful and timely endings to a life "ripe with age" can now commonly be defeated by medical intervention, often prolonging lives marked by great physical suffering, emotional despair, and utter debility. In 1898, for example, Dr. William Osler wrote that, "Pneumonia may well be called the friend of the aged. Taken off by it in an acute, short, not often painful illness, the old man escapes these cold gradations of decay so distressing to himself and to his friends."[2]

But today, we can often defeat pneumonia and other ailments that afflict the afflicted, and we can prevent the "acute, short, not often painful" death that these ailments once delivered. As the possessors of this medical power, we face a number of questions with no easy answers: Does curing pneumonia or other ailments for an elderly, debilitated, suffering person really benefit the person? Are there cases when pneumonia is in fact "the friend of the aged," such that curing pneumonia is not a form of care but an acquiescence in or imposition of future degradation? Does the power to cure pneumonia—without imposing new burdens in the act of treatment—create a moral obligation to do so?

The doctors and scientists who have brought us such welcome medical benefits did not, of course, intend to cause us these dilemmas; their goal remains a full life for all, lived to the natural end free of disability. But although medical progress is always made by human beings, the human makers themselves do not fully control its exact direction, or the ways new medical powers can affect the shape of human life. For example, it may be that our capacity to prevent or correct various types of organ failure will one day allow us to sustain the human body for much longer than we do now, without reversing severe cognitive decline from age-related dementia. For a disease like Alzheimer's, we may discover ways to radically extend the middle-stage, where the disabling cognitive and affective aspects of dementia have already arrived but the total breakdown of the body has not yet begun. Many of these interventions may work without burdening the patient in the act of treatment. But are these interventions necessarily good for the person entrusted to our care, and do we have a moral obligation to use them?

As devoted caregivers, we do not want to refuse or cease treatment *so that* the person will die, and we do not want to abandon care by excluding our patients or loved ones with dementia from the medical benefits enjoyed by the wider community. Yet we must also wonder whether repeated interventions to rescue the patient, yielding him years or decades of incontinence, minimal consciousness, and constant neediness, is really a human benefit and therefore a human obligation. At some point, we might be tempted to ask whether continued treatment seems more cruel than caring, not love but betrayal, a way of perpetuating degradation at the hands of merciless nature rather than benefiting a diminished but still worthy human life.

How we think about such questions depends largely on how we think about the character and limits of human agency, both in general and especially at the end of life. Although death surely announces the ultimate limits of human mastery, human beings will often exert considerable control over the shape of dying, both for themselves and for others. Intervention and non-intervention are both acts of orchestration, whether the aim is to extend life, to hasten death, or to relieve or prevent suffering. Of course, this power of orchestration is always limited by the inevitability of death and the unpredictability of even a well-studied and well-understood human biology. But in the end, we cannot avoid the responsibility to shape the life-course of those entrusted to our care, which is why we need some reliable moral guidelines for deciding when, how, and why to intervene or not intervene with the medical art. (We will consider these moral guidelines below.)

As providers of medical care for those who are aging, suffering, and nearing death, we must aim to cure when we can, but also recognize that in many cases cure in any strong sense is no longer possible. Medicine, which is ethically committed to cure when possible, is also committed *always to comfort* and *always to care*. Our duty is never to abandon those who are aging and dying—even and especially when, diminished by dementia, they are dependent on commitments they can no longer ask or demand of us. It is this obligation—not to betray or abandon those in our care—that is the most fundamental commitment of physicians, nurses, and all of us who participate with them in deciding how best to serve the well-being of those with diminished capacities. *We betray them if, even with the best of intentions, we subject them to treatments that cannot benefit them or that burden them. We abandon them if, even with the best of intentions, we do not do what we can to benefit the life they still have.*

Of course, this fundamental commitment not to abandon those who are ours to care for does not answer all the difficult questions we face. If it did, we would have no need to speak of the *art* of medicine and, thus, the need for discernment and prudent judgment. For example, medical ethics has generally held that withholding or withdrawing medical treatment is permissible only when that treatment yields no benefit or when it burdens a patient excessively; yet this restriction may seem less than fully satisfactory in the face of hard cases.

Imagine the case of an elderly person in constant terrible pain who contracts an ailment that is easily treated but deadly if ignored. As caregivers, we face a choice between prolonging the painful life, sedating the person constantly, or letting a patient die who may not otherwise have to die soon. None of these choices seems obviously best or especially satisfying. This hardly means that our choices were better when our medical powers were more limited: surely we can control pain much better now, and surely some might argue that life in pain or under heavy sedation is still better than death. But it suggests that sometimes life-sustaining interventions are morally ambivalent, even in situations where denying their use seems morally questionable. (We will examine this dilemma more fully in the next chapter, when we consider some cases in detail.)

Modern medical advance also raises a challenge to the traditional ethical principle regarding forgoing life-sustaining treatment. If the only morally permissible criteria for forgoing life-sustaining medical treatment is that the treatment itself is burdensome or ineffectual, then every affordable treatment that meets these criteria becomes a moral obligation. Every medical invention of such a sort creates a new moral duty—regardless of how the invention seems to affect the trajectory of life and death, and regardless of whether it seems to serve or undermine our considered understanding of what would be a more or less humanly fitting way to live and die. By such criteria, we seem, to some degree, bound by technological inventions that may not always serve what seems like the human good. And we often leave ourselves with a range of morally and humanly unsatisfying choices.

What we face here is a particularly poignant instance of the dilemmas modern technological advance brings to many areas of life. The combination of new medical powers (such as curing pneumonia with ease) and lasting moral duties (such as never withholding effective and non-burdensome treatments from patients who are not already irretrievably dying) may create a situation in which progress *constrains* human choice as much as it *expands* it. As caregivers, we are surely not responsible for the burdens of disease or the pain of ailments that we cannot ameliorate. We are not responsible for the burdens of nature that we cannot fully control. But we are responsible for the use of man-made medical powers, and it is this responsibility that creates the most puzzling ethical dilemmas—especially when sustaining another person's life means extending a life marked by great pain and worsening deprivation.

Modern medicine, although greatly blessing and enhancing our lives, has also sometimes made it harder to know how best and truly to care for those with diminished capacities and for those living with serious and eventually fatal illness. Often, we have the medical capacity to extend life or delay death but without the moral capacity to know that doing so is *really* a benefit to the person who needs us to speak and act on his behalf. This is, in a profound sense, the caregiver's dilemma: a successful but always limited medical art, a progressive disease that erodes the mind on the way to disintegrating the whole person, moral uncertainty about how best to care. The rest of this chapter addresses the caregiver's dilemma: it offers ethical analysis and guidance regarding the ends and means of caregiving, with special attention to decisions regarding medical treatments for patients with dementia who get sick in other ways.

III. THE ETHICS OF CAREGIVING

For a variety of reasons, national discussions about aging, dying, and caregiving have focused largely on "end-of-life issues," on those dilemmas that bring life, quite literally, to a point: Should we treat this deadly ailment? Should we discontinue this life-sustaining intervention? Is it ever permissible to take active measures to end a life, either with or without the person's consent? These questions are crucially important, and we shall address them in the discussion that follows. But we must also remember that caregiving involves not only those moments when life comes to a point, or only those decisions regarding the use of medical interventions to sustain or end life. Caregiving, especially for persons with debilitating illnesses like dementia, involves much more the daily activities of *being there* for the person in need: protecting them from harm, managing their affairs, comforting them in dark times, feeding and bathing them and changing their soiled garments, and deciding when best care requires placing them in a long-term care institution to be cared for constantly by others.

The decisions we make when a person's life does come to a point will be shaped by the manner of caregiving that brought us to that point. For even though most caregiving decisions are not immediately matters of life and death, caregiving always embodies tacit judgments about the worth of the person entrusted to our care and always displays the character of the caregivers. Caregiving always involves thinking about what we owe to those who need us to speak for them and stand with them, precisely when they can no longer speak for themselves or stand alone. Our ability to fulfill these obligations—not just heroically in times of crisis, but mundanely and regularly on a daily basis—will make the decisive difference in the everyday life of those for whom we care.

We will keep these broader considerations in mind as we now focus on the ethics of caregiving in the clinical context. Our exploration proceeds in three basic parts. First, we consider the *positive goals* that caregivers might serve—moving from respect for the person's prior wishes, to the well-being of the family, to the good of the larger society, and finally—and most importantly—to the "best care" of the person now present. Second, we consider some *moral principles and moral boundaries* that should guide and constrain caregivers, as they try to serve that goal. As we shall indicate, the ability to pursue the "best care possible" depends on erecting such boundaries, both against unethical options and (even more) against our weaknesses as caregivers, especially as we care for persons who try our patience and test our ability to serve them wholeheartedly. Third, in the next chapter, we consider how loving *prudence* might function in a series of concrete and difficult cases. In other words: ethical caregiving involves the *pursuit* and *promotion* of good; the *protection* against ill; and *prudence* in judgment, here and now.

A further word is needed about prudence, a central notion in our account. In everyday speech we sometimes call "prudent" those decisions or actions that compromise to some extent what is good or just. Prudence is sometimes seen as mere compromise or cleverness, or as settling for something less than the truly good or morally required. In our moral tradition, however, prudence is a high virtue, in no way opposed to justice or goodness. On the contrary, prudence is that excellence of heart and mind that enables us to see deeply and wisely into the truth of things— deeply enough to discern the goods that are present, wisely enough to identify the best means available for pursuing those goods, without violating the norms of right and justice. Thus, prudent human caretakers seek to discern concretely the patients' good, here and now, and in doing so, they also observe the boundaries that justice imposes on us.

As we will see, the obligation to seek the best care possible hardly means that there is an easy answer in every case, or that there is a single best decision in every situation. In circumstances that admit of no happy options, morally conscientious caregivers may disagree as to which course of action is least harmful to the patient. But a commitment to seek the best care possible under the circumstances will help ensure that some kinds of decisions or approaches to decision-making will remain morally off-limits, because they are antithetical to care itself. The pursuit of best care both guides and constrains us as we seek the good (or best possible) in hard, often tragic circumstances.

A. The Goals of Caregiving

1. Respect for the Person's Prior Wishes and Ideals.

As we noted in the last chapter, the guiding principle of the current *legal* arrangements governing caregiving for persons with dementia is the obligation to respect the wishes of the competent person the patient once was—what some scholars have called "precedent autonomy."[3] At the extreme, this idea seems to imply that only competent individuals command respect as persons, and, more subtly, that all individuals with dementia are objectively less worthy of care than they were when they were cognitively healthy; or it suggests, at the very least, that there is no obligation to consider their best interests as they are, here and now. But mainly, "precedent autonomy" means that all individuals should have the freedom to decide for themselves, while they are still competent, whether (later) life with dementia would have any meaning or dignity *for them*, and what kinds of treatment should be pursued or rejected on their behalf.

There is, as we have seen in Chapter 2, a partial wisdom in this approach: It aims to honor the distinctness of each individual as a person with a unique and continuous life-history, and it seeks to maintain a connection between the person one was when fully self-aware and the person one might become (or now is) with dementia. It acknowledges each person's claim to self-determination, sets some limits on the types of decisions caregivers can make on behalf of voiceless persons, and protects them against the dangers of unwanted under-treatment or over-treatment. It also offers some direction and protection to future caregivers, who might tremble at the prospect of deciding the fate of a loved one without any guidance, or fear ever "letting go" without some formal permission to do so. For all these reasons, it makes sense to suggest that one of the goals of caregiving is to honor the prior wishes of persons who are no longer able to make their wishes known.

But as we have also seen, respect for the wishes and values of the competent person once present is often an insufficient or poor guide for caregivers in the clinical setting. In many cases, the person's prior wishes are simply not clear or not known. Many people cannot fully envision what they would want in a situation they have never experienced or imagined; they cannot speak for a self that does not yet exist; or they do not wish to confront the prospect of dementia and debility while still in their prime. The moral scope of past wishes is also limited, because a person's interests can change over time and change dramatically with dementia.

More broadly, as discussed above, self-determination has intrinsic limits in a civilized and decent society. Even if the law allows it, there are strong *moral* reasons not to aim at our own death or to ask others to help end our lives by willful acts. Even a competent person's wishes should be limited by such moral boundaries and considerations, because sometimes one's own wishes do an injustice to the value of one's own life, or to the concerns of one's loved ones, or to the norms of the broader society. Our lives are intertwined with others, who are affected powerfully by our choices, and who are themselves conscience-bound moral agents. Our caregivers are not obligated to execute our wishes if those wishes seem morally misguided, nor obligated to enter into contracts that require them to violate important moral precepts that are binding on everyone.

In life as actually lived, the burdens of decision always happen here and now, in circumstances that past directives, written then and there, cannot always imagine. These decisions fall on caregivers and surrogate decisionmakers, who experience the loved one with dementia *as they are now*. These caregivers are no doubt saddened by the capacities that are gone, but they are also bound to the person still present, who is more to them than a breathing corpse and an inherited set of instructions. Caregivers need to consider the incapacitated person's present needs and satisfactions, not only the once-competent person's past wishes; and they are summoned to make decisions not only for the self that exists in memory, but also (and especially) for the self that exists now in embodied reality.

This does not mean that the character or wishes of the individual before the onset of dementia should be treated as irrelevant in deciding how to care for the person she now is: to treat the personal past as irrelevant would deny the continuous life trajectory of the individual; it would deny, in a different way, the reality of the embodied self. The caregiver should always strive to honor the ideals a person with dementia once self-consciously held even though self-awareness is now largely or entirely gone, and to honor her past wishes and past character without transgressing certain firm moral boundaries.* This requires, in the end, that we look also to aims and obligations beyond respecting precedent autonomy in making decisions for the incapacitated person now entrusted to our care.

---

* We will discuss some of these boundaries later in this chapter.

2. The Well-Being of the Family.

Primary (non-professional) caregivers and recipients of care are most often members of families, linked by bonds of affection and obligation (and sometimes affected, too, by the frustrations and resentments that often develop in family life).* In giving care to an especially needy family member, caregivers understandably and rightly worry also about the well-being of the family as a whole. A caregiving spouse, for example, might think about how continued care for a husband or wife with dementia affects the well-being of children and grandchildren. And a caregiving adult child might think about the good of her own family, and how the obligations of caring for an aging parent in her home will affect her ability to care for a growing child.

One approach to aiming at the good of the family might be strictly utilitarian, weighing the costs and benefits of sustaining a dependent person's life for everyone in the family: Does the living presence of a parent or grandparent, in his or her current condition of dementia, give more joy than heartache? Is the cost of care to the family compensated by the continued life that this expense makes possible? And when does this cost-benefit calculus change?

But such narrow utilitarianism seems out of step with our society's moral understanding of family life. Central to our ideals of family life are the bonds of fidelity it entails, both for better and for worse. We do not (or should not) enter into and out of families like contracts, where the only purpose is our maximum pleasure or advantage. Rather, we aspire to live in and through families—as parents, children, siblings, spouses, grandparents—in a spirit of unconditional mutuality, recognizing that just as others care for us, we may one day care for them, and recognizing that mutuality is not always the same as reciprocity: in families, we must sometimes give more than we seem to get. By reducing an individual family member simply to a source of benefit

---

* We are well aware that many people in need of home or institutional care have no family members—or no *dependable* family members—who are able to care for them. In these cases, family well-being is, of course, not a relevant goal of caregiving.

or pleasure for other family members, we risk undermining the very idea of the family that such a utilitarian calculus supposedly aims to promote. In the name of family happiness, we risk undercutting family fidelity and loyalty altogether.

Without question, family life is often hard and imperfect and, for some, a source of pain more than strength, heartache more than joy. But the suffering many people endure within families—especially the experience of feeling abandoned or betrayed—does not justify denying what family can be at its best or what people might reasonably aspire to in family life. And it does not require giving up the hope that some families in trouble can reconcile and renew the ties that bind, and with it the willingness to stand with those fellow family members in need.

But even within affirmed bonds of fidelity and mutuality, matters are rarely simple. A caregiver might ask how her father, always a good provider, would now seek—if he could—to benefit the family, even in his dependent and cognitively disabled state. A caregiving husband might be troubled by seeing his afflicted wife become so utterly reduced before the aging couple's children and grandchildren, and wonder what such long-term changes mean for the reverence and respect at the heart of family life. A caregiver might struggle with finding the proper balance between caring for her parents and rearing her children, and ask whether a particular ailment at a late stage of dementia is nature's way of restoring the balance, to be accepted rather than opposed. Or a caregiver might recognize the moral gift to her children of seeing firsthand what it means to care for an elderly person, what it means to love another in the gravest need, and what it means to appreciate the blessings of health in the face of disease and death.

There is no doubt that caring for a person with dementia imposes real burdens on the caregiving family—on the old, the middle-aged, and the young alike. But it is not always so easy to discern the meaning of those burdens, or to envision what would happen to the family bond if the old were left to die in the name of the young and promising, or the weak left to die in the name of the strong and flourishing.

3. The Good of Society.

Most individuals, when making decisions at the bedside about how to care for loved ones, do not decide what is best here-and-now by thinking about what is best for the whole society in general. But as we have noted, family members are rarely the only actors in this drama: there are the doctors, hospitals, and nursing homes who make recommendations about best care; there are insurance companies and governments that pay a large fraction of health care and long-term care costs for the elderly and that decide what they will pay for; there is the larger polity that must weigh these goods against other civic goods; and there are the fundamental values of society, such as nurturing the young, securing the equal rights of all, and protecting the vulnerable from harm. Thus, although individuals may not aim at the good of society in making decisions, society as a whole establishes conditions that powerfully influence and constrain those decisions—including the influence of law and culture on the ethical intuitions of the individuals who bear the responsibility of care.

Just as families face hard economic decisions and trade-offs, so too does the larger community. Wealthy societies may be able to build both nursing homes and nursery schools, but even the wealthiest societies cannot do everything imaginable for everyone; they cannot maximize the well-being of all individuals all of the time. Yet how our society deals with these hard choices will both reflect and shape our character, both for better and for worse. What kind of society would we be if we left the elderly with dementia (and their families) to fend wholly for themselves? But what kind of society would we be if public subsidies for long-term care or heroic medical interventions for the elderly were financed by drastic cuts in educating the young or securing the peace?

To the broad question of society's "contract" with the elderly, one can envision a broad range of answers regarding their medical care. Some might argue that society should enact certain mandatory standards for non-treatment or public rationing, on the grounds that we should not divert valuable health care resources to care for those with a "low quality of life" and little time left. Others might argue that, because respect for the equal dignity and worth of all persons is a central value of our democratic society, we must ensure that this value is publicly affirmed rather than undermined by age-based or capacity-based rationing of health care. Still others might argue that we should change our priorities for the elderly, shifting resources from heroic measures of emergency rescue to support daily programs such as Meals on Wheels and in-home care.[4] Finally, some might argue that the best way for society to deal with such ethically fraught matters is through a procedural solution—allowing individuals and families maximum possible freedom to decide what is best for themselves, while preserving tolerance for different worldviews and civic peace within society as a whole.

There is surely a partial wisdom in seeking to set social limits on treatment, say by deciding as a society what medical procedures we will not publicly fund for those nearing death. This policy faces up to the reality of mortality, the passing of the generations, the limits on our resources, and the interconnectedness of all social goods. It acknowledges the potential danger of neglecting the young in caring for elderly persons entering upon a long "second childhood." But rationing resources for debilitated or demented persons risks dehumanizing them—by treating them as public burdens, as non-members of society, whose claim on us is limited by their very weakness and dependence. Such a policy might directly or indirectly impose death as "the best treatment" even in cases where a simple medical intervention would benefit the life a person with dementia still has. It might unjustly burden the poor, by excluding certain treatments from Medicare or Medicaid coverage that the wealthy could purchase with private funds. Or it might perversely alter the role of the state, by making certain therapies illegal across the board for certain classes of patients, rich and poor alike.

Of course, as a society we need to reflect on how to set limits, lest we allow the urgency of life-and-death medicine for the elderly to always trump the seemingly less urgent but no less important obligations and aspirations of society as a whole. In the face of limited resources, growing needs for ever-more-expensive long-term care, and the dwindling ranks of voluntary caregivers, we will be unable to escape difficult choices in setting priorities. But the effort to set limits can also lead to some socially pernicious results, separating citizens, by state mandate, into the eligible and the ineligible, the "still worthy" and the "no longer worth it."

There is also a partial wisdom in seeking a procedural solution, one that leaves caregiving decisions as much as possible to individual families. And yet, as discussed above, a policy of autonomy without limits offers little guidance to patients and caregivers about *how to exercise* their freedom. And it fails to confront the potentially dehumanizing excesses of autonomy itself—including the possibility of seeing one's own life as less valuable than it truly is. Moreover, a policy built on self-determination alone offers little guidance about what society owes its dependent members, and what its dependent members owe society.

What we discern, in the end, is that setting social policy in this area is no easy task, especially as it bears on individual cases at the bedside, where prudent judgment about the particulars is always needed. The principle that persons with dementia possess human dignity equal to non-demented persons provides an essential moral foundation for a caring and caregiving society. It means that individual caregivers and public policymakers should not see the disability of dementia *by itself* as a reason for discrimination or as legitimate grounds for the denial of equal treatment. It means that certain kinds of actions—like active euthanasia or a system of rationing that discriminated explicitly against dementia patients—should be morally off limits.

But this principle of equality does not in itself settle the hardest practical dilemmas faced by individuals, families, and citizens. Equal human dignity does not mean identical treatment; it simply means treating every human being as equally worthy of care, and then discerning what this human being, under these circumstances, requires and deserves. For family caregivers and medical professionals in the clinical setting, the task of loving prudence is to sort out, within certain moral boundaries, what the best course of action or non-action is for the person now here. And for society as a whole, the challenge is defending the dignity of persons with dementia in a human world where resources are always limited and where caring for the needy is not the only human good. In addition, the principle of equal human dignity, in itself, says nothing about what obligations persons with dementia (in its early stages) may still have to the society of which they are part, including generosity toward and concern for generations yet to come.

Perhaps our greatest social obligation is toward the large number of people who do not have family caregivers and thus rely on the community to stand with them and speak for them. This obligation is all the more reason why a strictly legalistic solution, like advance directives or even durable power of attorney, will not be adequate. And this is why there is good reason to lay out, for strangers taking care of strangers, what "best care" for the patient here-and-now might require.

4. Best Care for the Person Now Here.

If the goal of caregiving is to provide the best care possible for the person with dementia now here, then it is important to try to see the world as the person with dementia sees it, and to ensure that we do not allow our own discomfort with his or her diminished capacity to become the scale we use to measure his or her worth. Surely, we need to improve our understanding of life-as-lived by persons with dementia; we need to probe the meaning of experiences that might make little sense to us—such as reading books without paying attention to the order of the pages—but often give persons with dementia experiential pleasure. More deeply, we need to see the person with dementia as more than simply an individual with interests for himself, but as someone whose life has meaning for others. Sometimes this means seeing the value of a disabled person's life even when being alive may no longer seem like a benefit to the disabled person himself.

People who contend that caregiving ought to serve the "best interests" of the patient rightfully seek to put the present patient at the center of caregiving decisions. But to speak of "interests" *alone* also seems somewhat impoverished: human beings are not simply collections of interests, but whole persons whose lives are intertwined with others, lives that have meaning even when their interests seem limited and even when their life options have shrunk significantly. In this, the proper aim is not simply "best interests" but "best care" for the *well-being* of this patient, under these circumstances, at this time.

Yet even as we try to empathize with persons who suffer dementia and see them as human beings with equal dignity and worth, we also cannot lose sight of the deprivations that dementia often or eventually brings: the loss of modesty and self-control; the outbursts of anger; the descent into mindlessness; the physical discomfort; the need for diapers or physical restraints. Seeing the good of a life with moderate or severe dementia often means seeing the worth of a life that has been stripped of many worthwhile and dignified things. We need to see both the dignity of the person and the indignity of the disease.

Approaching caregiving decisions in this way brings us to the core question: How do we benefit the life this person now has—even if it is not the life the person would have chosen for himself? This straightforward question does not always have a straightforward answer. Surely physical well-being is central to the obligation of best care, and so finding ways to ease suffering and treat physical ailments as they arise—broken hips, pneumonia, urinary tract infections—would have a strong moral claim. But there are other claims that must also be considered, going beyond the present good of the body. Does one benefit the life a person now has by trying to prevent an excessively painful or degrading death, even if it means accepting an earlier death? Does one benefit the life a person now has by extending an existence marked mostly by physical and emotional misery? Does one benefit the life the Alzheimer's patient now has by forgoing life-extending treatment, so that he might finish life with some remnant of past nobility and self-awareness intact and while his presence still awakens reverence rather than repugnance in his grandchildren?

Surely, different people will see the good of the person with dementia in different terms; they will value different factors differently. To repeat, best care does not always mean that there is only a single right choice in every case. But doing our "best" for each patient should always be our guiding aspiration, and thus a check on the tendency to lower our standards and seek only what is "good enough" rather than what is "best under the circumstances." Caregivers must resist the temptation to do what is best or most comfortable *for themselves* in the false name of doing what is best for the patient, and they must avoid projecting their own wishes, prejudices, or burdens onto the patient.*

Spirit and motivation matter in these decisions, and two decisions that look very similar may have a profoundly different meaning when seen in their totality. But in the end, all decisions should operate within a shared moral framework—one that recognizes the deprivations of dementia, the limitations on family and social resources, and the significance of a person's prior wishes, but which never defines life with dementia as "life unworthy of life" and never sees causing death as a morally choiceworthy means to the end of easing suffering. After all, it is self-contradictory to propose to "care" for any patient by making him dead; and it is hard to think wholeheartedly about best care if one morally eligible option is to ease the suffering person out of existence.

To sum up: Caregivers should be guided primarily by a moral obligation and an ethical disposition to care always, and by an appreciation of the particular current needs and circumstances of each person now in their care. We should seek to provide the best care possible, case by case, situation by situation, but always within certain universal moral boundaries. In what follows, we expand our consideration of the moral guidelines and moral boundaries that should guide caregivers, before taking up some difficult yet paradigmatic clinical cases.

B. Moral Guidelines

As we have already indicated, the discernment of best care for any particular patient, here and now, is the work of prudent deliberation and judgment. Because the variables are so numerous, person by person and circumstance by circumstance, it is impossible to reduce prudence to precise rules or to write programs for wise decision-making. Nevertheless, our tradition of medical ethics, reflecting on the character of human action and on the care-

---

* At the same time, potential patients should not seek a guarantee, long in advance, that they will "never be a burden" to their loved ones and thus look for ways to orchestrate an early exit, especially when those loved ones would rather bear the burdens of care than the burden of not being permitted to care.

giving dilemmas of interest to this report, has articulated certain crucial concepts and distinctions to guide prudent thinking: *negatively*, to set some moral boundaries beyond which prudence cannot rightly go; *positively*, to clarify the target at which prudence should rightly aim. Such ethical concepts and distinctions are both necessary and perilous. They are necessary, because we need to see ethical decisions in their proper light, and we need to erect certain protections against doing harm, even—or especially—with good intentions. But they are also perilous, because there is always a risk of turning a concrete human situation into an abstract case and of adhering narrowly to general principles without discerning the best care possible for each particular patient.

Below, we consider four moral distinctions or concepts that have been used to try to distinguish between what is morally required, what is morally forbidden, and what is morally optional. These are: (1) ordinary and extraordinary care; (2) acts of commission and acts of omission; (3) the motives, intended deeds, and results of a human action; and (4) the burden of treatment imposed by human action and the burdens of disability and disease imposed by nature.[5] Out of this analysis, we will then formulate the operative moral boundaries that should guide us in actual cases.

1. Ordinary and Extraordinary Care.

In formal discussions of medical ethics, the terms "ordinary" and "extraordinary" care have been commonly used to think about whether to initiate, continue, or cease particular medical treatments, ordinary care being considered mandatory, extraordinary care being considered optional. But defining these terms is something of a challenge. People sometimes apply these terms to the medical technique or intervention itself, where ordinary can mean *reliable* ("it works"), *common* ("part of standard medical practice"), *easy* ("not distressing to the patient"), *simple* ("unsophisticated and easy to administer"), *affordable* ("not unduly expensive"), or *easily available* ("near at hand, not requiring much travel to get it").

In the discourse of medical ethics, the terms "ordinary" treatment and "extraordinary" treatment acquired a more precise and technical meaning, referring specifically to the intervention as it relates to a particular ailing person.[6] Thus, the operative meaning of these terms becomes relative to each case, often differing dramatically for different patients. For example, it seems relatively "ordinary" for a vigorous middle-aged man with decent health insurance to get coronary artery bypass surgery at the first-rate medical center near his home; for a frail old man with the same heart condition but lacking medical insurance and living far from any medical center, bypass surgery would probably be deemed "extraordinary." For the first person, the surgery is readily available and affordable without upending his entire domestic life; for the second, the surgery would create burdens so great that it becomes virtually beyond reach. The surgery itself imposes physical burdens that are not exactly "ordinary" ("easy to take") even for the first person, but also not so "extraordinary" that living with and through them is too onerous to endure. As a person ages, however, the burdens of surgery and post-operative recovery increase, and the once "ordinary" treatment becomes increasingly "extraordinary," because it becomes increasingly burdensome and risky to the patient.

To generalize: A proposed treatment could be reliable, common, simple, affordable, and readily available, yet be regarded as "extraordinary" for a given patient. For despite being ordinary in all those ways, the proposed treatment could still be useless for the patient—or, even if possibly useful, quite burdensome. Treatments that are either "useless" or "excessively burdensome" for a particular patient, however ordinary they might otherwise seem, are in the ethical sense "extraordinary"—above and beyond what is morally required. As such they may be accepted or declined, and in some cases they should clearly be declined for the good of the patient.

At one time, medical ethicists relied a great deal on this distinction, and it was the staple of Roman Catholic casuistry on this subject.[7] Today, this distinction is much less frequently used by doctors and ethicists. And because "extraordinary"—meaning "ethically optional"—treatment really translates into "excessively burdensome" or "useless" treatment, we might be better off working directly with those terms, seeing as they focus our attention more precisely on the well-being of the patients and thus on the kinds of concerns that are always of central moral significance.*

2. Acts of Commission and Acts of Omission.

Another common distinction used in thinking about life-sustaining or life-ending treatments is that between acts of *commission* and acts of *omission*. Whereas "ordinary" and "extraordinary" focus on what counts morally in balancing benefits and burdens *for the patient*, this distinction focuses on the deeds of the *moral agent* who elects, provides, or forgoes the treatment. In the clinical context, acts of commission involve the deliberate, active use of some agent (like a drug, machine, or surgical technique) to alter the life-course of the patient. Acts of omission involve the deliberate decision *not* to intervene in the life-course of a patient.

Clear as this basic distinction may seem, however, its meaning is often far from obvious and its moral usefulness is, at most, partial. Analysis of the meaning of an "act" or "action" is an extraordinarily complex matter, to which we can hardly do justice here. A few observations are, however, especially germane. First, a human action is more than a spontaneous reflex or a slice of behavior. The description of an act itself—*what* the person *does*—is governed by the person's intention (by his "plan of action"), both as to ends and means. In addition, the same action (or plan of action) may be done from many different motives and in order to accomplish many different results. All of these aspects count in any ethical analysis of our deeds, and their evaluation depends on more than the distinction between doing and not doing: if undertaken with wrongful intention, all deeds—whether of commission or omission—may be judged adversely.

Second, if *not* acting is a choice made by conscious decision, this omission is itself a moral act with moral significance, and those who so choose are often as morally responsible for *not* doing as those who choose to act are responsible for doing. In cases such as the ones of interest to this report, people some-

---

* We take up the subject of "burdensomeness" below.

times take refuge in the distinction between omission and commission, as if it were an easy way of distinguishing between what
is morally permissible or praiseworthy and what is not. That is
probably more weight than the distinction by itself can bear.

Third, the moral meaning of the same act of commission (or
of the same act of omission) can differ, owing to *the predictability
or non-predictability of the outcome.* In some cases, we can know with
virtual certainty that intervening will sustain (or end) life or that
not intervening means that the patient's life will end. In other
cases, we can only know the likely, or probable, or potential outcome of acting or not acting. Where omitting an action is *certain*
to produce death (for example, not providing artificial nutrition
and hydration to a person in a coma), it will be evaluated differently than when the outcome of the omission is uncertain (for
example, not inserting a feeding tube into a dimly conscious person who can still be spoon fed).

Commission and omission seem to be ends of a spectrum
rather than either/or categories of action. There are *clear acts of
commission*—such as treating pneumonia with antibiotics or killing
a patient by administering some lethal agent. There are *clear acts of
omission*—such as allowing a patient to die of infection by electing
not to treat. In between are actions that are harder to classify as
commissions or omissions. Some actions *remove treatments already
underway*—for example, turning off a respirator or removing a
feeding tube. Others *cease periodic treatments*—for example, stopping blood transfusions or ceasing dialysis.

It scarcely makes sense to label every failure or refusal to act
as itself a form of action; our responsibility as actors depends on
the circumstances. Clearly, some behaviors—such as failing to
wish a stranger a happy birthday—are unlikely to be termed acts
of omission; for in almost all circumstances they would not be
regarded as *acts* of any kind. Other behaviors—like forgetting to
wish one's mother a happy birthday—may or may not be acts of
omission, and may or may not be blameworthy, depending on
the circumstances. In the medical context, a decision not to intervene—especially after clinical assessment of what intervention
versus non-intervention likely means for the patient—is not simply an omission but a *deliberately chosen* omission. Physicians have
a legally defined affirmative duty to act in medically appropriate

cases; in such cases their decision not to act when they are duty bound to do so becomes a culpable omission.

Despite these ambiguities and complexities, the distinction between commission and omission does still possess *some* moral significance, mainly in the two common situations in which the difference between acting and not-acting is thought to be especially relevant: (a) the difference between stopping and not starting treatment (where the distinction may make, morally speaking, only a symbolic and psychological difference), and (b) the difference between active killing and letting die (where the distinction makes considerable—but not complete—intrinsic moral difference).

a. Never beginning treatment versus ceasing/removing a treatment-in-process. Is there a moral difference between never beginning a treatment at all and ending a treatment already begun? (There may sometimes be a legal difference, but we limit ourselves here to the moral question.) We can imagine a case in which, though there might have been some initial reason never to begin a treatment, that reason ceases to be significant once the treatment has been in place for a time. For example, a patient might strongly resist the initial insertion of a feeding tube, but eventually grow physically accustomed or at least un-resistant to it. Conversely, there might be cases in which an intervention (believed to be temporary) is begun in the hopes of improving a patient's condition, but where improvement never comes and the continuation of the intervention, now necessary to sustain life, has become a serious burden for the patient.

There is surely symbolic and psychological importance to ceasing an ongoing treatment, especially where one knows in advance that the likely consequence of doing so is imminent death. If we withdraw treatment in such a case, we may more readily think of ourselves as having caused the patient's death or, at least, as having initiated the irreversible process of the person's dying. In forgoing a new treatment, one does not alter the status quo of the patient; in acting to end a treatment-in-process, one deliberately alters the status quo, and the consequence of such alteration may be lethal. In many cases, however, there is little or no *intrinsic moral* difference between these two kinds of acts—

never beginning treatment and ceasing treatment already be-gun—and in both cases, the actual *cause* of death is not the care-giver's action or non-action but the underlying disease-in-process.* Yet it is natural that we experience ourselves as causal agents more strongly when we withdraw a treatment already be-gun than when we decide never to begin a treatment at all. And it is surely important for all concerned that physicians not seem to be intending to cause a patient's death when they rightly elect to discontinue treatment that, after a trial, has become futile or ex-cessively burdensome.

But in the end, this distinction, though relevant, is hardly de-cisive, neither medically nor (especially) ethically. Much will de-pend on the condition of the patient, the nature of the disease, and the particular type of treatment in question: Is it burden-some? Will it work? Can we know before we try? What matters most is not whether a decision forgoes treatment in advance or removes treatment-in-process, but the moral and human aim of the decision to begin, cease, or never begin a particular treat-ment. Whether the action is leaving a disease untreated or ending a treatment already begun, the question is always: Am I benefit-ing the life the patient now has by acting in this way?

b. Active killing versus letting die. Medical ethics has long insisted on the moral difference between taking deliberate posi-tive measures to bring about the death of a patient and letting a patient die of "natural causes." To be sure, medicine generally seeks to oppose death by natural causes and to correct or restrain the biological causes of debility and mortality. But caregivers must also, eventually, "let die" those entrusted to their care, if only because every patient eventually dies, medicine or no medi-cine. "Letting die" is thus always part of caregiving.

---

* A good case can be made that a *deliberately limited* trial of therapy is morally better than not starting it, because it permits a realistic assessment—and not just a guess—of the merits of the treatment for the particular patient. To avoid the trap of not being able to stop what has been started, some physicians now place a time (or other) limit on the treatment *at the time it is begun.* For example, they order tube feeding "for three days," with evaluation to follow the trial. If it is then deemed unlikely to do good, it stops "automatically." (We owe this information to Dr. Joanne Lynn.)

The question, therefore, is not *whether* to accept natural death, but *how* and *when* to do so. What matters morally is discerning when it is appropriate to "let die," even in cases where the means to oppose death and extend life still exist, but where using such means may not benefit the life the person still has. Extending life is not the only way to benefit a person's life, and length of life is not the only good worthy of the caregiver's consideration. And so, in some cases, letting a patient die "earlier than necessary" is morally sound or even morally obligatory, if the available ways of extending life are themselves morally problematic.

By contrast, taking active measures to end a patient's life, even if such measures are taken with the best of motives, is always difficult (or impossible) to reconcile with the ethics of caregiving. Active killing, even when motivated by a desire to end bodily or psychic pain, makes caregivers the final masters and arbiters of life and death for the person entrusted to their care. It denies the patient's right to life. It breaks the state's monopoly on the legitimate use of lethal force. It makes some doctors sometimes executioners, calling into question their trustworthiness always to serve the patient's good. Wielding such power is deeply antithetical to the practice of medicine and the vocation of doctors, who are called to serve the patient until the very end. As the Hippocratic Oath already put it: "I will neither give a deadly drug to anybody if asked for it, nor will I make a suggestion to this effect. . . . In purity and holiness I will guard my life and my art."[8]

Serving the patient does not mean extending life at all costs; doctors are not only in the business of *curing* but also in the business of *caring*, which sometimes means accepting a shorter, more comfortable life. But even when doctors and caregivers surrender to death, this surrender honors our humanity best when it steadily affirms the *life* of even a dying person and when it steadfastly refuses to abandon the *person* in his dying. To end a person's life is to abandon that life. Active killing—even out of mercy—is not the giving of care.

Although the distinction between "letting die" and "active killing" is morally significant, it is not by itself morally decisive. For although active killing is always off limits, letting die is not always permissible or praiseworthy. As in all of our chosen actions, the moral quality of the action taken (or omitted) will be shaped by the *reasons* for taking it; hence, we must consider the moral weight of those reasons. If one deliberately omits treatment *so that* a patient will die, such a choice seems morally little different from intervening actively to end the patient's life. True, by not moving from deadly intention to overt deadly deed, an act of omission aiming at death does not put doctors and caregivers in the perverse position of being the actual cause of death. And, by leaving the patient at the mercy of nature and his diseases, it does not guarantee or manage with precision a particular moment of death, a death-on-demand. To this extent, the harm to all of us—as a society devoted to caring for one another—is much greater in the case of active killing. At the same time, however, the wrong done to the dying person may be morally the same, if, either by omission or commission, we betray the patient *by aiming at his death.* In the one case (active killing) we use a lethal agent of our own devising as the means; in the other case (letting die where death itself is the aim) we use disease as the means of achieving a death we seek but do not cause.

Nevertheless, even if the distinction between active killing and letting die does not solve all our difficulties (as just noted, it does not help us discern the difference between morally sound and morally problematic instances of letting die), the distinction remains morally important, and the condemnation of active killing that it implies is ethically crucial. For example, we might in good conscience remove a respirator from a patient in the final stages of brain cancer so that he can die a more peaceful death unburdened by the machinery. But we should not give a patient in the final stages of brain cancer a lethal injection so that he will die a more peaceful death. (Instead, we would rely only on improved pain management, including, if necessary, heavy sedation.)

A death resulting from "letting die" (withdrawing the respirator) and a death resulting from "active killing" (giving a lethal injection) might follow a roughly similar trajectory and would reach the same outcome, and they might therefore seem similar, at least from the perspective of the dying patient (or those for whom, mistakenly, only the end result counts). But for us, as a

society of caregivers, the two deeds would have a morally different meaning and morally different implications. We need to trust
that our healers will never turn into our killers; we need shared
limits to prevent deliberate harm to the vulnerable. We need to
cultivate a society of caregivers who will never think of eliminating a patient in order to avoid the trouble of caring for him. For
both ethical and prudential reasons, therefore, we must preserve
the line between active killing and letting die, knowing that this
distinction may not always be morally sufficient or morally satisfying in real-life cases.

Embedded in this distinction between (a forbidden) "active
killing" and (a permitted or approved) "letting die" is a deeper
distinction between *wrongs* and *harms*, and more precisely, between wrongs that *we ourselves commit* and harms that *"nature" in-
flicts*. It acknowledges that there are ills we cannot relieve as
quickly and completely as we might wish—at least without doing
injury in the process. There will, of course, be at least some moments—for example, when continued life of one who is suffering seems itself an unrelieved misery—in which we wonder why
we should respect the boundary (that forbids active killing while
approving letting die) firmly established in our medical and moral
tradition. Exactly when we ourselves are distressed by our own
inability to relieve suffering, we are understandably most tempted
to set aside this distinction and end suffering by "ending" the
patient who suffers. We might even try to persuade ourselves
that we are in fact not aiming at the patient's death but merely at
his suffering.

Such wrenching human situations often lead caregivers into
confusion and anguish, with mixed and complicated emotions:
we desire to keep a loved one alive yet want her suffering to end;
we fear that not doing "everything" means that we are guilty of
betrayal yet we worry that prolonging life in such a condition is a
form of torture; we want what is best for those we cherish but
we are exhausted and anguished ourselves. Under such circumstances, caregivers may find that the moral lines between love
and betrayal, between standing with the patient until the end and
forcing the patient to endure the worst kind of end, between
compassion and cruelty, between leaving the patient to suffer
and leaving the patient to die, seem profoundly unclear.

Yet in this murky world, the distinction between "active kill-ing" and "letting die" offers us one bright line—a line that keeps us from becoming killers ourselves. Fidelity to the life we care for requires that we not set ourselves resolutely against it, per-versely trying to help it by erasing it altogether. Caregiving that truly cares will not annihilate its beneficiary.

Although this moral boundary should be respected in all cases, its utility is, however, also limited. Even if we steadfastly refuse to kill our patients and loved ones, we often still find our-selves in morally difficult straits. Determining, for example, how and when to accept natural death or the circumstances in which one may ethically let a patient die requires that we attend care-fully to the motives, the intended deeds, and the goals of our ac-tions (and inactions), a set of distinctions to which we next turn.

3. Doing and Accomplishing: Motives, Intended Deeds, and Goals.

As already noted, every human action can be looked at and evaluated in several different ways. One way has to do with the agent's *motives*. Suppose a terminally ill man, dying of cancer, lies in his hospital bed in considerable pain and respiratory distress. Suppose also that another man enters the room and, in order to bring about the patient's death, gives him a fatal overdose of morphine.

Now consider this scenario from two different angles, with two different reasons that moved the giver of morphine to target the patient's life. In the first scenario, the "killer" is a close friend of the dying man. He fears for his friend the pain and anguish of the coming weeks, desires for him a relatively peaceful death, and gives him an overdose moved by these feelings of mercy and af-fection. In the second scenario, the "killer" is an ex-friend (and now an enemy) of the dying man. Cheated and betrayed in im-portant matters by the man now dying, this ex-friend is not satis-fied simply to see him die. He wants to have a hand in it, to be himself the agent who brings about the patient's death.

If asked to evaluate the character of the two "killers," we might find much to praise in the character of the first and much to condemn in the character of the second. Yet, despite their very different motives, each *does* the same thing: Each targets the life of the patient and aims at his death. Hence, whatever final moral evaluation we make of their actions, we should not deny that they *do* the same thing. It would be misguided to describe the second man's action as "killing an ex-friend" while re-describing the first man's action as "showing mercy to a friend." To do so blurs rather than clarifies the moral situation. Instead, if we want to approve the first man's action and condemn the second man's, we will have to argue that a praiseworthy motive (such as mercy) is more important than the chosen deadly deed itself—so important that, moved by mercy, we might rightly exercise a kind of ultimate authority over the life of a fellow human being. But if, on the contrary, we hold that the exercise of that kind of authority violates the equal human worth that we prize, we would probably think that such a motive in such circumstances should be characterized as a *temptation*—understandable, to be sure, but not praiseworthy if it moves one to perform deeds that are ethically unjustified.

We know that motives are important, and we want to give them weight in our moral judgment, but we quite properly are reluctant to let a praiseworthy motive *by itself* transform any deed, however questionable, into the *right* thing to do. For regardless of motive, what we do, and what we are willing to do, itself shapes our character. Over time, our deeds turn us into people of a certain sort. Judgments about what we do, therefore, carry their own independent moral weight and should not simply be re-described in terms of our motives.

But there is a further complication in the analysis of our actions. We act not only because we are moved by (praiseworthy or blameworthy) motives, but also because we have *goals* that we seek to achieve. What we do is related to what we accomplish or hope to accomplish by acting. Thus, moved by mercy, one might intentionally take a friend's life, hoping to achieve thereby the relief of the friend's suffering. What one does in this case is to kill; what one accomplishes (if successful) is an end to suffering (by means of the person's death).

The complicated connections between what we *do* and what we *accomplish*, between the intended deed itself and the direct or indirect results of our actions, constitute one of the enduring

problems for moral reflection.* On the one hand, we hardly want
to say that results count for nothing, that it matters little morally
what purposes we undertake, or what goals we try to accomplish,
or what outcomes actually result from our pursuing them. On
the other hand, we are also reluctant to say that desirable results,
in and of themselves, are alone sufficient to justify any deed that
may accomplish them. Moreover, some actions that are undertaken even with advance knowledge that bad things may result
can be morally justified, provided that the primary intention of
the action is good and that the bad consequences are not the intended aim or goal of the action itself. (This is the so-called principle of "double-effect": it sanctions, for example, the giving of
high doses of morphine to a terminally ill patient in order to relieve severe pain, even though doing so increases the risk of de-
pressing respiration and thus hastening death.) Some of the most
wrenching of life's circumstances—including and especially in
the clinical context—arise when we can find no way to *accomplish*
very desirable goals other than by *doing* what may be wrong, or
when *doing* what is right seems to *accomplish* undesirable results.

An act can be wrong even if it achieves good results, and an
act can be right even if some of its effects are evil. It would be
wrong to compel an unwilling and fully competent patient to receive treatment, even if the treatment turns out to cure him (and
even if he thanks us afterward). Likewise, it would be right to
give a 65-year-old man just diagnosed with early Alzheimer's disease antibiotics for his pneumonia, even if doing so results in
more years of worsening debility and dementia.

There are additional reasons why we should not be seduced
into making choices and evaluating judgments solely on the basis
of results. Doctors, nurses, and all caregivers daily confront the
many uncertainties that surround our attempts to accomplish
what is good for patients in need. Often we cannot say with certainty how a given disease like dementia will progress, what the
results of different possible interventions may be, whether the

---

* Strictly speaking, there is a difference between the *goals* and the *results* of our
actions: our goal (that is, our wished-for end) might be to accomplish a certain
desired result, but the actual result might turn out to be other than what we
wished for.

course of a (certainly deadly) disease will be swift or slow (or preempted by some other unforeseen cause of death). To be a caregiver is to live, day after day, with unexpected side effects, with desired results that turn out to seem undesirable, with a recalcitrant nature that resists our attempts to master it. These uncertainties argue for modesty on our part—and for a respect for moral limits on what we *do* in our endeavor to *accomplish* what we think would be good.

In any case, as will be readily apparent in the discussion of cases in the next chapter, thinking about the complexities of care for those who are aging, suffering from dementia, or dying will require us to pay attention to different aspects of moral analysis: to the motives that shape us and may sometimes tempt us, to the goods and goals we hope to accomplish in our work as caregivers, and to the nature of what it is we actually do (whatever our motives or goals may be). All these features of moral analysis will play a role in our discussion of cases; for they play a role in our effort to live well and do well for those who rely upon us.*

---

* This moral analysis is most difficult in those cases in which the relationships among our *motive*, our chosen *deed*, and our desired *result* are most complicated. In some cases, these different elements of human action are clear: The doctor who gives a patient a lethal injection clearly aims at the person's death in undertaking such an action. Death is the aim; compassion is the motive; and an end to the patient's suffering is the desired goal and the accomplished result (along with a dead patient). By contrast, the doctor who withdraws a life-sustaining but unbearably painful or distressing treatment foresees death as a possible (indirect) result of his action, but in seeking to remove the suffering his own treatment has caused, he *does not* aim at death. Stopping a painful treatment is the aim of action; benefiting the life the patient still has is the motive; and greater peace and comfort (notwithstanding the risk of an earlier death) is the desired result.

In other cases, however, the relationship between our motives, our chosen deeds, and the goals or results of our actions is far more complicated. This is especially the case in trying to describe and understand certain acts of omission, where caregivers elect not to treat a deadly or potentially deadly ailment even when the treatment itself is not burdensome and might be efficacious in treating the ailment in question. Confronted with a life marked by terrible suffering or in the end stages of disease, the motive for not treating may be the desire to provide the best care possible to the suffering patient as a whole, rather than pursuing the most effective strategy for acting against a particular treatable co-morbidity. But how, precisely, shall we characterize the *aim* of not giving treatment: "The death of the patient?" "The refusal to continue extending his miseries?" "A life with fewer burdens until its natural end?" (*Note continues on next page.*)

4. Burdens of Treatment and Burdens of Disease.

In our discussions so far, we have frequently mentioned but not yet explored in detail a crucial distinction: the distinction between the burdens of a medical intervention and the burdens of living with a disease or disability.

The burdens of medical interventions range both in degree and in type: from the minimal pain (for most people) of drawing blood, to the nausea caused by cancer treatments, to the pain of recovering from major surgery, to the excruciating suffering of being treated for major burns. Sometimes the burdens of therapy involve not bodily pain but various limitations on human action required by treatment or side effects caused by treatment—such as extended immobility, restrictions on eating, or impotence as the side effect of taking certain medications. Sometimes the burden of treatment is less the acute burden of a single intervention, more the accumulated exhaustion of being a permanent patient—of needing insulin shots daily or dialysis multiple times each week for the rest of one's life in order to continue living.

Moreover, sometimes the burdens of treatment are more psychic than somatic—the misery of being stuck in a hospital bed, removed from everyday life, unable to do the things one loves, temporarily or even permanently. For many patients—especially patients with dementia or other kinds of cognitive dysfunction—there is often the burden that comes with not understanding a given treatment, and therefore believing that caregivers are intervening against them rather than for them. And—though it must be evaluated somewhat differently if our practice

---

Do we necessarily aim at death by not treating? Is "aiming at death" really the best way to describe what loving physicians and family members do in such a case, especially those who are administering care simultaneously in many other ways? Or do caregivers aim at a life with fewer burdens until its natural end, a life where nature is allowed to take its final course, a life where excessive suffering is not unnecessarily extended by our own interventions? This is indeed the hardest kind of case. In one sense, it seems impossible to describe withholding such life-preserving treatment as anything other than aiming at death, on the tacit premise that the patient is "better off dead." And yet, the overall human description of such a decision to "let go" or "let die" *seems different* than taking active measures to kill. This is a dilemma we will confront in greater detail in the particular cases that follow in Chapter 4.

of medicine is to remain patient-centered—there are also the burdens of treatment endured by the caregivers: the personal burden of arranging for medical care, the economic burden of paying for medical care, and the emotional burden of continuing medical care, especially when there is little or no hope of recovery. Of course, the same treatment will burden different patients very differently—depending on age, strength, tolerance for pain, the level of support from friends and family, and the quality and skill of physicians and nurses. There is no simple formula for deciding which treatments are excessively or unduly burdensome. We cannot make such judgments based entirely on the treatment itself, but only the treatment as applied or not applied to a particular patient.

But what is crucial to remember about the burdens of treatment is that they—in contrast to the burdens of the disease or disability we treat—are always produced or imposed *by the caregivers themselves*, not by nature or chance. The treatment itself always aims to make things better for the patient. But sometimes the effort to improve a patient's long-term condition makes the patient's current condition notably worse; sometimes intervening to fight a deadly disease itself imposes such excessive suffering that the treatment harms the life the patient has now, even if it might delay the patient's death a little longer. As caregivers, decisions about treatment always fall within the realm of our moral responsibility; it is the realm in which we decide what we owe the patient. It is the realm in which we exert greatest control and therefore have greatest responsibility—if never perfect control (treatment is limited and often unpredictable) and never perfect responsibility (the obligation to care for the patient does not make us responsible for every burden the patient confronts).

As we think about what it means for a treatment to be "burdensome" and thus what our obligations as caregivers are, we need a more developed typology of different ways in which burdens may be related to treatments. Specifically, there are: (i) treatments that are excessively burdensome; (ii) treatments that are not excessively burdensome but prolong a life marked by the terrible burdens of current disease; (iii) treatments that are not excessively burdensome but prolong a life where the terrible burdens of a disease in-process seem likely to increase greatly in the near or distant future; and (iv) treatments that ease a current burden but prolong a life marked by other existing or likely future burdens.

One of the most difficult situations is precisely when a relatively non-burdensome treatment can prolong a life marked by great hardship or looming misery. From the patient's perspective, after all, suffering is suffering, and the burdens caused by nature and chance seem—*as suffered* burdens—no different from the burdens caused by intervention.* So why is it that medical ethics holds that it is morally permissible to withhold burdensome treatments but morally wrong to withhold useful, non-burdensome treatments *so that* a life marked by terrible burdens will more likely come to a swifter end? This difficult question prompts three kinds of answers or reflections.

First, medical interventions are concrete human acts for which we bear clear responsibility as human agents; by contrast, those diseases imposed by nature are not produced by human action. We are fully responsible for our acts; we are not fully responsible for the burdens life itself sometimes brings (even though we may be deeply dismayed by such burdens in our own life or that of others). In training ourselves to distinguish between the burdens produced by treatment and those brought by life, we are searching for a way to turn against burdensome treatments without simultaneously turning against the life of a fellow human being.

Second, although we are not responsible for the possible, probable, or likely future miseries that befall those whose lives we sustain by intervening medically to benefit the patient's present life, we must acknowledge that we act *knowing* and *accepting*

---

* Of course, a person's attitude toward the *fact* of his having to suffer would be different if he thought that he was suffering at the hands of his family rather than at the hands of nature or fortune. But as experienced bodily suffering, the clear difference in the cause would not manifest itself in a clear difference in the misery or distress. And for persons with advanced dementia, the capacity to distinguish between the burdens of disease and the burdens of treatment is already long gone. But as we have already indicated, one can mistreat someone even if the person cannot know that he is being mistreated. This is why, even if the source of his suffering matters not to the patient with dementia, the distinction among causes is relevant for assessing morally the actions and agency of caregivers.

the consequences or potential consequences of our interventions, even if we are not fully responsible for them.

Finally, we should acknowledge the frustration we may experience when we seem obligated to let a humanly indifferent nature "take its course" while prohibiting certain human acts— like actively ending a painful life or deliberately seeking the end of life by an act of omission—that might relieve the burdens of chance. We should expect that we will continue to be troubled by the fact that our medical and moral tradition holds that there are some burdens we cannot rightly relieve entirely (if the only means to do so is turning against not just a treatment but a life). We will and should suffer at the suffering of others to whose care we are committed. Yet we should remember that aiming at a person's death is always a kind of betrayal; standing with the suffering person, in the hardest times, is not—even if we might rage together with the patient at the God, or nature, or universe that permits such misery, and even if we pray with the patient for an end to a painful life that is nevertheless not ours to end.

C. Moral Boundaries

The foregoing discussion of these various moral distinctions has shown, we believe, why it is difficult to state precisely how to define "best care" when patients who are suffering greatly are candidates for treatments that might extend their life, especially when such patients cannot choose for themselves and are entirely (or largely) in the hands of their caregivers. There are no simple formulae to guide us, and no algorithms for calculating the relative weights of benefits and harms. Seeking the best care possible will always require the wise and prudent judgment of the people on the spot: spouses and children, guardians and friends, doctors and nurses, social workers and hospice professionals.

Yet prudence needs help from principle. Our ability to seek wholeheartedly for the best care possible under often very sad circumstances is immeasurably enhanced by the existence of certain moral boundaries that define the limits of possible choices and that prevent us from erring greatly when we are overcome with frustration, exhaustion, or moral confusion. These moral boundaries are in fact entirely in line with our medical-moral traditions, frequently renewed by reflection and adjustment through changing times. They are by no means the whole truth that prudence seeks to discern. Although they set boundaries to our deliberation and possible choices, they provide no formula for best care in particular cases. Further thought and reflection will be required to discern what we owe those for whom we must care.

We recognize that we are entering on perhaps unprecedented times, the age of a mass geriatric society, with hundreds of thousands of people no longer able to care for themselves and unable to decide what kind of medical care they in fact want. We also recognize that there will likely be great pressure to alter these boundaries, as frustrated and unhappy caregivers look for easier ways out of the sad fate of having to expend mountains of care on persons who will only sink further into their prolonged and degrading decline. But relying partly on the strength of the moral exploration just completed, partly on the evident good moral sense of the boundaries themselves, we present the following moral boundaries as rules to guide prudent caregivers in action:

- No active killing or assisted killing of another, no matter how painful or diminished a life has become
- No aiming at death as a purpose of action, whether by acts of commission or omission
- No imposing excessively burdensome treatments on others
- No obligation to do what we *cannot* do in the role of caregiver, but the obligation to see how much we *can* do without destroying or deforming everything else in our lives (we will analyze this moral precept more fully below)

We can also state the clear grounds for forgoing life-sustaining care:

- When the treatment itself is excessively burdensome for the patient
- When the treatment is useless
- When a better death is possible in circumstances where death is proximate (for example, by allowing an irre-

trievably dying patient to remain at home in the company of family rather than go to the hospital)

As we have already noted, respecting these boundaries does not suffice to reach the concrete conclusion of what constitutes best care in individual cases. And as we shall soon demonstrate, we recognize that there will be hard cases that put our ability to abide by these rules to the test. Still, we think that these boundaries will and should guide us as we struggle to keep faith with the duty to care and as prudence guides us to act affirmatively in the service of our loved ones' well-being.

Before leaving the general considerations of caregiving to examine concrete cases, we should emphasize that ethical caregiving is not primarily about following rules of right conduct or observing moral boundaries, important though these are. It is primarily about creating the disposition to care and cultivating the habits of caring, often in the face of great obstacles and at the cost of considerable time and resources. Ethical reflection of the sort engaged in here cannot, by itself, produce the requisite traits of character, neither in individuals and families nor in the larger community. But it can begin to sharpen the gaze and deepen the understanding, without which even a good heart can sometimes be led astray. By pointing us to the proper target—best care—and by showing us the limits of proper conduct, these theoretical discussions, admittedly far from both public policy and the daily practice of medicine and nursing, can improve our aim and limit our failings as we try to meet our obligations, case by case, thereby manifesting and acquiring the caring character so indispensable to the task ahead.

ENDNOTES

[1] Xenophon, *Apology of Socrates I.15*, translated by H. G. Dakyns, Project Gutenberg, January 1988. Available online at http://www.gutenberg.org/etext/1171 (accessed September 5, 2005).

[2] Osler, W., *The Principles and Practice of Medicine*. 3rd ed. New York: D. Appleton, 1898, pp. 108-137.

[3] See, for example, Davis, John K., "The Concept of Precedent Autonomy," *Bioethics* 16: 114-133, 2002.

[4] See presentation by Dr. Joanne Lynn at the March 3, 2005 meeting of the Council, the transcript of which is available online at http://www.bioethics.gov.

[5] These distinctions have been explored by many ethicists and some previous advisory commissions. We note especially Paul Ramsey's pioneering work, *The Patient as Person*, New Haven, CT: Yale University Press, 1970, Chapter Three, "On (Only) Caring for the Dying," and a report by The President's Commission for the Study of Ethical Problems in Medicine and Biomedical and Behavioral Research, Deciding to Forgo Life-Sustaining Treatment, Washington, DC: U.S. Government Printing Office, 1983. An earlier treatment of some of the issues covered in this report resulted in The Hastings Center's *Guidelines on the Termination of Life-Sustaining Treatment and the Care of the Dying*, Bloomington, IN: Indiana University Press, 1987.

[6] See, for example, Ramsey, *op. cit.*

[7] See, for example, Kelly, D. F., *Contemporary Catholic Health Care Ethics*, Washington, D.C.: Georgetown University Press, 2004, pp. 128-133. See also, Kelly, G., *Medico-Moral Problems*, St. Louis, MO: The Catholic Hospital Association of the United States and Canada, 1958.

[8] "The Hippocratic Oath," translated by Leon R. Kass, M.D., in *Being Human: Readings from the President's Council on Bioethics*, 2003. See also, Kass, L. R., "Neither for Love nor Money: Why Doctors Must Not Kill," *The Public Interest* 94: 25-46, Winter 1989.

4

Ethical Caregiving:
Principle and Prudence in Hard Cases

In this chapter, we move from general considerations and basic principles to consider ethical caregiving as it is actually practiced: in concrete human situations, with real patients, concerned family members, and an array of medical professionals intimately involved in providing care. Our goal in the following case discussions is to explore how devoted caregivers should approach treatment decisions in a range of complex clinical situations—always aiming at best care for the person now here, and always working within the ethical boundaries articulated above.

Every clinical case is unique, with innumerable medical and personal factors that need to be considered—factors that are always changing. With dementia, caregivers are rarely handling a single medical condition or personal problem; they are usually juggling multiple issues at once—ranging from ongoing ailments to worsening risk factors to acute diseases, and ranging from family struggles with day-to-day care to worries about finances to caregiver exhaustion and depression. In specific clinical cases, caregivers often need to make decisions based largely on probabilities—the probability that a given disease will progress without treatment, the probability that a treatment will work to the desired effect, the probability of complications and side effects, or the probability that the person's dementia will worsen quickly or slowly.

But ethically responsible caregivers also operate within certain firm moral boundaries—central among them the obligation never to seek a patient's death in making decisions about a person's care. This complexity requires us to think through many larger ethical issues in the context of particular cases—where the aim is always to care and never to kill, always to benefit the life the patient still has, even as the person's powers decline, dependence becomes total, life options are limited, and death looms ever closer.

In presenting these cases, we have three interrelated purposes. First, we wish to demonstrate by example what it means to think seriously about "best care," served by loving prudence, beyond the procedural solutions of "let each family decide" or "consult the advance directive." Second, we seek to show the great complexity and moral difficulty often involved in deciding how to provide best care, precisely because the best course of action is frequently far from obvious. And third, we aim to show how, even in hard cases where there is no obvious good choice, prudence can probe deeply how best to care for the particular individuals for whom we are responsible, all the while respecting those ethical boundaries that should be respected by everyone. At least as important as the "bottom line" in each case is the character of moral reflection and the manner of moral reasoning required to judge and act well.

In discussing cases of ethical caregiving, it is important to remember that we are addressing not only the professionals in hospitals, nursing homes, and hospices. We are also addressing audiences both more private and more public: family members and friends who participate in making decisions for loved ones; public policymakers, directors of caregiving facilities, and others who form the ideas and set the practices that shape how the more immediate caregivers think and act when called upon to do so. It is also necessary to remember that the "hands-on" caregivers, the principal actors in our caregiving cases, are not professional ethicists nor generally given to long discourses about the whys and wherefores of their recommendations and decisions. As human beings and members of our society, they have moral ideas and intuitions that guide them at the bedside; as professional caregivers, they have certain standards of care that they pledge to follow; as clinicians, they wrestle *concretely*—not at the level of abstract moral principle—with hard choices when values they hold dear are in tension. At the same time, however, it is also true that patterns of practice call for justification, especially when they are challenged by appeals to novel principles or demands for new procedures. Challenged or not, these patterns of professional care come to shape and reflect broader public judgments about how to think and what to do when the thinking and doing become very difficult. We trust that practitioners reading these case discussions will see the merit in trying to think things through and to offer discussable reasons for whatever course of action is under consideration. In matters this weighty, we need to generalize our experiences, in search for wisdom in the face of often tragic choices.

We offer two additional caveats: First, one central idea of this report is that caregivers in particular and society as a whole must never lose sight of the humanity of those persons with dementia entrusted to their care—which is to say, the unique histories and life stories that define the richness of the life now moving toward completion. Yet the following cases, presented in ways to permit exploration of moral problems that caregivers and patients may experience, risk losing the fine texture of the persons and lives they so minimally describe. We are aware that such an approach risks encouraging the very dehumanization of persons with dementia that we are in this report trying to combat, and we urge the reader to lean against any such apparent intimations or suggestions.

Second, these cases leave many precise clinical details undescribed: just as every life is unique, so is every medical situation. In trying to be somewhat paradigmatic, we risk losing or deforming the realities of the bedside, and risk leaving unexplored the clinical details that are often central in deciding what the best possible course of action truly is. With these caveats in mind, we nevertheless hope these case discussions might enrich our thinking about what "best care" really means in practice and how principle and prudence can operate together to do right by those for whom we are summoned to care.

We organize the discussion that follows thematically, by considering cases that highlight the following issues: (1) the distinction between deciding for oneself and deciding for others; (2) the significance of dementia and its stages; (3) the meaning of well-being for persons with dementia; (4) the significance of living wills; and (5) the well-being of caregivers themselves.

I. DECIDING FOR ONESELF
AND DECIDING FOR OTHERS

We begin by exploring the moral differences (and similarities) between *deciding for oneself* in a still competent state and *deciding for another* who has become mentally incapacitated. Consider, in this vein, the following case:

A married man, in his sixties, has two adult children who live far away. He has cared for two parents who have suffered and eventually died from Alzheimer's disease, and he begins to notice his own lapses of memory: forgetting to turn off the stove, losing track of the time, forgetting the names of colleagues, repeating himself in conversations. He suspects (and his doctor agrees) that he is probably in the very early stages of Alzheimer's disease, and he surmises from personal experience where he is heading and what his life will likely become. He knows he would prefer a shorter and still lucid life to a slow decline into total dependency—with the accompanying erosion of self-control and loss of shame, and with the possibility of behaving in sexually inappropriate ways as his father did or becoming incontinent and immobile as his mother did. For years, he has also been treated for high cholesterol and high blood pressure, and his doctors tell him that the blockage in his left-main coronary artery is severe enough that he is a candidate for bypass surgery. As his cognition begins to weaken, he is still aware of his overall condition. He decides to stop taking all his heart medication, and he makes clear to his doctor and family: no surgery—ever. How should his family and his doctor respond?

Whatever judgments we might make about the moral propriety of the individual's decision to *forgo* all treatment for heart disease, it would be a different matter if his family or doctor sought to *deny* him future care because of his probable diagnosis of early-stage Alzheimer's. Perhaps his reasons for declining treatment are sound; perhaps they are not; perhaps we can never know for certain. We will shortly explore the possible reasons why he does what he does, and consider the possible moral meanings of his choices. But clearly it would be morally misguided for *others* to deny treatment if the patient himself wanted it, and not only because of the coercion involved. In making such a decision, the individual's family and doctors would be sending the clear message that they would rather see him dead than suffer advancing dementia; that his coming life will be an unjustified burden to them and to society; and that he lacks all basic claims on care because of his probable diagnosis and looming decline. Such a denial of care is not only coercive, it is dehumanizing.

Denial of care, of course, represents an extreme. Further analysis would be required to show why it would be impermissible for family members or doctors to *suggest* to the patient, had he not thought of doing so himself, that he could, if he wished, stop taking his heart medications as a form of "Alzheimer's prevention." But neither denial nor discouragement of treatment is the issue here, but rather acquiescence: should the doctor and family endorse or accept the patient's decision to stop his medications and to refuse all further treatment of his cardiac condition?

In reality, of course, such a thought would not likely occur to them. In most such cases, the patient's family members and doctors would probably resist vigorously his decision to forgo all future treatment. They would urge him to continue his medications and perhaps even to undergo bypass surgery. Even the loving wife who admires her husband's nobility and self-command, or the family physician who knows what the individual went through in caring for his own parents, would likely balk at his seeking or inviting an avoidable and earlier death. But are there good reasons for the patient to resist their resistance, or for the individual to resist becoming a "patient" at all? What considerations determine whether his decision to forgo treatment is morally acceptable or morally sound? And should the range of morally acceptable choices be wider when the person decides to forgo treatment for himself, as opposed to when others decide to withhold treatment from and for him?

The most obvious difference concerns the absence or presence of direct coercion: The patient's decision is his own; it is not imposed on him against his will or without his full participation. The patient also makes what appears to be an informed decision, drawing upon his direct experience caring for his parents with Alzheimer's and extrapolating forward to what it might be like to live in their condition and to need the kind of care he once provided them. Not only is he not coerced, he knows his own inner life in a way even those closest to him arguably cannot. He knows what he values, what he thinks he can endure, and what he hopes the final chapters of his life story will look like.

It is, of course, possible that he has not reasoned this out, that he is reacting emotionally to the bad news, or that he is even, without knowing it, clinically depressed. But insofar as he has thought about his decision, any number of considerations might (alone or in concert) seem to him to warrant doing whatever he can to decrease the chances that he will have to endure the full course of Alzheimer's disease. Perhaps he knows that he does not want to die incapable of recognizing his wife in his final months, or that he does not want to die after years in a nursing home. One can also imagine the range of goods that his decision to forgo treatment hopes to achieve: Positive goods, such as leaving an education fund for his grandchildren rather than spending down all his assets on nursing home care, and negative goods, such as ensuring that he never behaves in ways that erode the code of honor and decency by which he has always lived. People with Alzheimer's sometimes do things that are normally considered shameful and offensive—such as making sexually inappropriate advances or undressing in public. Of course, the disease is the cause of the loss of inhibitions. Yet it is, in a crucial sense, still the person who acts, and seeking to avoid or preempt such behavior is a morally worthy goal, even if a particular means of doing so is morally questionable.

But the seemingly clear differences between deciding for oneself and deciding for others need to be examined and questioned. To what extent, we must ask, are such momentous decisions ever fully "one's own"? As Robert Burt explored in *Taking Care of Strangers*, people often make the choices that they believe others want for them.[1] Perhaps the patient imagines that his wife and children do not want to care for him, and perhaps his decision to forgo treatment reflects his assessment of their hidden wishes more than his own desires. Perhaps he does not trust his doctor to be able to guide him through the illness. Rather than confirming these suspicions by acquiescing in his decision, his family, friends, and physician should explore these matters with him, explicitly and thoroughly.

In addition, they should ask him to consider how his decision might affect the web of relations he most values. Has he considered that his choice to forgo treatment might send the message that he does not really trust his family members to be devoted caregivers or that he does not believe they are capable of caring for him? And has he given adequate thought to the potential moment of crisis—the sudden heart attack—that his decision to forgo treatment makes more likely and perhaps deliberately invites? Does he expect his loved ones or neighbors simply to watch him die rather than call the paramedics? Has he considered what it will be like for his family to suffer the ordeal of rushing him to the hospital, hoping to save him, living through the experience of triage, fearing and perhaps losing the possibility of saying goodbye? If he survives the heart attack, he might end up in a severely debilitated condition, or else die a lingering death from chronic heart failure, with shortness of breath and swelling of the extremities, rather than dying suddenly as he might have wished. If he does indeed die suddenly, has he considered how his choice to forgo preventive treatment might affect the way his wife and children will remember him?

In seeking to avoid the worsening degradations of Alzheimer's disease, he probably worries deeply about being remembered in a distorted way, not as the person he has long been but as the person whose self is hollowed out by dementia. But what about the potential distortion of being remembered as someone who sought an earlier death by deliberate acts of omission, or someone whose actions helped precipitate a death in crisis? Would this be seen as a sign of his noble willingness to accept an earlier death to prevent becoming wholly dependent on others, or as a mark of his timidity in the face of a difficult death by dementia?

In reality, individuals, though free to choose, never simply decide solely by and for themselves, even when they are fully competent. The present patient's decisions reflect, in part, his image of himself in the eyes of others, and his decisions affect the course of their lives. More generally, our identity and values always take shape within a network of human relations. The individual may know himself from the inside, but his inside knowledge is shaped by his understanding of how others understand him. And his inside knowledge, never final or definitive, is always open to transformations of self-understanding in light of new circumstances, at least as long as he is still self-aware. A discussion with those affected by his decision or with his trusted physician could very well lead to such a transformation of outlook, and they should certainly attempt it.

Beyond doubt, the competent individual should be accorded greater freedom of choice in making treatment decisions than should surrogates deciding for others. It is always possible that the individual knows aspects of his own life story that no one else can know, and with this privileged perspective his wishes deserve heightened respect. And surely, competent individuals should never be coerced to accept treatments they do not want, even after attempts at thoughtful persuasion have failed.

But the competent individual's greater freedom to decide does not mean that every permissible decision is morally sound, or that his loved ones should simply accept his choices as necessarily right or necessarily final. Moreover, this freedom of action operates within certain widely accepted moral limits: even if the law allows it, an individual is not morally justified to act deliberately to achieve his self-destruction. And although the individual deciding for himself rightly exercises greater freedom than surrogates deciding for others, the moral criteria for deciding for oneself and deciding for others are actually quite similar. In both cases, what matters most is what we *actually do in service to our goals* and the *reasons* for seeking or forgoing particular treatments in particular circumstances. And in both situations, the person or the surrogate is making a decision about whether the life in question is worthy of continued care and about whether the life in question requires protracted preservation.

Let us return to the case itself, and what the doctor might say to the individual in this situation: "Yes, you are probably in the early stages of Alzheimer's. But the trajectory of that disease is long and gradual, you have much good life left to enjoy, and you can count on me to help you negotiate your way. I will be with you, through good times and bad. But that it is not now my most pressing concern. Your heart disease is getting worse. You need to continue your daily medications. You need to begin a stricter heart-healthy diet. You need to exercise more intensively.

And you are a candidate for immediate bypass surgery, and I recommend that you have it very soon."

In speaking with the patient, doctors and family members must take seriously the moral reasons why the individual might seek a course of life that, although shorter than it need be, does not end in dementia. Perhaps he believes that suffering a heart attack is a more humanly fitting way to die—facing death with the powers of memory and self-awareness still largely intact, without the deformations that long-term care can sometimes impose on families. And perhaps he concludes that he has no moral obligation to accept medical care that seems likely to rob him of this more fitting death and condemn him instead to what he sees as a dehumanizing death by way of dementia. Why must he cede control of his destiny to the medical inventions and interventions of others? Why must he visit or call the cardiologist in the first place?

Yet there are sound moral answers to these questions. We are ethically free to accept a higher risk of death or expose ourselves to a foreseeable death in the course of choosing a particular kind of life—such as a soldier serving his country on the frontlines or a policemen working in a gang-infested neighborhood, where death by gunfire may be the likely cost of bravery, or a physician tending patients suffering from plague or performing surgery on patients with AIDS, where death by contagion may be the possible cost of compassionate care. But it is hard to see, in this case, how ceasing heart medication is essential for living a particular kind of life, a life in which being un-medicated is the necessary cost of living well in the present. It is hard to see the moral grounds for stopping such medication *now* (that is, upon learning the diagnosis of probable Alzheimer's)—assuming the drugs have no burdensome side effects, and assuming the economic burden of the drugs is minor.

The most likely reason for the patient to stop treatment *now* is *to increase his chances of dying earlier*, or of dying *this way* (heart disease) rather than that way (dementia). Taking heart medication does not preclude living now in the way he wants to live; the drugs are not a barrier to present goods or a direct cause of present distress. And unless an individual has an established pattern of resistance to taking such drugs—for example, for religious reasons, akin to those who reject blood transfusions—there seems to be no decisive moral difference between stopping medications in-process and deciding not to start medications that are newly indicated: in both cases, one forgoes treatment with an earlier death as the goal, or with an earlier death as the potential means of achieving other goals (such as never burdening loved ones or never becoming incontinent). Even if the individual rightly possesses the freedom of action to make such choices— that is, to reject needed medications—his loved ones are morally right to resist.*

It is, of course, possible that the person sees his choice not as expressing a desire to die sooner but as a desire to live out the remainder of his life in a certain way. He might even think or say something like this: "I am a person coming to the end of my life and its projects. I trust in God and I am reconciled to my fate. My obligations to my body are present but limited now. It is okay for me to decide about medical treatments in a way that makes it more likely that I'll live out my natural life in the family and home I love, aware of salvation and relationships. It is acceptable to all to make such choices. I am not a prisoner of medical advances that would condemn me to a more troubled course."†

This is a more difficult argument to answer. Yet even here, the patient's family and his physician could rightly argue back, making the case for the goodness of the life still at hand, reminding him of the burdens that his choice might be inflicting on those who love him, and reassuring the patient that a commitment to treatment now need not mean that he will in the future become a prisoner of unwanted medical innovations when he comes closer to his death. Persuading the patient to change his mind about taking his medications still seems to be the course of loving prudence.

The duty to exercise more frequently or to eat more restrictively is a different matter. If life's primary goal were merely optimizing health and longevity, then good diet and regular exercise

---

* To be sure, such resistance has its costs and, hence, its decent limits. The family should not resist to the point of driving themselves apart or of inflicting strife all around.

† We owe this insight and example to Dr. Joanne Lynn.

would be one's primary obligations. But we seek to be healthy in order to live well, not the other way around, and many of the things we rightly enjoy in life are—to say the least—not always conducive to maximizing longevity. It would be entirely understandable if our patient—mindful of his impending descent into dementia—would like to relax and enjoy life in his last years of lucidity more than he could under the heart-healthy regimen. Perhaps he wishes to spend more time reading and less time on the treadmill, or wants to enjoy large pasta dinners instead of dressing-free salads, or wants to continue his favorite pastime of shoveling snow even though his doctors recommend against it. In choosing to forgo the ideal regimen of diet and exercise, the individual is choosing one kind of life over another. He is choosing some goods (the pleasures of eating) over others (the greater chance of longevity). He is not simply acting so that he might die sooner, even if his actions make it more likely that he will.

The patient's choice to forgo bypass surgery also seems morally defensible, if not the only morally permissible choice under the circumstances. Bypass surgery is an experiential and physical ordeal—with serious risks, grave burdens, and various uncertainties. It disrupts personal life and family life. It requires hospitalization and a considerable period of recovery, in which being a patient is the core of one's existence for weeks and often months. It even carries a high risk of yielding a major drop in cognitive function. Although statistically it tends to extend healthy life, there are good reasons to opt against it, just as there are good reasons to opt for it. Another person, in the same situation, might rightly decide to have the surgery as soon as possible, so that he can recover and improve physically while his mental faculties are still relatively sound and the effects of Alzheimer's are still fairly limited. But the individual in this case is on solid moral ground in rejecting bypass surgery even if his doctors recommend it, and even if his family encourages him to have it.

Let us consider a slightly different case: What if, instead of being a person with heart disease, the individual was a (long-lived) type-1 diabetic, absolutely dependent on regular insulin shots? And what if, upon learning of his probable Alzheimer's, he decided to spend a few wonderful weeks with his family, say goodbye, and stop taking his shots, so that he lapses into a diabetic coma resulting in his imminent death. Unlike forgoing heart medication or rejecting heart surgery, this decision *makes very likely* a certain kind of death rather than simply altering the probable course of death. It ensures death now rather than awaiting a still unknowable death in the future. Although taking insulin shots is a marginally greater burden than taking heart medication, this marginal burden hardly justifies the decision to embrace death now by a deliberate act of omission. In this case, the individual's moral freedom should give way to the moral limits that rightly constrain that freedom. And although the competent individual cannot be forced to take insulin against his will, his family and doctors are justified in exerting every decent means to alter or reverse his death-seeking decision.

Consider yet another case: What if the patient with probable early-stage Alzheimer's gets diagnosed with a form of cancer that is treatable with a reasonable probability of cure but deadly if left untreated. The treatment of chemotherapy followed by radiation would require a disruption of his current life—regular trips to the hospital over an hour away, considerable discomfort and nausea, general fatigue—but not unendurable physical suffering. Untreated, the progression of the cancer would leave the patient largely unaffected for a while, with things getting worse toward the end, with a relatively swift decline and death in an estimated nine to eighteen months in the future. In this case, the individual sees two possible paths before him: the first path involves disrupting his current routine, possibly curing his cancer, and extending a life likely marked by worsening Alzheimer's; the second path involves enjoying the life he now has without disruption or burdensome treatments, living with a worsening cancer that will eventually kill him, and probably dying before his Alzheimer's hollows out all recognition of himself and his loved ones.

Unlike forgoing heart medications, a choice to forgo cancer treatment involves avoiding a burdensome treatment. And it involves accepting a relatively predictable progression toward death, rather than increasing the chances of having a deadly heart episode and thus inviting a future moment of crisis, for which his loved ones cannot really prepare. And unlike type-1 diabetes, an ailment that the hypothetical patient above had been treating throughout his life, with treatment already a part of his routine and not an impediment to it, the cancer diagnosis is new and the treatment will be a major disruption. In the end, this is a case where each individual should rightly decide for himself what is the best course—doing his best to make such decisions in concert with loved ones, and resisting the temptation to see cancer as simply a means to avoid the later ravages of advanced dementia. The decision to forgo cancer treatment in this case, if rightly made, will aim at a certain kind of life until the end, not at a certain kind of death sooner rather than later.

Finally, how would this ethical analysis change if the individual's dementia progressed to the point where surrogates had to make all medical decisions on his behalf? And what weight should be given to the preferences he expressed while he was still competent? The latter question we will take up more fully in the case below on advance directives. But in general, surrogates should make decisions that aim at best care for the person now here: They would have no clearly compelling reasons to withhold his heart medication, assuming there are no intolerable side effects and assuming the cost of the medications is not excessively burdensome to the family. They might even be morally justified in resuming the medications that the once-competent patient had previously chosen to stop. They should encourage those foods and activities that seem to promote and augment their loved one's happiness. They should almost certainly forgo heart bypass surgery, rejecting it as unduly burdensome, especially when the patient cannot be a full participant in his own treatment and recovery, and because by then his physical capacity to endure such a procedure has probably weakened along with his dementia. And they should surely continue insulin shots if the patient were to suffer from diabetes. To do otherwise is to seize an occasion for death, and thus to treat the life being cared for as unworthy of continued care. But they should not begin aggressive cancer treatments that the person himself knowingly chose to forgo.

II. THE SIGNIFICANCE OF AGE-RELATED DEMENTIA AND ITS STAGES

As we move now to consider the dilemmas of caring for those with dementia who can no longer direct their own care, we must first inquire more precisely about the significance of age-related dementia itself, and whether this particular condition differs from other forms of disability and dependence. That is to say: Is the presence of dementia a morally legitimate factor in denying or forgoing treatment? Is the person with dementia morally different from—and should she be treated differently than—the lucid elderly person with severe physical debilities, or the mentally incompetent younger person who did not lose his mental powers with age but never had them at all?

There is, of course, a difference between the never-competent person and the once-competent person, and this age-related transformation seems to matter, humanly speaking. The person who late in life develops dementia is no longer the wise father but the needy one; he is no longer the husband who remembers every wedding anniversary but the man who cannot recognize his wife; he is no longer the grandfather who takes the young to the zoo but the man who acts strangely in the nursing home. The question, however, is what these changes mean, if anything, for how we regard our loved ones *as patients*, and whether their *psychic loss* is a disability that makes their dependence *morally* different *in kind*.

In the case of total physical dependence, the person is no doubt also transformed, and his or her physical neediness may bring about significant psychic change. But even in a state of total dependence, such a person might still direct his or her own care, or at least be involved in many caregiving decisions. Moreover, the dependent elderly person who is still cognitively self-aware may still acknowledge his special attachment to the loved ones who now care for him—perhaps with a mix of gratitude for being helped, sorrow at lost pastimes, and shame at being so needy.

With advanced dementia, however, the situation is somewhat different. The beloved person is still present—still the same person in body, with a continuous life trajectory. But he is also, in a certain sense, increasingly absent. He is *both* always himself and no longer himself. And although the same thing might be said regarding all forms of decline and dependence—the great dancer in a wheelchair is also no longer as she once was, certainly not in the way that once defined her—cognitive loss seems to be existentially different. The great dancer in a wheelchair still knows she was once a great dancer (though whether such knowledge makes life better or worse, easier or harder, is not a simple question). The great mathematician, now demented, knows nothing of his former life.

In clinical situations, these puzzling theoretical questions of identity and personal continuity give way to urgent practical questions of how vigorously to treat the supervening or concurrent illnesses that the patient with dementia also suffers. There is no question but that physicians tend to be more aggressive in treating serious illnesses in thirty year olds than in eighty year olds, partly because younger patients generally tolerate treatments better, but also because everyone tacitly recognizes that the old patient is closer to the end and that, beyond good standard medical care, certain treatments that are probably regarded as obligatory in the young ("ordinary care") will probably be regarded as optional in the old ("extraordinary care"). But within this general approach to aggressive treatment at various stages of life and health, the relevant question before us now is whether the special changes in mentation and self-awareness that come with dementia should affect decisions about medical care. Does a person with dementia have a lesser claim on or lesser interest in essential medical treatment *solely by virtue of his dementia*?* Is he less a "person," and thus more ready for life to be over? And if the goal is providing the "best care possible" for the person with dementia, how does dementia itself influence or shape what best care requires?

---

* Alzheimer's disease is, of course, more than the dementia through which it most prominently manifests itself. As we indicated earlier, it is a progressive and ultimately fatal disease—unlike the multi-infarct vascular dementias that may or may not be part of a fatal picture. This means that differential treatment of patients with Alzheimer's might be based not on the presence of dementia as such but on the whole disease process. This fact becomes more relevant in thinking about treatment decisions in the middle and late phases of the disease.

The general answer seems to be two-fold: As argued above, the fundamental equality of human beings suggests that human worth, in the caregiving setting, does not depend on possessing particular capacities or particular qualities. To discriminate against patients *because* they suffer dementia is to violate this first principle. At the same time, as dementia advances, the systems of the body begin to shut down; and different choices might be made as the patient gets closer to death, even when death is not yet imminent.*

To consider these questions in concrete cases, we need to make three crucial distinctions: First, we need to distinguish between the *different stages of dementia*, and to ask whether a person's level of mental decline is in itself a relevant factor for shaping treatment decisions. Second, we need to distinguish between "good days" and "bad days," and pay close attention to the fluctuating cognitive capacities exhibited by many persons with dementia. And third, we need to distinguish between conditions and complications: Dementia is a *condition* that might be used (wrongfully) in itself as a moral ground to treat patients differently; but dementia is also a source of ethically relevant special *complications* that must be faced and evaluated by caregivers in the clinical setting, especially when dementia patients cannot understand the value or necessity of a given treatment.

---

* Compare the situation of advanced Alzheimer's with two other clinical cases: (a) the young person in a persistent vegetative state and (b) the middle-aged person in late-stage terminal cancer. In the case of the persistent vegetative state, the person lacks all cognitive capacity, but she is not suffering from a degenerative condition. In many cases, the patient is stable; the body is not shutting down, even if it requires artificial feeding to sustain it. In the cancer case, the body may be breaking down, but the persistence of self-awareness means that the struggle for life still continues in a unique sense; the personal will to fight on exists in contradistinction to the realities of bodily breakdown. With advanced Alzheimer's disease, however, there is neither stability as the body begins to fail nor the presence of a self-conscious patient struggling for life. This unique combination of cognitive and physical breakdown, this clinical instability combined with advanced age, raises questions as to whether the dying process has already begun and whether death should continue to be opposed. Perhaps some treatments are better seen not as preservation of life but as prolongations of the dying process, even if such prolongations last for a while.

To see how dementia might affect the decisionmaking of surrogates, let us consider how we should care for the following person, suffering from bacterial pneumonia, at five different stages of her life:

> *(1) As a healthy ten-year old child.*
>
> *(2) As a healthy middle-aged woman with three children of her own.*
>
> *(3) As a woman in her late sixties. She is showing the first signs of memory loss—forgetting to turn off the stove, getting lost on the way home from the market, forgetting to pay bills—but she still knows who she is and who her loved ones are.*
>
> *(4) As a woman in her early seventies. She remembers little, generally does not seem to recognize her children when they come to visit her in the assisted living facility, and does not seem to recognize the caregivers who see her day to day. But she seems generally happy and content, still knows how to say hello to those who greet her, and, although ambulatory, spends most of her time just sitting before the television.*
>
> *(5) As a woman in her middle seventies. She says almost nothing, and what she says makes little sense. She needs to be reminded to eat and requires feeding by others. She is bedridden and losing control of her bodily functions, but she is basically a calm and compliant patient, and seems to like having her hair brushed, though it is hard to tell for sure.*

Are there any moral grounds for treating the person's bacterial pneumonia differently at these different points in her life, and if so, why? Let us assume she has no living will, and that she has always trusted her daughters to take good care of her as she grows old. The decisions (in her later years) regarding medical treatment thus rest entirely on the daughters' judgment about best care for their elderly mother, a judgment that will depend in part on the moral meaning they ascribe to her worsening dementia and her increasing nearness to death.

In stage 1, the girl's parents are clearly deciding *on her behalf,* and they have a clear moral obligation to treat her pneumonia. In stage 2, the woman is deciding *for herself,* and one can see no obvious reason to forgo treatment (if the patient is not opposed in principle to all medical interventions, as are adherents of Christian Science). In stage 3, the woman is still able to understand the need for treatment once it is explained to her, but she probably needs assistance getting to the doctor, following through on her medications, and navigating among different health care providers. She is no longer the sole director of her own care, but she is still a full and active participant in her own treatment. She may be frustrated by her fading powers and growing dependence on others, but she still values life, and the good of treatment seems clear.

By stage 4, all her decisions need to be made for her, and explanations of her sickness and treatment are beyond her comprehension. She is a needy recipient of care, and the sufferings of her body may prompt physical expressions of dismay akin to a child's cry. But she is no longer a knowing seeker of care, and those who actually care for her—daughters, doctors, and nurses—are indistinguishable to her. Yet in the case as described, her health is not in rapid decline. Hence, the only apparent grounds to deny her treatment for her pneumonia would be that life without memory of the past or control of the future is simply not life worth living or that there are even worse futures coming, as indeed there are. In other words, dementia as a degenerative and debilitating condition would be the reason to stand aside in the face of a disease that is easily treated but potentially deadly if not treated. To say *no* to treatment in this case is to declare that death is preferable to life with this degree of dementia (or worse), or that dementia means being a "non-person" ready to die. But does saying *yes* to treatment depend entirely on the fact that she still seems to get some experiential satisfactions from being alive, even if she does not experience the present in connection to her personal past? In other words: Does the worth of being alive depend decisively on the enjoyment one takes in being alive?

This becomes an issue in stage 5, when even the limited experiential pleasures or experiential interests of her earlier dementia seem to be fading or gone. The caregivers must now distinguish between enjoying the present with little sense of the past (as in stage 4), and having apparently little or no active sense of the present itself (as in stage 5). Does the woman in stage 5 still have a life that we can benefit by treatment, and do we benefit that life by curing the pneumonia that assaults it? Does she have—or, even if we cannot be sure, *might* she have—levels of awareness (even if physiological more than cognitive) that recognize and respond to changes in how her family and her doctors and nurses choose to treat her?

Unless there are complications that make the very activity of providing treatment a burden, or unless there are other health problems that suggest that her systems are shutting down and that she is irreversibly dying, the only ground for denying treatment seems (yet again) to be the judgment that her life should now come to an end. Non-treatment seems to entail the view that the life she now has is no life at all, meaningless and degrading to her and not worth the labors required to sustain it. Such labors are surely great for the caregivers—emotionally, physically, and financially. And the patient's life experiences and life options are severely limited. But it is also hard to see how deliberately acting with the intent or hope that her life come to an end, however well-meaning one's motives, is actually a form of *best care for the person as she now exists*. And it seems hard to imagine how one could withhold treatment from the patient in stage 5 without intending that she die.*

Looking beyond this particular case, any decision to treat a person with dementia differently *simply because of the condition itself* seems to require accepting one of the following propositions:

---

* In order to focus only on the relevance of the degree of dementia, the case as presented supposes a simple case of community-acquired pneumonia, manifested in cough, fever, shortness of breath and general misery, but in the presence of adequate blood pressure and good enough cardiac and renal function. But if the patient were in shock or suffering kidney failure, and the pneumonia were just one manifestation of generalized breakdown and a harbinger of more or less imminent death, the benefits of treating the pneumonia would be highly uncertain. Antibiotic treatment would be less likely to succeed; and even if successful, the patient might be relegated to spending the rest of her life in the intensive care unit. Under these circumstances of vital organ system failure, treatment of the pneumonia would become optional, not only for the person in stage 5 but perhaps even for the person in stage 4.

(a) that human dignity resides foremost in our sustained mental capacities, and that a human being with severe dementia is no longer a person, but a body without a person; (b) that the person's wishes before becoming mentally incapacitated should always be honored, and that if the once-competent person stipulated the cessation of medical care in the case of dementia, this particular act of self-definition should always be respected, no matter how much a demented person may still seem to have a life, and even a seemingly happy one; or (c) that the experience of *becoming* demented is so horrible—different in kind from being mentally incapacitated throughout life—that the progressive and irreversible loss of one's powers justifies non-treatment. More specifically, to treat patients with dementia differently from other classes of dependent elderly persons, one must believe that dementia is *in itself* a special kind of disability or suffering; that treating intervening illnesses is a way of perpetuating the person's degradation (that is, a kind of torture, not caregiving); that a person with dementia lacks dignity not because of his dependence on others for everyday needs but because of his changed cognitive condition; or that it is legitimate for an individual to believe that life with dementia lacks dignity, and thus permissible to direct his surrogates in advance to cease all care if he becomes demented. But for those who judge that being worthy of care and worthy of life does not depend on possessing certain cognitive capacities, such comparative judgments about the comparative worth of different lives seem morally misguided. Discrimination solely on the basis of dementia seems incompatible with the moral demands of equal respect and best care, an incompatibility that includes discrimination by a past self against a future self with dementia.

In case situations like this one, in which the necessary medical intervention is modest, likely to be effective,* and does not

---

* Accustomed as we are to the miracle cures of antibiotics, unimaginable by our grandparents, we are prone to overlook the fact that, despite the high success rates, even the treatment of the common pneumococcal pneumonia is not guaranteed to succeed. It can be followed by lung abscess, bacterial meningitis or brain abscess, septicemia with shock, empyema, endocarditis, and acute respiratory distress syndrome. Some of these complications of treatment would require

require a struggle with the patient or a dramatic disruption of the patient's existence, treatment seems morally appropriate. But as the patient deteriorates and medical interventions become more complex and disruptive, that moral assessment will likely shift. We must ask whether aggressively treating the patient who can no longer be an active partner in her own recovery may turn the person entirely into an *object*, to the point where acting on the person no longer benefits the minimal life the person still has, but makes the person into a mere receptacle of technical intervention and the doctor into a mere technician. In cases like uncomplicated bacterial pneumonia, where treatment probably does not require a significant disruption of the patient's routine or physical coercion, the ethical demands of best care clearly point toward treatment. But in cases in which treatment would require sedation, physical restraint, frequent re-locations, or other complicating factors, dementia may become a factor leaning against particular treatments: not because being demented lessens one's moral claim on life, but because the treatment itself adds to the un-consenting and un-comprehending patient's miseries, burdens, or degradations. We will consider these complicated cases more fully below, as we consider what it means to promote the patient's well-being in the clinical context.

III. THE WELL-BEING OF THE PATIENT

In the collection of cases considered in this section, we explore in greater detail how concrete treatment decisions are related to the personal welfare of persons with dementia. But if caregiving aims to serve the well-being of the patient as person, we need some operative idea of what well-being means, and how the well-being of a person with dementia is both similar to and different from well-being for persons in very different physical and mental conditions. We also need in advance a more detailed account of the different types of treatment—with the various upsides, downsides, burdens, and uncertainties of different medical inter-

---

invasive, even heroic, measures. The simple treatment of simple pneumonia is not necessarily always simple.

ventions. Therefore, as a prelude to the cases themselves, we will briefly consider (a) dementia and well-being and (b) the nature of treatment and the trajectory of illness.

A. Dementia and Well-Being

For most of life, we live both *immediately* and *reflectively*. We experience the physical and emotional ups and downs of the present moment—the pleasures of eating a favorite food and the pain of burning a finger on the stove. We smile when we see a newborn child and shudder when we see a stranger get hurt. But our well-being also depends on how we see ourselves critically and self-consciously—on aspirations fulfilled and unfulfilled, on human attachments made and broken, on values affirmed and compromised.

With dementia, however, the reflective dimension of well-being fades and the person lives ever more immediately. The mature complexity of human relations is gradually replaced by the raw physical neediness more characteristic of an infant and the spontaneous (and not always appropriate) reactions to the presence of others and to their words and deeds. Life informed by thought about one's personal past and hopes for one's future gives way to life as a sequence of disconnected present experiences. As the individual's ability to see himself critically and self-consciously declines, the more complex psychological dimensions of well-being are eclipsed by the simpler psychophysical ones.

Responsible caregivers for persons with dementia aim at a series of overlapping human goods: the comfort of the person; the pleasures of activity as long as activity is still possible; a sense of connection to others; a stable, safe, reliable, and nurturing environment; and the good of being itself, of being alive rather than dead, even in a diminished condition. This does not mean, as we have often noted, that keeping the person alive is the caregiver's highest purpose. The probability or even certainty of an earlier death must often be accepted when life-extension involves painful or misery-inducing treatments. But for responsible caregivers, death itself will never become the means to relieving suffering, and life itself will never be treated as the burden to be relieved.

We cannot, after all, serve the well-being of a person's life by seeking his death.

Promoting well-being for persons with dementia often presents special challenges in the clinical context—distinct from caring for independent persons at the height of their powers or physically incapacitated persons who are still cognitively able. Consider, for example, what it is like for a cognitively healthy person to have blood drawn by venipuncture: He knows beforehand why this procedure is necessary—such as the medical value of diagnostic tests or the civic value of donating blood. His understanding of the experience gives him a reason to endure or reinterpret what is, in the immediate sense, unpleasant and painful—indeed, a violation of his body. This understanding does not make the needle hurt any less, but it makes the pain humanly comprehensible.

A person with advanced dementia, however, no longer has the capacity for such understanding. Drawing blood may serve the person's present interests—as critically assessed and understood by others—but a person with dementia cannot understand how or why. He experiences the needle simply as a threat, a violation, a source of pain. His immediate experience is uncorrected by reflective understanding. Skillful caregivers might sometimes find ways to have drawing blood "make sense" within the patient's impaired cognitive reality. But in many cases, the violation will be experienced as senseless, because it will be experienced uncritically—as an act committed against rather than for the patient's well-being.

The point, once generalized, becomes crucial for ethical analysis and prudent judgment: Certain treatments that are not excessively burdensome for comprehending patients may be excessively burdensome for patients with dementia. Dementia itself does not make the person less worthy of treatment, but the *complications created by the person's lack of understanding* often change the judgment of how best to serve his well-being.

Finally, although concern for bodily well-being is central to caring for the person with dementia, caregivers take care not only of the body but also of the whole person who is and lives as and through his body. They are caretakers of his personal past as well as his bodily present, of the life he has lived in addition to the life he is now living. In this light, caregivers always need to consider the significance of past values and past character—such as the ideas of meaningful life that the person once held, or the ideals of family flourishing and personal honor that he lived by when he was still an ideal-forming and ideal-seeking being. The person whose needs are eventually largely bodily also possesses enduring moral interests, even if he is no longer aware of them.

This insight cuts in multiple directions: It means that even those who might be oblivious to our care still have an interest in our care, because they still possess the dignity of being human; and it means that even those who no longer know the ideals they once held still have an interest in those ideals—an interest entrusted to us. This does not mean that we must always allow the past self to speak decisively for the present self, or that we should judge the worth of the present life entirely by the standards of a person's past existence. But it does mean that caregivers, in caring for the unique person the patient now is, must honor the unique person the patient once was—for example, by being less aggressive in pursuing optional treatments for a person who all his life treasured self-reliance above all else, or, conversely, by being more aggressive in pursuing optional treatments for a person who always held that any vestige of life was incalculably precious.* What such honor means and demands in any concrete case is often a puzzling question, especially when persons with dementia get sick in other ways, and especially when caregivers must begin thinking about not only the patient's continuing life but the patient's approaching death.

B. The Nature of Treatment and the Trajectory of Illness

To think clearly about how certain treatments or non-treatments might affect the well-being of persons with dementia in the clinical setting, we need a clear way of thinking about the complex character of "treatment" itself—with all its benefits, uncertainties, tradeoffs, and imperfections. The professional caregiver always begins with a *diagnosis* of the current situation: What is

---

* There are, of course, limits: Honoring the unique person the patient once was does not mean that we would be *obliged* to give hemlock to Dr. Kevorkian.

wrong with the patient, what are the options, and what will probably or likely happen if we leave the patient untreated? The diagnostician inquires about the *present* ("Is the patient suffering now?") and imagines the *future* ("How will the patient's condition change if we do or do not intervene?").* Perhaps without treatment the patient would die imminently and certainly; perhaps he would face persistent or worsening discomfort and suffering; perhaps he would be at greater risk of more severe complications or earlier death in the near future; or perhaps these greater risks will amount to nothing.

Once we have diagnosed the current problem or problems, we then ask what kinds of treatment are possible: Can we *cure* the given illness entirely—as we may reasonably hope to do with a urinary tract infection using antibiotics? Can we *manage* the illness with ongoing treatments—as with kidney failure using dialysis? Can we *slow down the progression* of the illness—as with radiation treatments for some forms of cancer? Can we *ameliorate the symptoms* without altering the course of the illness itself? Does the treatment involve a one-time intervention, a battery of interventions for a fixed period of time, or a permanent regimen of interventions until death? Does it involve a long and difficult recovery? Will it create temporary or permanent disabilities? What are the likelihood of success and the likelihood of complications? Answers to all these questions, whether given explicitly or tacitly, are germane to any decision to treat or not.

---

* It is hard to imagine a situation in which it is ethically sound for caregivers to tolerate physical suffering in the present when such suffering can be ameliorated with treatment or palliation—unless the medical intervention itself will cause suffering or impairments that are worse than the underlying ailment. What to do in cases where the burden of treatment in the short-term is very great but the long-term benefits are significant is a complicated question. Indeed, caregivers must make very complex judgments about the relationship between present goods and future harms and between present harms and future goods. For competent patients directing their own care, one could imagine avoiding treatments or forms of palliation that compromise self-awareness, and one could imagine patients who might prefer to suffer physically, to the degree such suffering is tolerable, in order not to affect their psychic state. But in dementia cases, such self-awareness is already compromised, partially or completely, and thus the obligation to ease physical suffering seems preeminent in most imaginable circumstances.

Different treatments obviously entail different upsides, downsides, and levels of uncertainty. The best treatments involve no pain or disruption with a high probability of cure; the worst involve physically invasive procedures with little chance of improvement. Some treatments involve virtually no burdens—such as taking pills with minimal side effects. Others involve increasing levels of burden—from minor surgery with a speedy recovery, to radiation therapy that leaves the patient weak and nauseated, to interventions that result in permanent disabilities or deformities. For persons who are elderly, the burdens of treatment are often more severe. And for persons with age-related dementia, there are the additional problems of confusion and disruption—because the patient cannot understand what is happening and why, and because altering the patient's familiar routines is often especially terrifying.

Ultimately, caregivers must compare the burdens, consequences, and potential complications of the *treatment itself* against the burdens, consequences, and potential complications of *nontreatment*; and they must compare the likely realities of *life after treatment* against the likely realities of *life without treatment.** This is where the true moral complexity of the clinical situation presents itself, especially because persons with dementia who get sick are often already sick in other ways. In many cases, the life of the patient is already filled with many physical burdens. The goal of treatment is always to reduce those burdens, never to add to them. But the dilemma, in many cases, is whether adding days, months, or years to such a burden-filled life—even if the life-extending treatment effectively eliminates a discrete threat—is morally sound. Good care often means accepting that the life now present is a life with burdens that cannot be eliminated by our actions. *The dilemma comes when we must decide whether to extend a burden-filled life in cases in which the life-extending treatment itself is not a burden or not a very great burden.*

---

* Though the account here focuses on the professional caregivers, especially the doctors, these people must also be able to explain these matters to family members or others who, as proxies for the patient, have the ultimate responsibility for deciding what should be done.

Especially perplexing are circumstances in which two ill-nesses are present simultaneously: an illness that would probably kill the patient relatively quickly and with minimal suffering (like bacterial sepsis), and an illness already under way and beyond cure, that will likely lead to severe physical distress on the way to certain death (like pancreatic cancer with metastases). In such a case, would the intervention against the curable disease bring suf-fering greater than the disease itself, by dramatically increasing the chance of additional suffering and a more difficult death? On the one hand, caregivers seek to benefit the life the patient still has by treating current problems; on the other hand, caregivers seek to avoid the prolongation of suffering and the most painful kinds of death. Do we benefit the life a person still has by ex-tending life with severe burdens? Do we benefit the life a person still has by intervening in ways that cause new disabilities in the process of eliminating present dangers to life itself? Is the moral calculus different for elderly persons who suffer from age-related dementia compared with mentally incapacitated persons at earlier phases of life or physically incapacitated persons whose cognitive powers are still intact? These kinds of questions—and more broadly, the relationship between treatment and well-being for persons with dementia—can be considered only in concrete cases, with due regard for both the moral principles that should guide all caregiving decisions and the irreducible particularity of every clinical situation.

C. Three Complex Cases

To probe these issues, we will consider three types of cases in this section: The first explores the relevance of a patient's subjec-tive well-being and outward behavior toward others; the second considers the burden of certain treatments and the significance of a patient's resistance to treatment; and the third considers the meaning of concurrent deadly illnesses, where a treatable super-vening disease would likely bring a quicker and more peaceful death.

1. The Relevance of Subjective Well-Being.

> *Patient #1: A seventy-five-year-old man with middle-stage Alzheimer's disease who usually does not recognize his family or his caregivers but enjoys being visited. He likes to "read" the same book over and over again—jumping randomly and uncomprehendingly from page to page. He wanders around the assisted living center, waving and smiling to the other residents, and he generally seems happy. He has a Stokes-Adams episode (temporary loss of consciousness due to transient interruption of electrical impulses in the heart, and the consequent failure of the heart to pump blood to the brain), and doctors say he needs a pacemaker immediately to prevent a possibly fatal episode in the future.*
>
> *Patient #2: A seventy-five-year-old man with middle-stage Alzheimer's disease who usually does not recognize his family or his caregivers but lashes out equally at his visitors. He is often angry and occasionally violent, and sometimes walks into other patient's rooms to scream at them for stealing his wallet. He has had competent examinations searching for a treatable cause for his erratic behavior and none was found. He cries and yells, and is already on mild sedatives to control his behavior. On a few occasions, caregivers have had to use physical restraints. He has a Stokes-Adams episode, and doctors say he needs a pacemaker immediately to prevent a possibly fatal episode in the future.*

Medically, both these patients have a similar heart condition requiring a similar treatment. Without a pacemaker, the danger of a cardiac arrest in the near future increases dramatically, and with it the likelihood of sooner and sudden death, or of a non-deadly but debilitating episode that leaves the patient in a considerably worse condition. But the two persons are also very different in the condition of their lives: one appears content and one does not, one is agreeable and one is difficult, one brings mostly happiness to others and the other brings mostly misery. Do these existential differences matter in deciding how or whether to treat?

For Patient #1, the moral presumption in favor of installing the pacemaker seems fairly strong, assuming the procedure itself is relatively non-burdensome and does not somehow disrupt the person's seemingly pleasant existence by permanently altering his everyday routine. With a pacemaker, this seems like a modest concern. But what about more demanding medical interventions that *would* disrupt the patient's happy existence?

Because the clinical possibilities are so wide-ranging, it is hard to generalize. If the medical condition in need of treatment is not painful in itself or life-threatening now, and if the treatment would likely disrupt the patient's current happiness, there are sound moral reasons to forgo treatment, even if doing so increases the likelihood of an earlier death. In such a case, the caregivers choose one kind of life (present happiness, with the possibility of a shorter lifespan) instead of another kind of life (present ordeal, with the possibility of a longer lifespan). With the pacemaker, the medical intervention seems morally desirable because the burden of treatment and the likely disruption are likely to be fairly minimal. With more burdensome treatments—such as chemotherapy or coronary-bypass surgery—the moral calculus clearly shifts, making treatment or non-treatment equally defensible options depending on the circumstances, or making non-treatment the morally preferable option in cases (such as the examples just given) where the burdens of treatment are severe. A dementia patient cannot comprehend the value or nobility of enduring painful interventions in the present for the sake of future goods, and this lack of understanding may in some cases provide grounds for forgoing certain treatments, either because of the burdensomeness of *imposing* an unwanted treatment on the patient or because of the danger of turning the patient into a mere *object*.

For Patient #2, the situation is more complex—especially if the individual strongly resists all efforts to undergo the procedure. We will consider the significance of a patient's resistance to treatment in our next case; for now, let us focus on the meaning of the patient's current discontent and bad behavior, and whether it deserves to be given any weight in making a treatment decision. The first question is whether the patient's apparent discontent and bad behavior are being caused by the caregiving environment itself or by poorly treated psychiatric problems. It may be that the behavior itself can be modified by better care. But let us assume, in this case, that Patient #2's situation cannot be dramatically improved short of constant heavy sedation. What then?

If the question for caregivers is how to benefit the life the patient still has, is installing the pacemaker a benefit to him? Certainly it is a medical benefit: it improves his bodily condition and decreases the likelihood of repeat episodes. But is it a benefit to the patient *as a person*? In this case, the person seems to experience life with dementia as a special kind of misery, and he certainly causes significant misery for others. Why intervene to help prolong such a life, if doing so means prolonging this misery? Let us assume that he was, before dementia, a thoughtful and decorous gentleman. Do we benefit the life the patient still has by prolonging his degradation and bad behavior? Can one choose not to treat out of fidelity to the person we once knew—that is, out of the loving desire not to prolong the deformation of his past character that merciless nature has now imposed upon him? Or would we be abandoning the patient if we treat his unhappiness and bad behavior as a reason to invite an earlier death, as disqualifying conditions for our ongoing care?

If the caregiver elected not to install a pacemaker, he would *not* be seizing an occasion to produce *certain* death (in the way, for example, that stopping insulin injections for a person with type-1 diabetes would). But the caregiver would deliberately leave the person in a condition where an earlier death of a certain sort is probably more likely. We cannot know for certain how the patient will change as dementia progresses; we cannot know for certain whether his apparent misery will get worse, or whether his mood might improve by changing his environment, or whether dementia will advance to the stage where his bad behavior will be eclipsed by further cognitive and physical decline. And we must ask whether our failure to treat now will only make his cardiac condition worse in the days ahead—with more cardiac episodes, more emergency situations, more falls from dizziness and perhaps permanent injuries as a result. We must ask whether non-treatment is also a kind of endangerment.

This case puts the dilemma of caregiving sharply before us: *Prolonging life seems like prolonging personal misery; forgoing treatment seems like courting death.* The strongest moral grounds for forgoing treatment seem to be the fear that the ordeal of even this minor procedure would make his catastrophic reactions and uncontrollable behavior even worse upon his return. One could argue that the complications caused by his dementia make treatment an excessive burden for this patient. But let us ask, by comparison, whether we would install a pacemaker in a similarly miserable, delusional, and disruptive psychiatric patient in his thirties, who could only be controlled with the use of heavy sedatives. If the answer is yes for the young psychiatric patient, then the reason not to treat Patient #2 would seem to turn on the age-related dementia itself: that is, on the grounds that he has lived a full life, that his disease is undoubtedly irreversible and progressive, that the process of *becoming* demented is an affront to his past dignity, or that he is ready to die precisely because he is both old and demented.

Perhaps the difference, in this case, is that the young psychiatric patient is physically strong enough to endure the ordeal of forced treatment, while the elderly patient is not. Or perhaps one would treat the younger psychiatric patient because there is a greater chance that medical progress will provide a future cure for his mental condition. These factors might make the two cases clinically and morally distinct.

But in the end, those who decide not to treat Patient #2 would need to think carefully about what they were really doing and why they were moved so to act. They would need to consider the unpredictable—and perhaps horrible—consequences of not treating: for example, a non-deadly heart episode that causes the patient to fall down and break his hip. Of course, they would also need to consider the human consequences of electing treatment—such as extending a life that appears miserable, a life that ends in a long dehumanizing decline. They might believe that they are under no moral obligation to act so as to make a person's fate worse. In this case, caregivers might feel a powerful moral intuition to forgo treatment, but it is hard to articulate the grounds for doing so without tacitly or explicitly declaring that the impairments of Alzheimer's disease are, by themselves, a legitimate moral reason to aim at death as the means of ending the individual's unhappiness.

As with Patient #1, one could surely envision many medical interventions for Patient #2 that would not be morally obligatory, including those that might be necessary to prevent an imminent and certain death. Certainly, one could decline a battery of treatments that required long-term physical restraints—treatments that necessarily treat the patient as someone trapped in a kind of medical servitude. But in this particular case, the moral analysis seems to lead in favor of installing the pacemaker in both patients—with sober recognition that doing so for Patient #2 may extend a life that exists with little or no present contentment. Often, with regret and anguish, we must opt for affirming what seems to be miserable or undignified life over death, and that choice should be at least the default position, in both law and prudence. In some situations, we are forced to recognize what Vergil called "the tears of things."[2] Recognizing this, we must aim for the choice that does not define individuals in distress as better off dead. And in this case, the patient's very misdeeds and apparent discontent are proof that there is life left in him, and that death is probably not imminent.

2. Burdensome Treatment and Patient Resistance.

A sixty-seven year old woman entering middle-stage of Alzheimer's disease is being cared for at home. She is still mobile but in no way self-sufficient; she is still talkative but lacks any reliable memory of who her family members are; and she has no real grasp of her own clinical condition. The caregiving is hard on the family, but the family is strong and lovingly devoted to her, and the daily routine is at least moderately stable. Bathing has begun to be a struggle, and she needs increasingly to be watched to ensure that she does not get herself into trouble around the house. But in general, day-to-day life is as good as one might expect given the circumstances. The most distressing episodes occur when her daily routine is altered. For example, she physically resists being put into the car, and so the family doctor has agreed to check on her periodically at home. But then a series of tests determine that her kidneys are failing badly and discussion ensues about whether to give her renal dialysis. With treatment, her kidney disease can likely be managed but not cured; without treatment, the patient will likely survive for a few weeks and then die a fairly swift and relatively peaceful death. Although the physician was hesitant to recommend dialysis, the family members asked that it be undertaken. They go a few times to the renal dialysis center twenty miles away, but the struggle is making both the patient and the caregivers increasingly miserable. Should the treatment be continued?

This case permits us to examine the relevance, for deciding about best care, of the burdens of receiving treatment—both the physical burdens of the given treatment itself and the burdensome effect that administering treatment might have on the patient's lived experience. It also permits us to look at the significance of patient resistance as a factor in deciding about treatments that might otherwise be medically and ethically indicated.

Before coming to the question about *continuing* hemodialysis, we first review the decision to *initiate* it: Was this decision compatible with ethical caregiving, an example of best care? The answer is not obvious.

On the one hand, it is likely that dialysis would preserve the patient's life for an indefinite period of time. In the absence of treatment, her kidney disease is probably deadly, sooner rather than later. In purely physical terms, hemodialysis is less taxing than, say, major surgery or chemotherapy. It would almost certainly be medically recommended for a younger patient with renal failure, or for a non-frail person of similar age who was not suffering from Alzheimer's disease.

On the other hand, dialysis is not happy treatment. Studies show that the majority of patients do not think that their life is good on dialysis (even when they are glad to be alive because of it). Sometimes too much fluid is taken off, sometimes too little. The shunts clot and get infected. Although it saves lives short-term in patients with end-stage renal disease, it often causes death from heart disease in a few years. Virtually no patient wants to stay on dialysis, and some patients, tired of waiting for a kidney transplant that often never comes, elect to discontinue their treatment rather than continue living under its burdens.

Unlike mentally competent patients facing the prospect of hemodialysis, a patient with moderate dementia cannot knowingly elect to seek its benefits despite its burdens, or to forgo those benefits because of those burdens. In one sense, our dementia patient's burden of treatment might in fact be less than usual: owing to her lack of self-awareness, she might not suffer the psychic distress that often accompanies living through the ordeal of never-ending treatment, contemplating death hovering over her all the time. In another sense, however, because she cannot choose or understand the treatment or its purpose, she cannot willingly understand or accept its physical discomfort or the alteration of her relatively comfortable and familiar daily routine at home.

In the present case, the physician apparently regarded hemodialysis as optional for the patient, extraordinary rather than obligatory, thinking the benefits did not outweigh the burdens in her case. Ethically, we think that this is a defensible judgment. But her family members, eager not to lose her and perhaps hoping also to keep her alive for a special family occasion already planned for the following year, opted for treatment, and the doctor readily obliged. Ethically, we think that this too is a defensible judgment. Both the doctor and the family caregivers were seeking to benefit the life the patient still had; neither was pronouncing judgment on its worthiness.

But after a trial of treatment, people have cause to reconsider. The treatment, especially the human ordeal it entails and the physical coercion it seems to require, turns out to be much more burdensome than anticipated. Should it now simply be stopped? Or are there things to be considered and tried first before reaching such a conclusion?

One proper avenue is to see whether there might be ways to reduce the burdens and to dissolve the patient's resistance to treatment—ways to make the necessity of treatment "make sense" to the patient or at least seem less burdensome, or ways to make the patient a more willing (or less resistant) participant in her own care. If the resistance is caused, for example, by the way the patient is being treated by her caregivers at the dialysis center, a change in their behavior or approach might ease the current ordeal. If the patient might now also be suffering from depression, antidepressant medication might improve the patient's behavior. Because traveling by car to and from the treatment is especially distressing, peritoneal dialysis—less effective than hemodialysis but administrable in the home—might well be considered. Alternatively, one might think of moving the patient into an assisted living facility where dialysis is available onsite, and where perhaps a new, stable life routine can be established—though one should not underestimate the stress such a move might well produce.

It is possible that some combination of new medications and new caregiving strategies will still make hemodialysis possible without imposing an excessive burden and without radically altering existing caregiving arrangements. It is possible that the patient will tolerate peritoneal dialysis at home. But if these new strategies do not help the situation, it may be that ceasing treatment altogether and restoring (if possible) her pre-treatment routine is what best care requires, even knowing that the consequence will be an earlier death.

The decision to cease treatment can never be made lightly, especially in a case where death is hardly imminent so long as treatment continues. But in cases such as this where patient resistance makes the very activity of getting treated a great burden—not simply physically in terms of pain, but humanly in terms of the patient's overall well-being—the decision to cease treatment and accept an earlier death seems morally permissible once other alternatives fail, and it may even be the best choice among a range of imperfect options. Forgoing treatment might allow the patient to live out her last days with the happiness that her relatively stable and peaceful home life still permits—with minimum disruption or struggle, and without being treated as a mere object of care requiring permanent coercion.

As in all cases, the obligation of caregivers here is to ensure that they do not choose the path that benefits their own lives and well-being at the cost of the patient's life and well-being. Every avenue of easing the burden of treatment should be pursued before coming to the conclusion that treatment in this case, for this person, is an excessive burden that should not be continued. But in the end, there is a highly principled and prudent case for forgoing treatment: One is seeking to serve the patient's well-being here and now. One is not using death as the means to end suffering; one is not seeking death deliberately by one's own actions or omissions; one is simply seeking the best life possible under the circumstances, even if the best life now possible is a shorter life.

We would probably think differently about the problem of burden and resistance if the patient were not an elderly person with dementia but a resistant child or a middle-aged psychiatric patient who believed being taken to dialysis was a form of despotic control. Caregivers will and probably should give patient resistance different weight in these alternative cases, and there seem to be at least some moral grounds for choosing differently based on the person's age and underlying condition. In the case of the child, one imagines that he will one day appreciate the parental coercion that kept him alive. In the case of the psychiatric patient, his life trajectory is longer than the incapacitated person with age-related dementia, and the possibility of benefiting the patient's life in novel ways remains a greater possibility. But for the elderly dementia patient, it is almost certain that the person's dementia—and thus her inability to understand the need for dialysis—will never get better and only get worse. And there is little hope for improvement from medical progress.

The potentially greater obligation to treat the psychiatric patient is not because the younger person's life has greater dignity than the older person's life; it is because the different clinical conditions of the two individuals alter what it means to benefit the life each patient currently has. In both cases, the bar for forgoing treatment should be set high—but even higher in the case of the psychiatric patient, because the possibility of a significant future improvement is also being forgone if and when hemodialysis is stopped.

The ethical dilemma in all these cases—where the patient resists for reasons that do not make sense or for reasons that do not necessarily serve the patient's best interests—is deciding what weight to give such resistance. There are some who believe that resistance on the part of dementia patients is autonomy's subconscious way of expressing itself—that is to say, it is the incapacitated person's way of expressing a will to die or the willingness to surrender to the inevitable. But more likely, this resistance is the activity of an individual living purely and spontaneously in the present—unable to fathom past wishes, unable to fathom the future consequences of non-treatment, and fearing in some instinctual way what it will mean to lose the experienced goods of the present, such as staying at home where things are familiar and not scary.

In such cases, the incapacitated person's well-being is entrusted to surrogates acting on her behalf. The ethical dilemma is that intervening medically on behalf of the patient seems to require acting against the patient, and in some cases the present burden of a given intervention—an intervention that is burden-some in part because of how it is seen by individuals who cannot see things clearly—outweighs the future benefit. In such cases—and the specific case here presented seems to be one of them—caregivers can morally choose a path that ends in an earlier death, because such a path is the best life possible for the patient under the circumstances. But they should always seek the fullest range of life-sustaining alternatives that do not wreak undue havoc on the goods the patient still has in the present.

3. The Trajectory of Death.

> *A woman with middle-stage Alzheimer's disease—disordered speech and some disorientation, sometimes emotionally overwrought, sometimes withdrawn, and only occasionally able to recognize her close family members—is also suffering from a rare form of cancer, already widely spread. There is no hope of cure, invasive treatments aimed at slowing down the disease are no longer an option, and the patient is already experiencing pain from the bony metastases. The cancer will almost certainly lead to a painful decline and excruciating death over the next three to six months, where pain can be controlled only by constant and heavy sedation, and even then not completely short of inducing coma. Concurrently, the patient contracts a treatable bacterial pneumonia, and a decision needs to be made about whether to treat it.*

This case forces us to confront a very difficult question: Do we benefit the life a person still has by extending a life marked by terrible physical suffering and with worse physical suffering still to come? More broadly, how do we balance the obligation to heal the sick with the obligation to ease the pain of those who suffer? Thinking clearly about this case requires assessing the progression of her cancer, the nature of her suffering (both here-and-now and looming ahead), and the significance of the person's dementia, which forecloses the patient's freedom to direct her own care without eliminating her experience of physical misery. It also confronts us concretely with the moral difference between the burdens we produce by our acts of medical intervention and the (possibly even greater) burdens we (indirectly) make possible by extending an exposed life to the looming miseries of a disease-in-process.

The patient in this case is clearly heading toward death but probably not yet irretrievably dying. As the disease progresses and death looms closer, the case for not treating the pneumonia surely seems more compelling. At some point, we might say that the patient has become a "whole ensemble of diseases," that death is too close to fight any longer, that treating a particular treatable disease no longer benefits the patient in her totality as a person. With possibly six months left to live, one must be hesitant about seizing an occasion for death by leaving the pneumonia untreated. But as six months becomes six weeks or six days, the case for surrender strengthens, especially as the debility of the cancer gets worse.*

Obviously, at every stage of care, physicians should do what is medically possible to control, lessen, or ameliorate the patient's physical pain. In most cases, pain relief (or partial relief) is possible, if one pursues it diligently. But in some cases, short of permanent sedation that itself brings increased risks of earlier mortality, adequate pain relief is not possible. And so it is worth taking up the case precisely as written: with death from cancer looming three to six months ahead, with the person suffering from advancing dementia, with pain present now and likely to get significantly worse day by day, and with a decision in the hands of caregivers about whether to treat a concurrent bacterial pneumonia.

As in the case described earlier, using antibiotics to treat her pneumonia would most likely be effective—though it is important to recognize, first, that any readily treatable pneumonia has a substantial chance to resolve itself spontaneously, and second, that any pneumonia likely to be lethal is potentially dangerous

---

* Of course, one of the great dilemmas faced by caregivers is the inability to know with certainty how much longer a given patient will live, or whether death is finally arriving, no matter what we do to fend it off. Such uncertainty could lead us in either direction regarding treatment. But it should induce a certain modesty before the awesome choices forced upon us in this dance with death, even as we unavoidably must make them despite our imperfect knowledge.

even if treated.* And in the immediate, physical sense, the treatment itself is non-burdensome: it does not involve moving or violating the patient, or causing her new kinds of discomfort or distress. As caregivers, however, we must think about the future as well as the present, about future burdens as well as present needs. In treating her pneumonia—even if we assume it is the right thing to do—we make it more likely that she will endure more future pain than she would were the pneumonia to take her life. We cannot avoid that stark reality.

Accordingly, compelled to choose whether to give antibiotics, we must wonder whether doing so is really doing good—especially for a patient with advancing dementia whose existence is defined almost entirely by physical experience. The dementia patient lacks the self-conscious loves and longings that might give a competent person a reason to fight on, a reason to endure terrible physical suffering, a reason to live because there is something knowable to live for. The demented person may reach a point—if she is not already there—where the pain is so awful and her cognitive capacities are so limited that life with cancer is sheer and incomprehensible misery, with nothing positive in her subjective experience to compensate or sustain her.

So why might we decide to treat? As caregivers, we do not want to refuse treatment as a way of getting the patient to die. (Indeed, were that our plan of action, we might have difficulty explaining why we should not simply end her life now, pneumonia or no pneumonia, and spare her the ordeal of the next three to six months.†) Thus, even assuming the best and most merciful of motives, we should still draw back from acting in a way intended to bring about her death.

But there is more to be said. In such difficult circumstances it is always right to be suspicious of our own motives. The human psyche is extraordinarily complex, and what we tell ourselves is mercy can sometimes be something quite different.

---

* Antibiotic treatment usually increases the odds of curing pneumonia by some middling percentage, roughly 30 to 60 percent; neither treatment nor non-treatment have certain yes or no effects.

† But on this point, see our earlier discussion in Chapter 3 of the partial moral relevance of the distinction between deliberately killing and allowing to die.

Made uneasy by this woman's dementia, seeing in her a sign of our own vulnerability and mortality, suffering at our own inability to relieve her suffering as much as we would like, we may prefer that she simply go away as soon as possible.

If we treat her pneumonia, this does not mean that we want her to suffer or that we cruelly impose suffering upon her. If we have been her caregivers up to this point, we might well hope— or pray—that she die soon and suffer no more. Nevertheless, part of honoring our commitment to the equal dignity and worth of every human being, irrespective of condition or circumstance, is to accept the demands of solidarity even in suffering.

Our most fundamental commitment is not to minimize suffering but to maximize care—never to abandon care for another human being. In many, perhaps most, instances these two obligations amount to the same thing. But there may be occasions— and this case may be such an occasion—in which maximizing care, never abandoning care, means that there is at least some suffering we cannot relieve.

The reasons to treat depend, finally, on a judgment that this woman is not yet irretrievably dying—though, to be sure, she is terminally ill. Six months is not a short time; it allows for her life to be touched by loved ones (though her capacity for interaction is already severely limited by her dementia), or it gives time to enjoy whatever simple pleasures (if any) still mean something to her. At some point—hard to calculate—this ceases to be the case. The range of life's possibilities narrows so greatly that forgoing treatment is not minimizing care but lovingly accepting the natural conclusion of a life. Even when we argue for treatment, therefore, we should recognize the limited scope of the argument in this instance. Perhaps we are not yet at the time for stopping such treatments, but we are surely approaching it, and it would be foolhardy to make assured judgments about it.

How might we make the argument against treating her pneumonia—even now when she may have as much as six months to live? We might judge that this woman has come to a point where we can find few or no ways to benefit any longer the life she has. We might conclude that we should let nature take its course and acquiesce in her dying, being present with her and comforting her as best we are able. We might conclude that extending her life, even if medically possible, is not humanly wise. This would not be an attempt to get her to die, justified by an appeal to merciful motives; we would not think ourselves to have failed as caregivers should she survive the pneumonia without treatment. On the contrary, it would be the best way we could find—in what are admittedly very difficult circumstances—to remain committed to her life and well-being. And even as we leave her pneumonia untreated, we should do everything we still can to care for the person in her final trial; forgoing this particular treatment does not mean forgoing all treatments, since some interventions may still make her existing life better even as death looms closer.

A further reason not to treat lies in what we might think of as a humanistic understanding of medicine. The point of medicine is not to treat or cure a disease, such as pneumonia. The point of medicine is to treat human beings—persons who are ill and suffering. What we want to treat here is not so much pneumonia as it is *this woman*—and, hence, we deal with the pneumonia as a way of caring for her, not simply in order to overcome a disease. Yet, she has now become, as we put it earlier, an "ensemble of diseases." If antibiotics are not useless for treating the pneumonia, they may now be useless for treating *her*. If we can find no ways to benefit the life she has, then we should step back from attempts to treat. Here again, however, we should not be too confident of our judgments. We should be wary of how mixed our motives may be, and we should be reluctant to decide that we have reached the point where treatment is no longer a benefit to the living person still with us. Nevertheless, our patient must always remain the woman, not simply the diseases that afflict her.

This is surely a hard and puzzling case with no easy answers. It appears to be a case in which the distinction between "active killing" and "letting die" might take on real significance: which is to say, we appear to possess the moral discretion, as caregivers, to let pneumonia take its course, but (as always) never the moral freedom to kill the patient directly.

In trying to decide what to do in such a hard case, the particularity of the patient as a person might also take on greater significance. If the patient's children lived far away and wanted to be with her before she dies, that may be a reason to treat. If the patient was or is a religious person with a redemptive understanding of suffering, this fact might move loving caregivers to treat. Conversely, if the patient had an especially low tolerance for pain, or believed that generosity toward the next generation means accepting death after a long life whenever death arrives, then permitting pneumonia to be this "old woman's friend" might be the way to do our best as her caregivers. Ideally, loving family members and caring doctors would come together to make a prudential judgment in such a case, a judgment that would depend not only on the particularity of the clinical situation but also the particularity of the patient as a person with a past, a present, and an (albeit short) future life.

In the end, we believe that the moral *argument* could go either way in this case, depending in part on many personal and medical particulars, those just mentioned among them. Even those who lean toward treating the pneumonia should recognize that the wisdom of treatment diminishes as the cancer and its accompanying pain worsen and as death looms closer. This is a case in which, notwithstanding which side gets the better of the moral *argument*, it seems wise to leave family members and doctors some leeway to decide, lovingly and prudently, when to surrender to nature—but not the right to actively kill, even with supposedly well-meaning motives. As we struggle with our awesome responsibilities in heart-wrenching circumstances, we should remember that even our perfect desire to see another's suffering end does not make us the absolute master over that suffering or the authoritative arbiter of that person's life. Sometimes, the best we can do is stand with those who suffer and make sure they know and feel that they are not alone.

IV. THE SIGNIFICANCE OF LIVING WILLS

A man entering middle-stage Alzheimer's disease lives in an assisted-living facility in a wealthy suburb. He is still ambulatory and talkative, though his stories do not make much sense. He is generally cheerful and well behaved—more so, it seems, as his memory has declined: He enjoys watching television, looking out the window, and attending weekly concerts performed by local students. His daughter lives close by and visits regularly—at least three or four times each week. He does not usually recognize her, but a little conversation often leads to stories about taking her to camp last summer (really 35 years ago). His nurses discover that he has blood in his stool, and x-rays reveal that he has an operable tumor in his sigmoid colon which, if not removed, could lead to a complete obstruction of his bowels. While making plans for the recommended surgery, the doctors discover in his file that he has written a living will stating very clearly that he wants no invasive treatments of any kind once his dementia has progressed to the point where he is no longer self-sufficient and can no longer recognize his family members. He does not seem overly resistant to the treatment, and he has never resisted basic treatments since entering the assisted-living facility. His daughter remembers discussing treatment preferences with her father a few years ago. At the time, the possibility of not recognizing her seemed so remote that she agreed to honor his preferences, mostly just to make him happy, and she helped him prepare his advance instruction directive. But now she feels that she should proceed with the surgery.

In caring for the person the patient now is, caregivers should never ignore the wishes and values of the person the patient once was. This requires respecting more than their written instruments; it obliges caregivers to consider the reasons that animated the person who wrote them. It would be important, in this case, to know whatever we could about why the patient chose to write an advance directive of this kind, with blanket instructions to forgo *all* invasive treatments: perhaps it was the desire never to burden his daughter; or the belief that life with dementia would not be worth living; or the desire not to exhaust all his resources on end-of-life care; or the fear that he would lose control of his behavior and act in inappropriate ways; or the worry that extending life indefinitely would be physically painful; or the belief that he should be allowed to die peacefully rather than being hooked up to machines. But absent such knowledge of his reasons—and it is often not easy to come by, even for close family members—caregivers are obliged to take seriously the instructions as such.

Seriously, but not slavishly. For past wishes, as we have explored, are not always morally decisive in such cases. They are a crucial point of consideration, but not the only or even the most important one. No individual can foresee every future circumstance in his or her life; an individual's best interests and true needs can change over time; and medical situations are so complex that we can only judge wisely what to do case-by-case and in the moment. Only by making an all-encompassing determination that his life with (more than minimal) dementia would never be worth sustaining might the competent individual rule out in advance *all* future treatments should he become demented. But such a blanket assertion about the worth of a future self denies the intrinsic dignity of embodied life even when one's cognition is impaired; it discriminates against an imaginary future self long before the true well-being of that future self is really imaginable. And although there are genuine reasons to tremble at the prospect of life with advanced dementia—and to wonder whether even non-burdensome treatments simply impose prolonged degradation—responsible caregivers should not acquiesce in denying the worth of the person entrusted to their care, just as competent individuals should resist making a priori negative judgments about the disabled person they might become.

The primary moral obligation of caregivers is to serve the well-being of the patient now here, and to ask not only what the patient would have wanted but what we owe the person who lies before us. This means paying attention to an advance instruction directive if one exists, but not following its orders *regardless of all other circumstances.* If the patient seems miserable because of his dementia, there might be greater cause to respect his living will. If he physically resists treatment, there might be cause to forgo further interventions and accept an earlier death. Yet, neither of these conditions is present in the case as we have it. When the individual in question wrote his living will, perhaps he could not imagine the desire of his daughter to care for him, or the fact that he would be so cheerful with dementia, or that he would be willing to endure surgery of this kind. All of these factors, so difficult to anticipate beforehand, should make us hesitate simply to apply his instructions in a mechanical and thoughtless manner, as if we were not ourselves reflective moral agents responsible to do the best we can for the man now before us. In this case, there seem to be clear and compelling reasons for caregivers to override the terms of the advance instruction directive and proceed with treatment, understood by both the daughter and the doctors as the best way possible to benefit the life the patient still has.[*]

The same would be true in an opposite kind of case: where the advance directive (written in the past) demands every possible treatment to keep the person alive, but where all possible interventions (in the present) would be excessively burdensome or would prolong a painful process of dying. In such cases, caregivers would also have significant moral grounds to override an advance directive and forgo certain interventions.

Our case might be further complicated by certain economic considerations. Suppose that the daughter knows that her father wrote the living will primarily as a means of preventing the spending down of assets he wanted to leave to his children and grandchildren. Yet the daughter, although mindful of his intentions, would much rather spend her father's money (her own prospective inheritance), and even her own money, to ensure that he receive the best medical care. Under these circumstances, she would be justified in exercising discretion, overriding his wishes where treatment is clearly beneficial and not exorbitantly expensive, although perhaps avoiding costly treatments in circumstances in which treatment is ethically optional.

In raising these complications, we hardly mean to suggest that the presence of a living will is irrelevant in deciding the best course of care. In many cases, there will be no reason to resist its

---

[*] Those who disagree with this judgment because they oppose overriding the living will should ask themselves whether they would also object to surgical pinning of a fractured hip, should the patient fall and break it, leaving him in pain and unlikely to walk again.

instructions, either because they accord with what lovingly prudent caregivers would recommend anyway or because they recommend a course of treatment (or non-treatment) that is among the justifiable options. In other cases, caregivers will disagree about what to do, especially when the demands of best care are ambiguous, with compelling reasons either to treat or not to treat. In cases such as the one presented here—involving a not excessively burdensome treatment, a cheerful and physically strong patient, and the fact that forgoing treatment will lead to a painful and imminent death—prudent judgment points toward overriding the living will, even when caregivers disagree. But in many cases, where the best interests of the patient are not so clear and where caregivers disagree, there is solid moral ground to defer to the living will.

Consider, for example, the two cases discussed earlier: the patient with kidney trouble who physically resists being taken to treatment and the patient with deadly cancer who contracts pneumonia. In those cases, caregivers face wrenching choices about what best care requires, and they might rightly turn to an advance instruction directive, if it exists, for guidance in deciding what to do. In such complicated circumstances, where loving caregivers are not certain what best care requires, an advance instruction directive might provide the moral authority or needed permission to fight on or let go, knowing how hard either path will surely be. But, as we have emphasized throughout, the authority of living wills should always be limited by the obligation to serve the patient now living among us, by always seeking the best care possible under the circumstances.

V. THE WELL-BEING OF CAREGIVERS

A physician is contacted by one of his patients whose mother has advanced Alzheimer's disease. The mother is in her late eighties, incontinent of urine, and unable to recognize any family member. She is being cared for at home by her daughter without outside help and has no major medical problems other than her advanced dementia. When the physician makes a house call, he finds the mother on a bed in the dining room. She is unable to communicate or answer questions. On physical examination, she looks her age, but has no ulcers or other skin breakdown, indicating excellent care. Her daughter is in tears and tells the doctor that her husband and three teenage children all wish to have her mother transferred to a long-term care facility. She cannot stand the thought, but she acknowledges the cost her life as a caregiver has entailed for her marriage. Her husband seems increasingly distant and they have not had marital relations for several months. The physician speaks with her for about an hour and urges her to move her mother. He reassures her that her mother would not recognize the change, and that she (the caregiving daughter) is in danger of losing her family because of emotional neglect. Three weeks later, the mother is moved to a nursing facility with an Alzheimer's unit. Three months later, she dies.

In this case, the demands of caring well for a person with dementia have taken an enormous toll on the caregiver's family; and the decision to transfer the patient to a nursing home may have altered the trajectory of her final days—though exactly how we can never know for sure. How do we judge the behavior of the caregiving daughter, the husband and sons, and the attending physician?

The true caregiver always aims to do his or her best for the person being cared for, especially when the dependence of the needy person is absolute. But the moral obligation of best care always exists alongside many other roles and obligations: for example, one's role as a nurturer and provider for young children; as an employee at a company; as a volunteer in the community; as a spouse for better and for worse; as a person with aspirations of one's own. Caregivers are not caregivers *only*. Of course, they should always strive to make decisions aimed at the well-being of the person with dementia—asking what is best for the patient, not what is best for the caregiver. But caregivers should also see the obligations of caregiving in light of life as a whole, with its many attachments, many burdens, and many purposes. This is why caregivers rightly ask: What do *I* as a caregiver owe *him* or *her* as patient and person? For this is a question that encompasses both the unchanging worth of the life being cared for and the genuine limitations of being *human* caregivers. Those with unlimited resources might owe their loved ones more in terms of medical care; those nations with greater wealth might owe their citizens more public assistance and support. Prudence requires honestly making such assessments, both as individuals and as a community.

As a simple rule of thumb, caregivers should do the best they can do; they are never compelled to do what they cannot do, but they are obligated to see how much they can do without deforming or destroying their entire lives. But in practice, this rule of thumb rarely leads to any fixed rules, because every person faces different demands and has different capacities. And inevitably, we cannot do our best simultaneously in every area of our life: that is to say, we cannot do our best for everyone all the time; we cannot be there for everyone all the time; we cannot devote resources to everyone equally all the time.

To be a caregiver is to confront not only the limitations of the person with dementia who relies upon us entirely, but our own limitations as human beings who are more than just caregivers or who are caregivers in multiple ways for multiple people. In doing so, we need to avoid two kinds of dangers: the danger of not working hard enough for the person with dementia who needs us, by saying too early or too easily that the burdens of care are too great; and the danger of betraying everything and everyone else in one's life, by saying too often and too persistently that the burdens of caregiving can be shouldered alone, or that caregiving for the person with dementia always trumps every other obligation or good.

Life, of course, comes in many phases, with obligations and opportunities that shift over time: As a mother of a newborn child, an adult daughter may be more limited in the time she can devote to caring for a parent with dementia; as an adult son struggling to provide his teenage children with a college education, he may be more limited in the resources he can give to his parent with dementia. Alternatively, the successful corporate lawyer may need to put his or her career on hold when a parent becomes dependent; the phase of life in which the pleasures and obligations of career are dominant may need to give way, for a time, to a period of life during which caregiving becomes dominant. In all situations, the presence of myriad obligations requires prudential discernment about which obligations place the greatest claim on our time, our resources, and our very lives at particular moments. This challenge presents itself to caregivers day after day, not only when persons with dementia get sick in other ways, and not only when life-and-death decisions need to be made about medical care.

In this case, the daughter is heroically trying to care for her mother—a mother who could not survive, living at home, without her care. Her husband and children also need her as a mother and a wife; and though they could endure without her, they increasingly feel abandoned, and increasingly see the grandmother/mother-in-law as too great a burden to keep at home. All individuals, in this case, need to ask themselves probing questions: The caregiving daughter should ask whether she is paying attention to the genuine needs of her children and husband: Is she showing interest in their lives? Is she available to them as a source of guidance or strength in hard times at work or at school? Is she paying attention to the education and moral development of her children? The husband and children need to ask whether they are being selfish: Are their own problems and needs so great that they cannot endure them a bit longer, and comfort their mother/wife by supporting her in her role as caregiver? Can these needs wait until later—when the life of the grandmother/mother-in-law has ended, and this phase of the caregiving daughter's life has ended? Are they meeting the obligations of fidelity toward the wife/mother they miss so much?

These burdens and tensions are often not only emotional but economic: Should the funds set aside for the children's college tuition be used to pay for an in-home health care aid or for a private assisted living facility? What if the choice is between an inferior nursing home covered by Medicaid and superior nursing care paid for out of the tuition fund? Or what if the choice is between working longer hours to pay for optimal care and working fewer hours to provide care oneself?

Without question, caregivers should never seek the death of the person being cared for in the name of other familial goods. But they will almost certainly make caregiving decisions in light of other family realities—such as whether to keep the person at home or put her in a nursing home, whether to keep working and hire outside help or leave work to care for a dependent parent themselves, whether to scale back children's extracurricular activities to spend more time at the nursing home or to carry on as usual. In making such decisions, both families and societies face the most fundamental kind of ethical dilemma: a dependent person with immeasurable worth who depends on finite people with many other obligations. On the one hand, we wish to ensure that care for persons with dementia is the best possible; as persons of incalculable value, they deserve no less. On the other hand, we need to confront the fact that best care for the person with dementia may mean less-than-ideal care for everyone else who needs us, and it may mean doing less than our best in those activities of life where we aspire to excellence. Because the person with dementia often cannot survive without our care and often teeters between life and death, we are moved to put everything else aside to meet the demands of caregiving. We live, with them, in a perpetual state of near-crisis or real crisis. At the same time, because the person with dementia seems to have such a diminished life, we might be tempted "to put them aside," so to speak, so that everything else can flourish. The moral challenge is finding the best possible balance among these competing obligations, while operating within the fundamental moral boundaries articulated above: never seeking someone's death in the name of other goods, always doing the best one can for the person entrusted to one's care.

Finally, the physician in this case understandably wants to help the family as a whole, and he may have offered sound advice in recommending that the patient be moved to a nursing care facility. From a strictly therapeutic perspective, it may be that the patient has been at home too long, without ready access to regular professional care. But it also seems far too simple to say, as the physician does, that the patient "would not recognize the change." As a matter of cognitive understanding, this is surely true: the patient no longer recognizes her daughter or the home she lives in. But although it may not be obvious or evident to observers, persons with dementia often do "recognize" when the kind of care they are receiving changes—not cognitively, but experientially or physiologically. Moving the patient to a care facility may have been the right thing to do, and perhaps the caregiving daughter should have done so even earlier. But we also cannot ignore the fact that doing so sometimes means a degradation, not an improvement, in the quality of care; and it sometimes leads to a shortening of the person's life—not by aiming at her death or leaving life-threatening illnesses deliberately untreated, but simply by weakening her basic "urge to live" by leaving her in the care of strangers or in a foreign environment. This fear is what makes putting a loved one in a nursing home so difficult for many families, especially those without the economic resources to pick whatever care facility they want. The gravest decision faced by many families is often not whether to treat or not, but whether caring for a family member at home is the morally sound thing to do—for the patient, the caregiver, and the caregiver's entire family.

*   *   *   *   *

The cases presented in this chapter illustrate the difficulties conscientious caregivers face in trying to provide the best care possible for people who can no longer care for themselves. Our discussions have explored what ethical caregiving might require in such cases, suggesting ways of thinking and acting sufficient to the task of benefiting patients with dementia in the clinical context, often in circumstances that admit no perfect options or happy outcomes. Although the goal is clear—to serve the true welfare of the patient here and now—loving prudence must often struggle to find the right means of serving it. Caregivers should always seek to benefit the life the patient still has, even when they elect to stand aside because further interventions would only make matters worse and even when they recognize that surrender is the path of loving care.

To deal with the ethical complexities found under even the best of circumstances, our discussions throughout have assumed the presence of competent and caring physicians and loving and engaged family members, all of them trying to do their best. Needless to say, these ideal conditions are not always present, perhaps not even usually present. We are mindful of the temptations to treat patients with dementia as second-class human beings or "non-persons"; we are aware that doctors are often impatient or inattentive, that nurses are overworked, and that family members are easily tempted to put their own interests first, sometimes even rationalizing betrayal of the patient as the course of mercy. For these reasons we worry lest our counsel of "allowing to die" in a few of these difficult cases may serve to encourage less than loving caregivers to betray and abandon their charges or encourage society at large to move down the slippery slope toward the moral pit of euthanasia. Nevertheless, it remains our obligation to develop the outlines of what ethical caregiving requires here and now, in the hope that such knowledge can itself help protect against the dangers that lie ahead and enable us all to treat the vulnerable among us according to the better angels of our nature.

ENDNOTES

[1] Robert Burt, *Taking Care of Strangers: The Rule of Law in Doctor-Patient Relations.* New York: Free Press, 1979, p. 11.
[2] This passage appears in Vergil's *Aeneid*, I.462: "*Sunt lacrimae rerum et mentem mortalia tangunt.*" ("*These are the tears of things, our mortality cuts to the heart.*")

5

Conclusions and Recommendations

This report has been, in a sense, three reports in one, unified by a concern for, and a line of argument about, ethical caregiving in our emerging mass geriatric society.

Chapter 1 provided an *overview of our aging society*. We looked at the demographic trends, the effects of modern medicine on aging and dying, and the novel opportunities and social challenges now before us as the baby boomers age and retire. We also looked at individual aging and the lifecycle, and explored the many factors that shape how different people age and die. We paid particular attention to age-related dementia, especially Alzheimer's disease, and to the special burdens that this increasingly common form of debility imposes on both patients and caregivers. In the end, we concluded that we may face, in the coming years, a genuine caregiving crisis, with many more dependent persons in need of long-term care and fewer available people to care for them.

Chapter 2 looked more specifically at *advance directives*, a much heralded remedy for dealing with difficult decisions in long-term care. These legal instruments enable individuals to leave written instructions about future treatment preferences should they one day become incapacitated ("living wills") or to appoint a trusted proxy to make such treatment decisions on their behalf ("durable power of attorney for health care"). We examined the principles behind these two types of advance directives and the evidence of how they are working in practice. In the end, we concluded that appointing a proxy decisionmaker is almost always sensible, while trying to dictate the precise terms of one's future care is often misguided or ineffective. Living will or no living will, there is no substitute for human caregivers on the spot, who will regularly be called on to make treatment decisions for those who cannot make them for themselves and whose numerous and evolving everyday duties of caregiving simply cannot be specified in advance.

Chapters 3 and 4 then considered *how ethical caregivers should decide and act*, in giving care to persons with dementia. These chapters examined several ethical dimensions of caregiving: the aims of care and the moral boundaries and guidelines that should govern caregivers (Chapter 3); and the work of principle and prudence in reaching sound caregiving decisions in a range of ethically difficult clinical cases (Chapter 4). The goal of caregiving, we concluded, should always be *to serve the well-being of the person now here*, always trying *to benefit the life an individual still has*, even when that life has been diminished by disease, debility, or dementia.

Taken as a whole, our primary aim in issuing this report is to help spark a national conversation about aging and caregiving, and to enrich the nation's thinking about what it means, in practice, to age well and care well. Our purpose is not to provide a detailed policy program or extensive policy recommendations, but to spur and guide those who must undertake this grave and pressing responsibility. We aim to ensure that future policymaking will always take into account the ethical and humanistic aspects of aging and caregiving, not merely the economic and institutional ones. And we aim to give aid to caregivers, familial and professional, struggling to do their best in hard, often tragic circumstances. The challenges of aging are challenges for all of us—as citizens, family members, and individuals looking ahead to our own inevitable decline. We offer this report to help us serve and preserve our humanity in our new world of longevity.

In this concluding chapter, we summarize some of our key findings and present some modest recommendations. We offer guidance to caregivers and their advisers regarding the care of their patients and loved ones; we suggest ideas for legislators, judges, professional policymakers, and ethics committees regarding advance directives and the need for other possible policy initiatives; and we present one major suggestion for mobilizing sustained research and serious national attention to meeting the needs and responsibilities of caregiving in our aging society.

I. LIFE, HEALTH, AND DEATH
IN OUR AGING SOCIETY

A. Our Unprecedented Situation

Barring major unforeseen developments, we are entering an unprecedented phase of our history—indeed, of human history—featuring (1) a new age structure of society, (2) longer and more vigorous old age for millions, (3) new modes of dwindling and dying, and (4) a likely shortage of available caregivers.

1. The New Demography.

In the decades ahead, the age structure of the American population will almost certainly undergo a tremendous and unprecedented shift, continuing and accelerating a trend toward an older—and, increasingly, also an "old-older"—population, with the oldest segments of the population growing fastest, both in absolute numbers and percentages of the whole. One projection gives the big picture: Between 2000 and 2050, the population of Americans age 45 to 64 is expected to grow modestly from 61 to 85 million while the population 65 and over is expected to grow from 34 to 79 million, with the cohort 85 and above *more than quadrupling*, from 4 million to 18 million. These dramatic shifts are the result of improvements in public health and preventive medicine and of modern medicine's success against many causes of premature death; of the relatively high birth rates of the baby-boom years of 1946 to 1964; and of the relatively low birth rates that have persisted in the years since then. This society-wide increase in personal longevity is a remarkable human achievement, but it also creates an unprecedented social situation, with novel challenges and uncertainties.

2. Healthy Old Age.

In many ways and for increasing numbers of people, this is a wonderful time to grow old. More people are living longer and staying healthier. Premature death is in decline, and so are certain kinds of chronic disability for the population over 65. More peo-

ple are able to enjoy a true period of retirement, with the resources and leisure to pursue their avocations. Unfortunately,
many people still struggle economically, physically, and personally in old age, and many people still have their lives tragically cut
short. But compared to even the relatively recent past, when
growing old was rare, when healthy old age was rarer, and when
poverty in old age was the rule, the current situation is an aston-
ishing achievement. We are already, as it were, staying younger
longer, and we can look forward in the years ahead to still more
advances and improvements in healthy and vigorous aging.

3. Debility and Dementia, Death and Dying.

Living longer has also changed the patterns of illness during old
age, especially the illnesses that lead toward death. Although
most of us seem likely to enjoy a greater period of healthy old
age, many of us are also destined to experience a longer period of
chronic illness and dependency before we finally die. Already,
only a minority of us dies suddenly, without prior chronic illness.
Already, the most common trajectory toward death is the path of
"dwindling," of progressive debility, enfeeblement, and dementia,
often lasting up to a decade. Special challenges arise for patients
suffering from the various age-related dementias, especially Alzheimer's disease, a condition whose prevalence is now high (an
estimated 4.5 million sufferers in the United States) and increasing. This progressive, degenerative, and fatal disease, lasting typically between five and ten years, begins with weakening memory
and everyday forgetfulness, moves to progressive loss of basic
life skills, speech, and self-awareness, and concludes with severe
bodily breakdown, in total dependence on others for all activities
of daily life. An unprecedented number of people will need long-
term care, not just for months but for years. Through much of
that time, they will not be able to participate in caregiving decisions, and caregivers will often face critical decisions about
choosing or forgoing life-sustaining or death-postponing treatments, in addition to the daily efforts of providing ongoing care.

4. *The Availability of Caregivers.*

While the need for long-term caregivers and proxy decisionmakers appears to be increasing, the supply of readily available caregivers appears to be shrinking. Because families are smaller, there are fewer adult children to care for their aged parents. Many more old people are childless and alone. Increased family instability and greater geographic mobility mean that, in many cases, fewer caregivers are willing or available to care. Once the typical caregiver was a woman who did not work outside the home; today the typical caregiver, still a woman, is employed outside the home, and often obliged in addition to care for her own young children. At the same time, there are already shortages of professional caregivers—nurses and geriatricians—and caregiving jobs such as nurse's aides often lack the levels of compensation and benefits that might attract sufficient numbers of workers. The cost of care is rising, the ratio of workers to retired persons is falling, and many other social goods compete for scarce resources. Looking ahead, we may face a situation with more people needing extended long-term care, with more prolonged periods of debility en route to death, but with fewer qualified people willing and able to act as caregivers. This is an issue demanding urgent social attention.

B. Our Uncertain Future

Although we know much about the aging of American society, there is much we do not know, especially about possible future developments, medical and social. We have good reason, therefore, to be both alert and cautious. Economic growth or economic setbacks may increase or decrease the resources available to families and state governments for providing care in old age. New instruments such as long-term care insurance may expand the caregiving options available to families. Changed work patterns or levels of compensation may alter the availability of both voluntary and professional caregivers. Policy changes or new programs might reduce the costs of care or lead to better and more suitable kinds of care. Free societies are creative societies, and in the years ahead we should expect to see several now-unexpected ways of addressing the challenges of caring for the disabled elderly.

In addition, major biomedical advances—say in the prevention, delay, or amelioration of Alzheimer's disease—could modify these current projections, by altering average life expectancies, changing the prevailing patterns of health and illness, and transforming the most common trajectories toward death. (Conversely, major breakthroughs in the treatment of cancer or heart disease could increase the proportion of people whose death comes only after a decade of dwindling.) New technologies to facilitate basic care and improved practice standards within medicine and nursing could also make caregiving more effective and easier.

Yet even in the best-case scenarios—with healthy aging until the end, family caregivers ready and willing to care, and public policy that supports caregivers and care-receivers—we still face definite challenges ahead. These include, for example, the costs of financing long-term care or expensive medications for the elderly, or decreases in economic productivity should more workers in their prime devote more energy to the "non-productive" activities of caring. And it is by no means assured that we will get the best case scenario rather than something much less ideal: increased incidence and prolonged periods of dementia and enfeeblement, fewer family caregivers ready and willing to care, and a public policy that regards growing expenditures on the elderly as unwarranted or unaffordable. Under such circumstances, it may prove more rather than less difficult to do right by our parents and spouses in their long, last act of life. Yes, the future is unknowable and uncertain, but we know the stakes and they are surely high.

C. Ethical Commitments and Wise Public Policy

As we chart our uncertain course into an equally uncertain future, not everything is or should be up for grabs. Certain moral aspirations and moral boundaries—always to care, never to abandon or betray those entrusted to our care—should guide us in the days ahead. But these moral aspirations always take shape in real-life circumstances, where resources are limited, people are tested, and competing human goods call out for our attention and devotion. We cannot do without awareness of the likely perils. We cannot do without ethical guidance.

Looking ahead, American society needs to avoid two grave dangers: We need to prevent the worst kinds of betrayal and inhumanity toward the dependent elderly—such as relying on institutions that "warehouse" elderly persons, promoting assisted suicide as an answer to disability, and embracing euthanasia as a solution to the perceived social and economic burden of dependent persons. At the same time, as we aim at the best care possible for the elderly, we must avert the danger of intergenerational conflict over scarce resources, meeting our obligations also to our children and grandchildren, sustaining other social goods, and avoiding a major new drag on the economy that would (among other things) weaken the economic capacity of working families to provide care for their loved ones. Put positively, we need to encourage families and local communities to become *responsible* caregivers and *to sustain one another* in giving care, while recognizing the role of the state in providing a safety net of decent care for those who lack adequate economic resources or a network of family support.

Many Americans continue to believe that people should be self-reliant and care for themselves and their families without state intervention or support. But the looming crisis in long-term care may challenge these beliefs, unless government provides additional assistance to support caregiving families. We are rapidly moving into a situation in which—due to the genetic lottery and the vagaries of disease, and through no fault of their own— nearly half of society's families will face a demand for long-term care that they simply will not be able to meet without expensive professional help, while the other half will not. In a society of ethical caregiving, the government must accept a duty to find, encourage, and institute measures that would help share the economic part of this burden more equally.

II. CONCLUSIONS AND RECOMMENDATIONS

We come, then, to a summary of our conclusions and recommendations, some concerning individual caregiving, some concerning procedures and policies regarding advance directives and advance care planning, and a final recommendation to promote further national attention to the subject of aging, dementia, and caregiving.

A. Individual Caregiving

Human beings who are dwindling, enfeebled, or disabled in body or in mind remain equal members of the human community. As such, we are obligated to treat them with respect and to seek their well-being, here and now. We should always seek to benefit the life incapacitated persons still have, and never treat even the most diminished individuals as unworthy of our company and care. Their well-being in the present is of course related to the ideals and wishes of their earlier life, but those past wishes and ideals do not alone determine what we owe them today. We should seek their *present* good, avoid doing them present and future harm, and make every effort—in the light of their own special circumstances and ours—to find the wisest and best form of care possible.

Caregiving always takes shape in the particular—involving distinctive individual patients and caregivers, in unique and often complicated circumstances—and there can be no single principle or invariable formula for discerning the best care possible in each and every case. In decisions large and small, loving prudence is required to discern the most beneficial course of action. But, as we argued in Chapter 3, there are certain moral guidelines and boundaries that should guide all caregivers, as they strive to do their best for the person now relying upon them. We highlight three crucial teachings.

1. Euthanasia and assisted suicide are antithetical to ethical caregiving for people with disability. These practices should always be opposed.

If we are to care well for the needs and interests of persons incapable of caring for themselves, we must erect and defend certain moral boundaries that prevent us from violating the people entrusted to our care: No euthanasia, no assisted suicide. These practices should be opposed for many reasons, and not only because of our moral (and legal) opposition to seeking the death and taking the life of innocent human beings. These taboos are also indispensable for giving good care: one cannot think wholeheartedly about how best to care for the life the patient now has if ending his or her life becomes, for us, always an eligible treatment option. This holds true not only in the vexing end-of-life cases discussed in Chapter 4. It is also indispensable for fulfilling our everyday obligations and performing our everyday ministrations in their care. It is indispensable to serving faithfully and loyally, deserving of the trust that has been reposed in us, whether as family members or as doctors, nurses, and hospice workers. A decent society will not seriously consider abandoning and betraying its most vulnerable and disabled members. A prudent society will not weaken those necessary restraints that prevent even the most devoted caregivers from yielding—out of weakness or frustration—to the temptation to abandon or betray those in need of their care.

Try as we may to be devoted caregivers, we are not saints, and—under the pressure of trying circumstances—even our best motives may lead us to betray or abandon altogether those who in their vulnerability depend on our care. Hence, we all need a shared moral world in which certain actions that undermine the solidarity of the human community are firmly beyond the pale. Or, to put the matter positively, it is only as we deny ourselves the option of "solving" intransigent social problems by ridding ourselves of those who manifest the problem, that we can train ourselves to cultivate with greater clarity and wisdom the capacities we have and the virtues we need for caregiving. A society that sets its face against abandoning those whose lives are in decline has a better chance of being a society that thinks creatively about the trajectory of life and the bonds between the generations, of remaining a society in which to live long is also to live well together.

2. The goal of ethical caregiving in the clinical setting is not to extend the length or postpone the end of the patient's life as long as is medically possible, but always to benefit the life the patient still has.

In caring for those who cannot care for themselves, our primary goal is to do everything we reasonably can to *benefit* their lives— from meeting basic needs and sustaining life, to easing pain and curing ailments, to offering comfort in difficult times and, in the end, keeping company in the face of looming death. Medical interventions that sustain life are, of course, often a benefit to those whose lives they sustain. But extending life and delaying death are not the only or primary goals that should guide caregivers, and there are times in which pursuing those goals would require imposing new and unjustified burdens on the patient. Caring well for the patient does not require *always* choosing interventions that would prolong his life or delay his dying, and sometimes best care requires forgoing treatments that may sustain life at the cost of imposing undue misery or offering palliative care that accepts an increased risk of an earlier death. Some interventions, even if life-sustaining, do not benefit the life the patient now has. Some interventions, aimed at benefiting the patient's present life, may not be life-extending.

Moreover, in caring for the life the patient now has, we care also for the manner and humanity of his dying. Feeding tubes and respirators are not always obligatory. Neither is hospitalization or the intensive care unit. And if these measures are used for a time, there are circumstances when it is morally permissible— and even, perhaps, morally required—to desist. Dying as well as possible—or, more modestly, in as little misery as possible—is also one of our concerns and cares. Even as we must never seek or aim at the patient's death, so we are also under a positive obligation not to impose treatments that would unduly burden the patient, make his dying more difficult, or otherwise deprive him of a more peaceful end of life or of final hours in the company of those who love him. Dying, like living, is a human matter, not merely a medical or technological one.

3. The clearest ethical grounds for forgoing life-sustaining treatments are an obligation to avoid inflicting treatments that are *unduly burdensome to the patient being treated* and an obligation to avoid treatments that are not at all (or not any longer) efficacious in attaining their desired result.

As caregivers, with necessarily limited powers to fix what is broken, we must distinguish between the burdens of disease (which we cannot always control) and the burdens of treatment (for which we are fully responsible). There are some burdens and some forms of suffering that we cannot make disappear, despite our best efforts. Because our powers of cure are limited, sometimes all we can do is stand with the patient in her days of trial, always seeking to minimize those burdens we cannot fully eradicate. But *where we do intervene* with medical treatments or dislocations required to obtain them, we are under an obligation not to add unduly to the patient's existing miseries and troubles. And, of course, we are also under an obligation not to intervene uselessly. Those interventions that cause undue burden or fail to benefit the life the patient still has can be, and often clearly should be, forgone. Judging when this is the case is always the task of prudent caregivers, making conscientious decisions in particular circumstances for particular patients.

B. Procedures and Policies: Ethics Committees, Professional Societies, Judges, and Legislators

The ability to care well for people who can no longer care for themselves depends on many factors—economic, medical, social, cultural, institutional, civic, legal, and ethical—many of which are also influenced directly or indirectly by policy decisions. Most of these matters lie beyond the scope of this report, which is devoted mainly to the ideas and practices of ethical caregiving. In the realm of public policy, we have confined our attention to examining critically the legal instrumentality of written or formal advance directives. We here summarize our key findings and of-

fer some forward-looking recommendations to ethics committees, professional societies, judges, and legislators involved in developing or interpreting policies and procedures relevant to advance directives. In the end, we recommend also the search for
alternatives that focus more directly on creating an economic,
civic, and institutional environment in which best care for the
patient now here is the moral and medical aim and in which the
chances of providing such care can be significantly increased.

**1. Advance instruction directives (or living wills), though
valuable to some degree and in some circumstances, are a
limited and flawed instrument for addressing most of the
decisions caregivers must make for those entrusted to their
care.**

Living wills, although much talked about and recommended by
many people, are not a panacea. They address, at most, but a
small fraction of the decisions caregivers must make for incapacitated persons. Even if everyone executed a living will, and even if
the instructions were followed as written, the big questions of
long-term care and ethical decision-making would not disappear
or become readily manageable: there are too many situations in
which following orders is not the best way to give care, and giving care always requires more in terms of resources, character,
support, and judgment than any legal instrument can possibly
provide. We firmly believe that the American people—both potential patients and potential caregivers—should not be misled or
encouraged to think otherwise. Moreover, in addition to the
practical difficulties with living wills that we exposed in Chapter
2, the duties of actual—as opposed to imagined—human
caregiving always arise within concrete situations experienced in
the present, not conjured situations imagined in the past.
Precisely because the obligation of caregivers here and now is
always to the patient before them here and now, instructions
written long in advance can rarely be simply authoritative or
dispositive. To be sure, a few of the difficulties with living wills could be
ameliorated by improved and more prudent drafting: for example, every writer of a living will should be asked to consider writing into such a document—after, of course, discussing it with the

relevant parties—a provision acknowledging that the wishes expressed in the document are based on incomplete information and explicitly authorizing family members and clinicians to override the specific instructions if they judged it would serve the patient's present welfare to do so. Also, rather than write blanket exclusions of specific kinds of potential treatment interventions, advance instructions might explicitly allow for *temporary* trials of certain treatments, permitting the patient's caregivers to see if the treatments might actually be beneficial without creating a situation in which the treatment cannot be easily stopped. But even such improvements do not address the fundamental limitations and shortcomings of advance instruction directives, which can never replace prudent judgment by devoted caregivers about what a patient now needs. Ethics committees, drafters of professional guidelines, policymakers, and legislators at both the state and federal levels should address these failings and search for more practical and responsible alternatives.

2. Advance proxy directives are much more valuable and should be encouraged.

Instead of attempting to specify *what* should be done, advance proxy directives specify *who* should make crucial decisions on our behalf. These instruments ratify our fitting desire to be placed in the hands of loving caregivers whom we trust with our well-being when we can no longer act to promote it ourselves. Naming of proxy decisionmakers provides clear identification of who shoulders responsibility to act for the patient and makes it clear to physicians and others with whom they must deal. Such knowledge makes it much more likely that there will be the desirable discussions between family and professional caregivers at all important junctures of treatment and care.

3. Beyond legal instruments drafted and devised by individuals, we need to develop policies and procedures that encourage ongoing discussion and coordination among all relevant parties—including family members, health care professionals, social service providers, and, where possible, the patients themselves.

More important than the execution of such legal instruments is a process of advance care planning and full discussion, covering not only "end-of-life" decisionmaking but the whole range of caregiving realities—including questions about assisted-living, home care, medical preferences, finances, scheduling of available caregivers and respite care, and possible eventual transfer to a skilled nursing facility. Such planning in the early stages of illness can often include the patient, who can make known his greatest hopes and fears and who can gain much needed reassurance that he will have loyal care and company throughout his illness. Such planning should not be regarded as a rigid set of prescriptions for future care, since flexibility is always necessary. But wise planning in advance can sometimes improve the circumstances in which caregivers eventually make evolving and often unpredictable decisions, by thinking ahead about the range of caregiving options that may one day become relevant or necessary.

4. Ethics committees called upon to give advice to doctors and families, and judges obliged to adjudicate difficult and often tension-filled cases involving decisions about life-sustaining treatment, should do everything possible to ensure that surrogate decision-making focuses as much as possible on the best care for the incapacitated patient in his or her current condition.

Hospital-based ethics committees are frequently called on for advice regarding ethically difficult treatment decisions, often about the use of life-sustaining treatment. Professional societies often formulate practice guidelines for physicians treating incapacitated patients. Guideline drafters and ethics committees should always focus on the present welfare of patients. They should be concerned less with trying to figure out what the incapacitated patient would want done, were he now to be consulted in his own case, and concerned more with discerning what the incapacitated patient now needs in order to serve best the ongoing, if dwindling, life he now has. Judges who must hear cases in which there is an unresolved dispute about best treatment would also do well to make sure that the course of action recommended does not overvalue "precedent autonomy" or past wishes and pays proper regard to what best care owes this human being in his current situation.

Moving from individual cases to general policy in this area, state legislators should be cautious about putting more state authority and resources behind advance instruction directives. They should focus instead on standards governing decisions for patients who lack such directives. State law should be responsive to the reality that decisions at the bedside are almost always guided by proxies seeking to do what they believe the patient would have wanted or what they believe now best serves the patient's welfare. Lawmakers should give proxies, families, and other informal surrogates the necessary authority and discretion to resolve treatment dilemmas, while always encouraging those proxies and surrogates to seek the best care possible for the patient now here and always treating best care as the primary aim in disputed cases. Congress should revisit the Patient Self-Determination Act of 1990 and consider amendments and revisions that recognize the authority of informal surrogates to decide on behalf of incapacitated patients and that promote the "best care possible for the present patient" as the basic standard for clinical decision-making. This federal statute, which requires health care providers to notify patients about advance directives, was intended to increase patient involvement in treatment decisions, chiefly by providing patients with the opportunity to express their wishes ahead of incapacitation. Experience has shown, however, that these well-meant measures have not had much practical impact and have been ineffective in promoting better care for incapacitated patients.

5. Good long-term care requires willing and able caregivers, community supports, caregiving institutions, and social policies that go beyond advance directives and beyond even responsible advance care planning. Public policy must address these issues directly.

Improved legal instruments for decision-making, and more capacious and comprehensive forms of advance care planning, will not *by themselves* enable even the most devoted family members to do their work well. The ability of family caregivers to give proper care to persons with dementia depends greatly on the economic, social, and communal resources available to them and to their professional caregivers: for example, public and private health insurance that fits their special needs; affordable long-term care insurance; personnel and funds for respite-care; appropriate institutional housing and care-giving facilities; home care services; technologies devised to assist in giving basic bodily care; faith-based or civic support groups for patients and families; the availability of health care providers who can give continuity of care and comprehensive oversight of medical attentions; and, of course, vigorous support for biomedical research into the prevention and treatment of the various forms of dementia. Not having explored any of these issues in any detail, the Council is not now in a position to make legislative or policy recommendations in these areas, either about what should be tried or about how it should be paid for. However, our recognition of the importance of tackling these matters is one of the reasons for our next and final recommendation.

C. Presidential Commission on Aging, Dementia, and Long-Term Care

This report on ethical caregiving began by calling attention to the challenges our society may soon face as the population of elderly persons in need of long-term care grows. With the impending retirement of the baby boom generation, we see an urgent need to begin planning for the likely strain on families and institutions that may very well result from the unprecedented combination of greater longevity, increased incidence of dementia, the decreasing ratio of active workers to retired persons, the increasing cost of care, and the looming shortage of paid and unpaid caregivers.

We hope that our report has performed an important public service by heightening the visibility of the problems that can be expected to arise, by drawing attention to their often-neglected ethical dimensions, by pointing out the limited value of advance directives, and by suggesting some guidelines for what should be considered good care in a decent society.

And yet peering into this, our future, leaves us more humbled than certain of what course to take. We have offered key and, we think, quite critical advice in those areas for which our Council is best suited to give guidance. But our work has also opened up before us a series of questions touching upon areas that must be taken up by and in conjunction with others—by experts in demography and economics, and above all by policymakers. Intensive study and planning are required if the nation is to avoid a destructive conflict between generations and the neglect or abandonment of the frail elderly. We also recognize that the ethical analysis we have provided is of limited value in the absence of adequate caregiving institutions and familial caregivers with the requisite character and resources. **Therefore, we are recommending as a next step the establishment of a Presidential Commission on Aging, Dementia, and Long-Term Care**.

To meet the challenges of our aging society, we need first to face up to their existence. Although most American families are already all too familiar with this subject in poignant personal ways, we as a nation have not yet addressed this topic squarely in our public discourse. It is time for public acknowledgement, at the national level, of the seriousness of the challenge. More important than raising consciousness, it is time for careful research, sustained inquiry, creative innovations, and responsible collective action. A Presidential Commission on Aging, Dementia, and Long-Term Care could launch such an effort by undertaking a careful and comprehensive study of this entire subject—in all its aspects—and by offering feasible and sensible recommendations for innovation and reform.

The first mission of such a body would be to collect *reliable data* and to commission *empirical research* (1) to understand and assess the demographic, economic, and policy realities of the present, (2) to make reasonable projections about the challenges of the future, (3) to review and evaluate the economic and human resources available to meet them, paying attention to the hard questions about priorities, and (4) to identify and assess as models the best practices that are currently in use or in development in various communities around the country. The body should pay special attention to the social challenges of providing long-term care for persons with dementia and debility, once the baby boomers enter old age.

The second mission would be to develop and recommend feasible policy reforms, whose primary aim would be to improve the capacity of families to care for their loved ones, rewarding and supporting their efforts by promoting institutions and practices—such as long-term care insurance, community-based respite care programs, and a flexible menu of long-term care options—that can assist caregivers in their task. It should pay special attention to the needs for continuity of care and the importance of fostering cooperation among families, professional caregivers and caregiving institutions, and faith-based communities. At the same time, the commission should look for ways to improve the existing safety net for those who lack adequate resources to care for themselves.

The challenges ahead are ethical, social, economic, and medical. Accordingly, the Commission's members should include persons knowledgeable in these fields. Where it lacks the expertise, it should take testimony and seek advice from people with knowledge and experience in all the relevant areas, including, among them, the following: the demography of American society; the changing prevalence of chronic disease and trajectories toward death; biomedical research into the diseases and disabilities of old age (especially Alzheimer's disease and the other senile dementias); the design and management of long-term care institutions; best practice standards for clinical care for the frail elderly, especially those with dementia; nursing and paraprofessional recruitment and training; the changing structure of modern family life, with special attention to effects on available and likely caregivers; ethical caregiving at the end of life, including the experience of hospice care; the economics of old age; the wealth of baby boomers as they reach retirement; options and costs of private long-term care insurance; the effects of tax policy on incentives to save for old age; the rules governing Medicare reimbursements and Medicaid eligibility; the role of faith-based institutions in caregiving at the end of life; community based respite-care programs for caregivers; and local, ethnic, and religious differences in expectations and practices regarding eldercare.

We are well aware that Presidential commissions, like advance directives, are not a panacea. They have their occupational hazards and their temptation to grandiosity and radical "solutions." The commission proposed here should therefore proceed boldly but modestly, mindful especially of the fact that *old age and dying are finally not problems to be solved, but human experiences that must be faced.* The commission should also always bear in mind that the demands of long-term care exist alongside many other civic goods, and that what is practically possible and publicly responsible will fall short of some imaginable ideal that could be pursued if resources were unlimited or if our society faced no other serious challenges. Indeed, the commission's charge should require it to assess the potential unintended long-term costs of providing public long-term-care benefits, to make sure that any public benefits go to the truly needy, and to see that nothing is done to undermine familial and intergenerational responsibility and self-sufficiency. Our goal is to strengthen caregiving by loved ones, not to replace them.

We also recommend that the commission avoid any temptation to propose a complete reworking of the entire American health care system or wholesale reform of Medicare and Medicaid. Rather, in developing its recommendations, it should target those focused but crucial reforms that could have a large, cumulative effect in reshaping existing policy and behavior. The targeted reform, which seems small today, is often the best reform—both because it is the only practical reform possible in a society resistant to radical transformation and because responsible small steps taken early can lead us on a path toward permanent and sustainable improvements.

The challenges of caregiving in our aging society deserve and demand the attention of our nation's leaders at the highest levels. They will soon confront every American family, and we would be most wise to give them careful and most serious thought before they are fully upon us.

*   *   *

Aging, dementia, and dying, we are well aware, are not the cheeriest of topics. We recognize that it would be much more pleasant to look the other way and perhaps much easier to treat the topic in purely economic terms. But denial is not an option, and much more than money is at stake. Millions of American families already know the score and are struggling, often magnificently, to do the right thing for their loved ones, all on their own. It remains for the nation to acknowledge the need and rise to meet it. A mature and caring nation, concerned about staying human in a technological age, will not shy away from its responsibilities. If asked, "Who cares?" the answer must be, "We do."

APPENDICES

PERSONAL STATEMENTS

The preceding text constitutes the official body of this report; it stands as the work of the entire Council. In the interest of contributing further to public discussion of the issues, and of enabling individual members of the Council to speak in their own voice on one or another aspect of this report, we offer in this Appendix personal statements from those members who have elected to submit them:

Personal Statement of Professor Dresser

Bioethics often focuses on the speculative, the symbolic, the exotic developments that have little direct impact on people's lives. *Taking Care* departs from this model. Many, many families face the formidable task of deciding about medical treatment for older relatives unable to make their own decisions. And many not now in that situation worry that it will happen at some future point. Besides being a personal and family problem, this is a big and expanding social problem. There is a large and soon to be larger population of people affected by dementia and we are far from ready to cope.

In this report, the Council adds its voice to those calling for more systematic and sustained attention to the caregiving demands presented by an aging society. *Taking Care* offers ethical analysis and guidance, as well as a few rules to govern caregiving decisions. It represents our effort to move the conversation, to promote a richer and more robust examination of the distinct issues characterizing medical care for dementia patients.

Navigating a proper course between extending life and accepting death is never easy, but discerning that course is particularly difficult in the context of dementia care. People with dementia are vulnerable to the other health problems that accompany aging. At the same time, they can live for many years after they lose the ability to make their own choices. And they remain conscious and able to experience burdens and benefits from treatment interventions. These facts join to present special challenges to those who must decide on the patients' behalf.

The standard legal and ethical approaches to treatment decision-making for incapacitated patients supply insufficient guidance to loved ones and clinicians responsible for dementia patient care. In the dementia setting, advance instructions are of limited use. Indeed, dementia care is not a problem that we as individuals can manage on our own. If we are among the many people affected by dementia in the coming decades, others will inevitably determine how we live and die.

Best care for dementia patients includes ascertaining how they could experience a proposed medical intervention. Assessing an intervention's burdens and benefits demands attention to detail. Families and clinicians responsible for caregiving must look closely at the patient and possible treatment options. For confused and frail dementia patients, interventions often create new distress and discomfort, and this must be part of the benefit-burden analysis.

The case studies in *Taking Care* offer in-depth examination of specific treatment questions. Although individual Council members (and readers) will favor different resolutions in particular cases, what is most important is the careful and precise inquiry into the nature of appropriate care for dementia patients. The case analyses identify central features of good care and examine a range of permissible choices for those at the bedside.

Dementia caregiving is not a happy topic for biomedicine and bioethics. It does not offer opportunities for optimistic speculation about a future in which human mortality and suffering are absent. For this reason, many would prefer to ignore it and concentrate instead on the hypothetical benefits of various forms of cutting-edge research. This seems to me irresponsible and indefensible. Attention to everyday clinical problems should be part of the bioethics agenda. Delivering good care to patients suffering today should be the primary goal of medicine and health policy. For too many dementia and other patients in this country, we fall short of this goal.

With this report, the Council draws attention to today's unmet needs and to the larger problems that await us. We must respect and protect dementia patients, but we must also recognize medicine's limits, our status as mortal creatures, and our obligations to the other people in our lives. Giving due regard to all of these concerns will be hard to do, and without a concerted effort, we are certain to fail.

Rebecca S. Dresser

Personal Statement of Professor Gómez-Lobo

The report affirms two important philosophical principles that should govern our care of aging patients. The first one states that it is wrong intentionally to cause the death of a demented patient (or of any patient, for that matter). The force of this principle rests upon several considerations deeply rooted in our common morality. Life is the grounding good, the good that sustains all other human goods. Since the function of morality is the protection of the human goods, it is natural to uphold the universal principle that enjoins us to respect every human life, no matter how diminished it may appear to be. A demented person is a severely handicapped individual who does not thereby cease to be a person. To think otherwise is to embrace a radical form of dualism that leads to the positing of two deaths: one for the mind and one for the body. But this does not match our unified experience of ourselves and of others. A demented person is a human being with an organ failure just as a blind person is a human being whose eyes have failed. Basic forms of communal care and respect are due in both cases.

The second principle states that in certain circumstances it is morally permissible to let a patient die of natural causes if a treatment has become futile or excessively burdensome. This interpretation of the traditional ordinary-extraordinary means distinction also rests on considerations derived from our common morality. Life is the grounding good, but it is not the sole good, nor the highest good. Moreover, it is a fragile good and attachment to it in certain circumstances becomes irrational. We have to learn to let go, especially at a time when the imperative of relentless use of the available technology becomes the default position. Because of it, withholding or withdrawing treatment often requires an act of exceptional courage. In considering the burdens to be relieved by the decision to withhold or withdraw treatment we should not restrict ourselves to the patient, but should also take into account how the family, the immediate caregivers, and the surrounding community are affected. Their goods matter too. This traditional view is also rooted in the philosophical conviction that morality is not primarily an individualistic but rather a communal enterprise.

Alfonso Gómez-Lobo

Personal Statement of Dr. Rowley

For me, this report on the care of the demented aging is a scary document for a number of reasons. First, it is vehemently opposed to assisted suicide, saying it is behavior beyond moral bounds, although it is legally permitted in Oregon (never mentioned) and a bill for "Compassionate Choice" is currently being considered by the California legislature. This report takes a very draconian view of dying. The more painful it is made to be by applying rigid ethical rules, the more ennobling it is for both the patient and the caregiver. In the last case history in Chapter 4, the report explicitly says that very clear advanced directives written by an intelligent, mentally competent individual can be overridden by his daughter when he is no longer competent because he is happy in his demented state and his daughter wants to take care of him. So much for the moral or legal force of an individual's advanced directives! The report emphasizes repeatedly that the caregiver's primary responsibility is to the patient "here and now", and the advanced directives can and should be ignored depending on the situation at the time. The clear message from this report is, if you feel strongly about not living in a decerebrate state, you better kill yourself while you have control over your fate! Compassion (the term is used only 5 times, in Chapter 3 and never in Chapter 4) as a human virtue to be cultivated gets short shrift as well! "Compassion" may lead to acts that are ethically evil, so says the report, and under no circumstance should that suspect "virtue" be allowed to becloud the ethical issues. The irony between the Report's view of "compassion" and the bill before the California legislature, "Compassionate Choices," could not be more evident.

So what do those of us who are aging owe our families and friends and our society? As has been pointed out by Garrett Hardin in "The Tragedy of the Commons", in *Science* some years ago, greedy individuals often take more than their share from the common pool, in his case the common grazing land in England used collectively by many livestock farmers, thus destroying it for everyone. Unfortunately, the American political scene is rife with greedy groups, corporations and farmers, and now the AARP! This report from the President's Council on Bioethics comes with no price tag and I'm not competent to guess at how many billions of dollars it might cost to implement. Where will that money come from? Might it not come from programs that help needy infants receive better health care and early childhood education so that some of the disadvantages associated with being born in poverty might be ameliorated by an enriched early childhood? If you asked them bluntly, would grandparents really want to steal from their grandchildren? It is an interesting question. Maybe we do not wish to know the answer?

My Recommendations:

1. What is the responsibility of the patient to his/her family, friends, and society?

a) Virtually everyone regardless of age should have a will. Certainly when individuals apply for Medicare, the application process should be modified so that individuals are very strongly encouraged to have a will. Given the costs of probate, etc., it would likely be cheaper to have the government offer to pay some minimal fee for completing a will.

b) Individuals should also be very strongly encouraged to discuss planning for multiple eventualities including the level of medical care desired if mentally incapacitated, disposition of one's body, organ donation, etc. Thus although advanced directives may not have been effective in the past, their implementation could be substantially improved relatively easily. These decisions should be part of an electronic personal/medical record, that is protected for privacy, but available to caregivers, physicians, and hospitals in case of an emergency so that the person is treated in accordance with his/her wishes.

2. The questions raised in Chapter 3, about whether we benefit or harm the person by extending a life that is terribly painful or extremely burdensome to those the person loved most, are difficult, and they do not have a single answer. We need guidelines for caregivers of individuals with a variety of medical problems, but especially of the infirm elderly. The Department of Health and Human Services should commission the Institute of Medicine to develop guidelines regarding the use of various levels of treatment based on benefit to the patient, difficulty of the procedure and likely complications, and cost, for patients in various stages of dementia. What are the criteria and considerations for selecting or for recommending against certain procedures at different stages?

3. There should be a National Commission composed of members with very diverse views (not just the conservative right) to discuss and recommend guidelines about how health care resources should be distributed. At a time when parts of some of our large cities have infant mortalities rivaling the third world, and obesity in infants and young adults is skyrocketing, especially among the poor, how should the total national health expenditure be allocated among different groups? Once a portion has been allocated to elderly individuals, how should that resource be divided to fund the various categories of care, including that of the demented elderly individuals?

These are very serious issues. The report of the President's Council on Bioethics provides answers from a very restricted perspective and thus it, unfortunately, cannot serve as an enlightened guide as we try to cope with these critical challenges.

Janet D. Rowley

GLOSSARY

Advance (treatment) directives: Written or oral declarations, by individuals capable of making informed and voluntary decisions, indicating preferences regarding future medical treatments. For example, they may indicate a preference for or against certain medical interventions in specified clinical situations. Or they may specify surrogate decisionmakers, in the event that the individual becomes incapacitated. Advance directives are of two kinds: instruction directives and proxy directives. (See below)

Alzheimer's disease: A progressive degenerative disease of the brain that causes impairment of memory and dementia, manifested by confusion, visual-spatial disorientation, inability to calculate, and deterioration of judgment; delusions and hallucinations may occur. The most common degenerative brain disorder, Alzheimer's disease makes up 70 percent of all cases of dementia. Onset is usually in late middle life, and death typically ensues in 5-10 years. (Stedman's Medical Dictionary)

Best care: A standard for caregiving that always seeks to serve the patient's current welfare. It emphasizes benefiting the life the person now has, while considering also his own earlier ideals, preferences, and values as an integral part of his current well-being.

Best interest: A legal standard of caregiving for incompetent patients, defined by the courts in terms of what a "reasonable person" would decide in the same situation. A consideration of best interests generally attempts to weigh the burdens and benefits of treatment to the patient *in his present condition*, when no clear preferences of the patient can be determined.

Caregiver: Any person who cares for an individual needing help taking care of himself, in ways that range from meeting the basic needs of everyday life to offering medical, nursing, or hospice care. Caregivers may be paid or volunteer; they include family and friends as well as doctors, nurses, social service providers, and hospice professionals.

Dementia: The loss, usually progressive, of cognitive and intellectual functions, without impairment of perception or consciousness; caused by a variety of disorders including severe infections and toxins, but most commonly associated with structural brain disease. Characterized by disorientation, impaired memory, judgment, and intellect, and a shallow labile affect. (Stedman's Medical Dictionary)

Extraordinary care: Generally used to refer to medical treatments that, in the particular circumstances, impose undue physical or personal burdens on the patient or that are not likely to substantially improve the patient's condition but merely prolong his dying. Extraordinary care is considered ethically optional, rather than obligatory.

Healthcare power of attorney: A legal form of written proxy directive. (See below)

Hospice: An institution that provides a centralized program of palliative and supportive services to dying patients and their families, in the form of physical, psychological, social, and spiritual care; such services are provided by an interdisciplinary team of professionals and volunteers who are available at home and in specialized inpatient settings. (Stedman's Medical Dictionary)

Instruction directive: This form of advance directive is a written or oral statement of treatment preferences created to guide the choices of physicians or other decisionmakers when the patient is no longer able to indicate his preferences. It can be very specific, indicating specific treatment preferences for specific medical circumstances, or it may be more general, stating only (for example) that the patient does not wish to undergo "extraordinary" treatment measures when recovery is improbable and death is near. The written form of an instruction directive is also referred to as a **living will.**

Ordinary care: Generally used to refer to readily available medical treatments whose benefits to the patient are likely to outweigh the burdens and risks and that have a reasonable possibility of improving the patient's condition. Ordinary care is considered ethically required.

Principle of double effect: A traditional principle in ethics that aims to provide specific guidelines for determining when it is morally permissible to perform an action in pursuit of a good end in full knowledge that the action will also bring about certain bad results. It generally states that, in cases where a contemplated action has both good and bad effects, the action is permissible only (a) if it is not wrong in itself, and (b) if it does not require that the agent directly intend the evil result. For example, the principle of double effect is used in medical ethics regarding end-of-life care to justify giving morphine to relieve intense pain (the intended effect), even though doing so increases the risk of respiratory arrest and an earlier death (the second effect), *provided that one is not intending to produce death by administering the drug.* In contrast, attempts to relieve the pain by deliberately killing the patient cannot be justified, because the action is wrong in itself.

Proxy directive: This form of advance directive is a written or oral appointment of one or more specific individuals to serve as the surrogate decisionmaker(s) for a person when he is incompetent to decide for himself.

Prudence: An ethical excellence of heart and mind, displayed in an eagerness to seek and an ability to find the "just right" course of action, attaining the best outcome possible in the light of present circumstances. It is sometimes also known as practical wisdom.

Stokes-Adams episode: A temporary loss of consciousness due to transient interruption of electrical impulses in the heart, and the consequent failure of the heart to pump blood to the brain.

Substituted judgment: A legal standard of decisionmaking on behalf of incompetent persons that seeks to make treatment decisions by trying to discern or guess what the patient himself would decide were he capable of doing so. It may be informed by the patient's verbal instructions or the surrogate decisionmaker's recollection of the patient's values and attitudes during his years of competence.

Surrogate decisionmaker: A person appointed either by the patient, or, if the patient fails to appoint someone, by the courts, to make medical decisions on behalf of an incompetent patient.

THEMATIC BIBLIOGRAPHY

Resources for professionals, the elderly, and caregivers.

Contents

THEMATIC BIBLIOGRAPHY

Readers newly interested in this subject area may find the items noted with asterisks most useful.

Advance Directives / Legal Instruments

Books and Articles

Alexander, G. "Durable Power of Attorney as a Substitute for Conservatorship."4 *Psychology, Public Policy, and Law* 653, September 1998.

American Psychological Association, Inc. "Optimal Use of Orders Not to Intervene and Advance Directives." 4 *Psychology, Public Policy, and Law* 668, September 1998.

Boxx, K. "The Durable Power of Attorney's Place in the Family of Fiduciary Relationships." 36 *Georgia Law Review* 1, Fall 2001.

Brett, A. "Limitations of Listing Specific Medical Interventions in Advance Directives." *Journal of the American Medical Association* 255(6): 825-828, August 14, 1991.

Cantor, N. *Making Medical Decisions for the Profoundly Mentally Disabled.* Boston, MA: MIT Press, 2005.

Cantor, N. "Making Advance Directives Meaningful." 4 *Psychology, Public Policy, and Law* 629, September 1998.

Cohen, I. Glenn. "Negotiating Death: ADR and End-of-Life Decision Making." 9 *Harvard Negotiation Law Review* 253, Spring 2004.

Coppola, K., et al. "Accuracy of Primary Care and Hospital-based Physicians' Predictions of Elderly Outpatients Treatment Preferences With and Without Advance Directives." *Archives of Internal Medicine* 161: 431-440, 2001.

Culver, C. "Advance Directives." 4 *Psychology, Public Policy, and Law* 676, September 1998.

Danis, M. "A Prospective Study of Advance Directives for Life-Sustaining Care." *New England Journal of Medicine* 324(13): 882-888, 1991.

Degenholtz, H., et al. "Brief Communication: The Relationship Between Having a Living Will and Dying in Place." *Annals of Internal Medicine* 141: 113-117, 2004.

Ditto, P., et al. "Advance Directives as Acts of Communication: A Randomized Controlled Trial." *Archives of Internal Medicine* 161: 421-430, 2001.

Dresser, R. "Dworkin on Dementia: Elegant Theory, Questionable Policy." *Hastings Center Report* 25(6): 32-38, November-December 1995.

Dresser, R. "Missing Persons: Legal Perceptions of Incompetent Patients." 46 *Rutgers Law Review* 609, Winter 1994.

Dresser, R. "Precommitment: A Misguided Strategy for Securing Death with Dignity." 81 *Texas Law Review* 1823, June 2003.

Dresser, R. "Schiavo: A Hard Case Makes Questionable Law." *Hastings Center Report* 34(3): 8-9, May-June 2004.

Dresser, R. "The Conscious Incompetent Patient." *Hastings Center Report* 32(3): 9-10, May-June 2002.

Eakes, M., et al. "Planning Lessons Learned from End-of-Life Disputes." 17 *National Academy of Elder Law Attorneys Quarterly* 21, Summer 2004.

Eiser, A. and Weiss, M. D. "The Underachieving Advance Directive: Recommendations for Increasing Advance Directive Completion." *American Journal of Bioethics* 1: W10, 2001.

Emanuel, L., et al. "Advance Directives for Medical Care—A Case for Greater Use." *New England Journal of Medicine* 324(13): 889-895, March 28, 1991.

Fagerlin, A. and Schneider, C. "Enough: The Failure of the Living Will." *Hastings Center Report* 34(2): 30-42, March-April 2004.

Gallagher, E. "Advance Directives for Psychiatric Care: A Theoretical and Practical Overview for Legal Professionals." 4 *Psychology, Public Policy, and Law* 746, September 1998.

Garas, N. and Pantilat, S. "Chapter 49: Advance Planning for End-of-Life Care." *Making Health Care Safer: A Critical Analysis of Patient Safety Practices.* AHRQ Evidence Report No. 43. July 20, 2001. http://www.ncbi.nlm.nih.gov/books/bv.fcgi?rid=hstat1.section.62397 (accessed August 24, 2005).

Goodman, M., et al. "Effect of Advance Directives on the Management of Elderly Critically Ill Patients." *Critical Care Medicine* 26: 701-704, 1998.

Hamann, A. "Family Surrogate Laws: A Necessary Supplement to Living Wills and Durable Power of Attorney." 38 *Villanova Law Review* 103, 1993.

Hammes, B. and Rooney, B. L. "Death and End-of-Life Planning in One Midwestern Community." *Archives of Internal Medicine* 158: 383-390, 1998.

Hawkins, N., et al. "Micromanaging Death: Process Preferences, Values, and Goals in End-of-Life Medical Decision-Making." *Gerontologist* 45: 107-117, 2005.

Holley, J., et al. "Factors Influencing Dialysis Patients' Completion of Advance Directives." *American Journal of Kidney Diseases* 30: 356-260, 1997.

Jeffreys, J. "Advance Directives: Are They Worth the Paper They're Written On?" 27 *Colorado Lawyer* 125, June 1998.

Karnath, B., and Vaiani, C. "When a Family Member Changes Their Mind Regarding the DNR Order: The Importance of Documentation." *Ethics & Medicine: An International Journal of Bioethics* 20(2): 31-34, Summer 2004.

Lieberson, A. *Advance Medical Directives.* Deerfield, IL: Thomson Legal Publishing, 1992.

Longnecker, R. "Health Care Proxies, Living Wills, and Durable Power of Attorney." Proceedings from American Bar Association Continuing Legal Education. *American Law Institute*, September 12, 1991.

Lynn, J. "Why I Don't Have a Living Will." *Law, Medicine, & Health Care* 19: 101-104, 1991.

Meisel, A. and Cerminara, K. *The Right to Die: The Law of End-of-Life Decisionmaking.* 3rd ed. New York: Aspen Publishers, 2004 (2005 Supplement).

Morrison, R., et al. "The Inaccessibility of Advance Directives on Transfer from Ambulatory to Acute Care Settings." *Journal of the American Medical Association* 274: 501-503, 1995.

Schaefer, K., et al. "The Advance Directive: An Expression of Autonomy, But Also of Care." *Ethics & Medicine: An International Journal of Bioethics* 18(1): 15-19, Spring 2002.

Sehgal, A. "How Strictly Do Dialysis Patients Want Their Advance Directives Followed?" *Journal of the American Medical Association* 267(1): 59-63, 1992.

Shapiro, M., et al. *Bioethics & Law: Cases, Materials and Problems.* 2nd ed. Eagan, MN: West Publishing, 2003.

Teno, J. "Advance Directives: Time to Move On." *Annals of Internal Medicine* 141: 159-160, 2004.

Teno, J. "Do Advance Directives Provide Instructions That Direct Care?" *Journal of the American Geriatrics Society* 45: 508-512, 1997.

Zimring, S. "Multi-Cultural Issues in Advance Directives." 13 *National Academy of Elder Law Attorneys Quarterly* 12, Summer 2000.

Zingmond, D., et al. "Regional and Institutional Variation in the Initiation of Early Do-Not-Resuscitate Orders." *Archives of Internal Medicine* 165(15): 1705-1712, August 8, 2005.

Case Law & Statutes

Rather than attempt to provide a comprehensive list of case law and statues related to advance directives, we reference here only those items reviewed during the writing of this report. We refer legal researchers to the seminal work in this field by Alan Meisel and Kathy L. Cerminara, *The Right to Die: The Law of End-of-Life Decisionmaking.*

Federal

Cruzan v. Director, Missouri Dept. of Health, 497 U.S. 261, 110 S. Ct. 2841 (1990).

Pain Relief Promotion Act of 1999, H.R. 2260, S. 1272 (not enacted), available online at http://thomas.loc.gov/cgi-bin/query/z?c106:S.1272.

Patient Self-Determination Act of 1990, §4206 and §4751 Omnibus Reconciliation Act of 1990, Pub L No. 1010-508 (November 5, 1990).

Ulrich, L. *The Patient Self-Determination Act: Meeting the Challenges in Patient Care*. Washington, D.C.: Georgetown University Press, 1999.

State

Conservatorship of Wendland, 110 Cal. Rptr. 2d 412 (Cal. 2001).

In re Martin, 538 N.W. 2d 399 (Mich. 1995).

Matter of Conroy, 486 A. 2d 1209 (N. J. 1989).

Matter of Edna M. F., 563 N.W. 2d 485 (Wis. 1997).

Matter of Spring, 405 N.E. 2d 115 (Mass. 1980).

Matter of Quinlan, 355 A. 2d 647 (N. J. 1976).

McKay v. Bergstedt, 801 P. 2d 617 (Nev. 1990).

Superintendent of Belchertown State School v. Saikewicz, 370 N.E. 2d 417 (Mass. 1977).

Model Codes and Directives

Alexander, G. "Time for a New Law on Health Care Advance Directives." Symposium: Legal Issues Relating to the Elderly. 42 *Hastings Law Journal* 755, March 1991.

Bok, S. "Personal Directions for Care at the End of Life." *New England Journal of Medicine* 295(7): 367-369, August 12, 1976.

Emanuel, L. and Emanuel, E. "The Medical Directive: A New Comprehensive Advance Care Document." *Journal of the American Medical Association* 261(22): 3288-3293, June 9, 1989.

Kutner, L. "Due Process of Euthanasia: The Living Will, a Proposal." 44 *Indiana Law Journal* 539, 1969.

Martin, D., et al. "A New Model of Advance Care Planning." *Archives of Internal Medicine* 159: 86-92, 1999.

McLean, E. "Living Will Statutes in Light of Cruzan v. Director, Missouri Department of Health: Ensuring that Patient's Wishes Will Prevail." 40 *Emory Law Journal* 1305, Fall 1991.

Modell, W. "A 'Will' to Live." *New England Journal of Medicine* 290(16): 907-908, April 18, 1974.

Stavis, P. "The Nexum: A Modest Proposal for Self-Guardianship by Contract: A System of Advance Directives and Surrogate Committees-At-Large for the Mentally Ill." 16 *Journal of Contemporary Health Law and Policy* 1, Winter 1999.

Uniform Health-Care Decisions Act (1993).

Uniform Rights of the Terminally Ill Act (1989).

Reports

American Bar Association Commission on Law & Aging. *Health Care Power of Attorney and Combined Advance Directive Legislation.* Chicago, IL: ABA, September 2004.

American Bar Association Commission on Law & Aging. *Health Care Surrogate Decision Making Legislation.* Chicago, IL: ABA, June 2001.

American Bar Association Commission on Law & Aging. *Surrogate Consent in the Absence of an Advance Directive.* Chicago, IL: ABA, July 2004.

American Bar Association Section of Real Property, Probate, and Trust Law. *The Uniform Health-Care Decisions Act and its Progress in the States.* Chicago, IL: ABA, May/June 2001.

Last Acts. *Means to a Better End: A Report on Dying in America Today.* Washington, D.C.: Last Acts, 2002.

*New York State Task Force on Life and the Law. *When Others Must Choose: Deciding for Patients Without Capacity.* New York State Task Force on Life and the Law. December 1992.

Sample Forms

Aging with Dignity. "Five Wishes: The Easy Way to Help You and Your Loved Ones Plan for the Unexpected." Tallahassee, FL: Aging With Dignity, 2001. (www.agingwithdignity.org)

Legal Counsel of the Elderly, Inc. "Planning for Incapacity: A Self-Help Guide—Advance Directive Forms for Connecticut." 12th Annual Elder Law Institute Representing the Elderly Client of Modest Means, June 2000. Practising Law Institute, 2000. (This state provided as one example of many.)

Schuster, M. "Planning for Incapacity: A Self-Help Guide—Advance Directive for New York." Proceedings of 11th Annual Elder Law Institute: Representing the Elderly Client of Modest Means, July 1999. Practising Law Institute, 1999. (This state provided as one example of many.)

Alzheimer's Disease

Costs

Johnson, N., et al. "The Epidemic of Alzheimer's Disease. How Can We Manage the Costs?" *Pharmacoeconomics* 18(3): 215-223, 2000.

Martikainen, J., et al. "Potential Cost-Effectiveness of a Family-Based Program in Mild Alzheimer's Disease Patients." *The European Journal of Health Economics* 5(2): 136-142, 2004.

Prigerson, H. "Costs to Society of Family Caregiving for Patients with End-Stage Alzheimer's Disease." *New England Journal of Medicine* 349(20): 1891-1892, 2003.

Riggs, J. A. "The Health and Long-Term Care Policy Challenges of Alzheimer's Disease." *Aging & Mental Health* 5(Supp. 1): S138-S145, 2001.

Taylor, D. H., Jr. "Alzheimer's Disease and the Family Caregiver: The Cost and Who Pays?" *North Carolina Medical Journal* 66(1): 16-23, 2005.

Diagnosis

Aguzzi, A. and Haass, C. "Games Played by Rogue Proteins in Prion Disorders and Alzheimer's Disease." *Science* 302(5646): 814-818, October 31, 2003.

Arnaiz, E., and Almkvist, O. "Neuropsychological Features of Mild Cognitive Impairment and Preclinical Alzheimer's Disease." *Acta Neurologica Scandinavica. Supplementum* 107(179): 34-41, 2003.

Bennett, D., et al. "Mild Cognitive Impairment Is Related to Alzheimer Disease Pathology and Cerebral Infarctions." *Neurology* 64(5): 834-841, March 8, 2005.

Clark, C., et al. "Alzheimer's Symptoms May Strike Latinos Years Before White Americans." Presented at 9th International Conference on Alzheimer's Disease and Related Disorders of the Alzheimer's Association. July 21, 2004.

DeKosky, S. T. "Epidemiology and Pathophysiology of Alzheimer's Disease." *Clinical Cornerstone* 3(4): 15-26, 2001.

D'Esposito, M., and Weksler, M. "Brain Aging and Memory: New Findings Help Differentiate Forgetfulness and Dementia." *Geriatrics* 55(6): 55-58, 61-62, 2000.

Fujii, D., et al. "Dementia Screening: Can a Second Administration Reduce the Number of False Positives?" *American Journal of Geriatric Psychiatry* 11(4): 462-465, 2003.

Graff-Radford, N., et al. "Plasma Aβ Levels as a Premorbid Biomarker for Cognitive Decline, Mild Cognitive Impairment (MCI) and Alzheimer Disease (AD)." Presented at First International Conference on the Prevention of Dementia of the Alzheimer's Association. June 18-21, 2005.

Gualtieri, C. T. "Dementia Screening Using Computerized Tests." *Journal of Insurance Medicine* 36(3): 213-227, 2004.

Higuchi, M., et al. "^{19}F and ^{1}H MRI Detection of Amyloid β Plaques in Vivo." *Nature Neuroscience* 8: 527-533, 2005.

Kukull, W., et al. "Dementia and Alzheimer Disease Incidence: A Prospective Cohort Study." *Archives of Neurology* 59: 1737-1746, 2002.

Marx, J. "Play and Exercise Protect Mouse Brain from Amyloid Buildup." *Science* 307(5715): 1547-1547, March 11, 2005.

Mathis, C. A., et al. "Imaging Technology for Neurodegenerative Diseases." *Archives of Neurology* 62: 196-200, 2005.

McKhann, G., et al. "Clinical Diagnosis of Alzheimer's Disease." *Neurology* 34(7): 939-944, 1984.

Mosconi, L., et al. "Hippocampal Metabolic Reductions in Mild Cognitive Impairment and Alzheimer's Disease: Automated FDG-PET Image Analysis." Presented at First International Conference on the Prevention of Dementia of the Alzheimer's Association. June 18-21, 2005.

Neergaard, L. "Scientists Find Early Signs of Alzheimer's." June 20, 2005. http://www.wtopnews.com (accessed June 20, 2005).

Pilcher, H. "Alzheimer's Disease Cause Identified?" January 8, 2004. http://www.nature.com (accessed January 12, 2004).

Selkoe, D. "Alzheimer's Disease is a Synaptic Failure." *Science* 298(5594): 789-791, October 25, 2002.

Small, G. W., et al. "Diagnosis and Treatment of Alzheimer's Disease and Related Disorders: Consensus Statement of the American Association for Geriatric Psychiatry, the Alzheimer's Association, and the American Geriatrics Society." *Journal of the American Medical Association* 278: 1363-9271, 1997.

Tierney, M. C., et al. "The NINCDS-ADRDA Work Group Criteria for the Clinical Diagnosis of Probable Alzheimer's Disease." *Neurology* 38(3): 359-364, 1988.

Symptoms / Trajectory (including Personal Accounts)

Beard, R. L. "In Their Voices: Identity Preservation and Experiences of Alzheimer's Disease." *Journal of Aging Studies* 18(4): 415-428, 2004.

Campbell, C. "The Human Face of Alzheimer's." *New Atlantis* 6: 3-17, Summer 2004.

Davis, R. *My Journey Into Alzheimer's Disease.* Carol Stream, IL: Tyndale House Publishers, 1989.

DeBaggio, T. *Losing My Mind: An Intimate Look at Life with Alzheimer's.* New York: Free Press, 2003.

Dyer, J. *In Tangled Wood: An Alzheimer's Journey.* Dallas, TX: Southern Methodist University Press, 1996.

Espiritu, D. A. V., et al. "Depression, Cognitive Impairment and Function in Alzheimer's Disease." *International Journal of Geriatric Psychiatry* 16(11): 1098-1103, 2001.

Feinberg, L. F. and Whitlatch, C. "Are Persons with Cognitive Impairment Able to State Consistent Choices?" *Gerontologist* 41(3): 374-382, 2001.

Gareri, P., et al. "Neuropharmacology of Depression in Aging and Age-Related Diseases." *Ageing Research Reviews* 1(1): 113-134, 2002.

Gillick, M. *Tangled Minds: Understanding Alzheimer's Disease and Other Dementias.* New York: Dutton Books, 1998.

Henderson, C., et al. *Partial View: An Alzheimer's Journal.* Dallas, TX: Southern Methodist University Press, 1998.

*Hoffman, D. "Complaints of a Dutiful Daughter." New York: Women Make Movies, 1996 (video).

Hurley, A. C., and Volicer, L. "Alzheimer Disease: 'It's Okay, Mama, If You Want to Go, It's Okay.'" *Journal of the American Medical Association* 288(18): 2324-2331, 2002.

James, I. A. and Sabin, N. "Safety Seeking Behaviours: Conceptualizing a Person's Reaction to the Experience of Cognitive Confusion." *Dementia* 1(1): 37-45, 2002.

Keri, S., et al. "Categories, Prototypes and Memory Systems in Alzheimer's Disease." *Trends in Cognitive Sciences* 6(3): 132-136, 2002.

Lockwood, D. "Alzheimer's Seen in the Living Brain." March 14, 2005. http://www.nature.com (accessed March 15, 2005).

Menne, H. L, et al. "'Trying to Continue to Do as Much as They Can Do': Theoretical Insights Regarding Continuity and Meaning Making in the Face of Dementia." *Dementia* 1(3): 367-382, 2002.

Nagaratnam, N., et al. "Some Problematic Behaviors in Alzheimer's Dementia." *Archives of Gerontology and Geriatrics* 32(1): 57-65, 2001.

Nagourney, E. "Aging: Alzheimer's on the Road." *New York Times*. September 14, 2004, p. F7.

Pearce, A., et al. "Managing Sense of Self: Coping in the Early Stages of Alzheimer's Disease." *Dementia* 1(2): 173-192, 2002.

Rosen, H. J., et al. "Neuropsychological and Functional Measures of Severity in Alzheimer Disease, Fronto-temporal Dementia, and Semantic Dementia." *Alzheimer Disease and Associated Disorders* 18(4): 202-207, 2004.

Sabat, S. *The Experience of Alzheimer's Disease: Life Through a Tangled Veil.* Oxford: Blackwell Publishing, 2001.

*Shenk, D. *The Forgetting, Alzheimer's: Portrait of an Epidemic.* New York: Random House, 2001.

Snyder, L. *Speaking Our Minds: Personal Reflections from Individuals with Alzheimer's.* New York: WH Freeman & Co., 1999.

Sterin, G. J. "Essay on a Word: A Lived Experience of Alzheimer's Disease." *Dementia* 1(1): 7-10, 2002.

Zlokovic, B. V. "Neurovascular Mechanisms of Alzheimer's Neurodegeneration." *Trends in Neurosciences* 28(4): 202-208, 2005.

Treatment & Research

"Alzheimer's Vaccine Shows Promise." July 21, 2004. http://www.cbsnews.com (accessed July 28, 2004).

Bedard, M., et al. "Health Impact on Caregivers of Providing Informal Care to a Cognitively Impaired Older Adult: Rural Versus Urban Settings." *Canadian Journal of Rural Medicine* 9(1): 15-23, 2004.

Belle, S. H., et al. "Use of Cognitive Enhancement Medication in Persons with Alzheimer Disease Who Have a Family Caregiver: Results from the Resources for Enhancing Alzheimer's Caregiver Health (Reach) Project." *American Journal of Geriatric Psychiatry* 12(3): 250-257, 2004.

Borenstein, A., et al. "Consumption of Fruit and Vegetable Juices Predicts a Reduced Risk of Alzheimer's Disease: The *Kame* Project." Presented at the First International Conference on the Prevention of Dementia of the Alzheimer's Association. June 18-21, 2005.

Brauner, D. J., et al. "Treating Nondementia Illnesses in Patients with Dementia." *Journal of the American Medical Association* 283(24): 3230-3235, 2000.

Bryden, C. "A Person-Centred Approach to Counselling, Psychotherapy and Rehabilitation of People Diagnosed with Dementia in the Early Stages." *Dementia* 1(2): 141-156, 2002.

Craft, S., et al. "Therapeutic Effects of Intranasal Insulin in Patients with AD and Amnestic MCI." Presented at the First International Conference on the Prevention of Dementia of the Alzheimer's Association. June 18-21, 2005.

De La Monte, S. and Wands, J. "Review of Insulin and Insulin-like Growth Factor Expression, Signaling, and Malfunction in the Central Nervous System: Relevance to Alzheimer's Disease." *Journal of Alzheimer's Disease* 7(1): 45-61, March 3, 2005.

Durga, J., et al. "Effect of 3-Year Folic Acid Supplementation on Cognitive Function in Older Adults: A Randomized, Double Blind, Controlled Trial." Presented at First International Conference on the Prevention of Dementia of the Alzheimer's Association. June 18-21, 2005.

"Estrogen Replacement Linked to Dementia." *Nature Medicine* 10: 765, 2004.

Garfield, F. B., et al. "Assessment of Health Economics in Alzheimer's Disease (Ahead): Treatment with Galantamine in Sweden." *Pharmacoeconomics* 20(9): 629-637, 2002.

Gatz, M., et al. "Potentially Modifiable Risk Factors for Dementia: Evidence from Identical Twins." Presented at First International Conference on the Prevention of Dementia of the Alzheimer's Association. June 18-21, 2005.

Gaugler, J. E., et al. "Adult Day Service Use and Reductions in Caregiving Hours: Effects on Stress and Psychological Well-Being for Dementia Caregivers." *International Journal of Geriatric Psychiatry* 18(1): 55-62, 2003.

Haan, M. and Wallace, R. "Can Dementia Be Prevented? Brain Aging in a Population-Based Context." *Annual Review of Public Health* 25: 1-24, 2004.

Hara, H., et al. "Development of a Safe Oral Aß Vaccine Using Recombinant Adeno-Associated Virus Vector for Alzheimer's Disease." *Journal of Alzheimer's Disease* 6(5): 483-488, October 2004.

Hurley, A., et al. "Effect of Fever-Management Strategy on the Progression of Dementia of the Alzheimer Type." *Alzheimer Disease and Associated Disorders* 10(1): 5-10, 1996.

Margallo-Lana, M., et al. "Prevalence and Pharmacological Management of Behavioural and Psychological Symptoms Amongst Dementia Sufferers Living in Care Environments." *International Journal of Geriatric Psychiatry* 16(1): 39-44, 2001.

Marx, J. "Prevent Alzheimer's: A Lifelong Commitment?" *Science* 309: 864-866, 2005.

Maslow, K., et al. "Guidelines and Care Management Issues for People with Alzheimer's Disease and Other Dementias." *Disease Management & Health Outcomes* 10(11): 693-706, 2002.

Monsonego, A., and Weiner, H. "Immunotherapeutic Approaches to Alzheimer's Disease." *Science* 302(5646): 834-838, October 31, 2003.

Petersen, A. "Brain Imaging Study Is Launched for Alzheimer's." *Wall Street Journal.* October 14, 2004, p. D2.

Petersen, A. "Longer Use of Alzheimer's Drugs Gets Boost." *Wall Street Journal.* September 7, 2004, p. D4.

Ritter, J. "Rush Uses Gene Therapy in Alzheimer's Battle." *Chicago Sun-Times.* September 22, 2004, p. 8.

Sager, M., et al. "Wisconsin Registry for Alzheimer's Prevention: Prospective Cohort Study of Preclinical AD." Presented at First International Conference on the Prevention of Dementia of the Alzheimer's Association. June 18-21, 2005.

Santaguida, P. S., et al. *Pharmacological Treatment of Dementia Summary, Evidence Report / Technology Assessment No. 97.* AHRQ Publication No. 04-E018-1. Rockville, MD: Agency for Healthcare Research and Quality. April 2004.

Selkoe, D., "Alzheimer Disease: Mechanistic Understanding Predicts Novel Therapies." *Annals of Internal Medicine* 140(8): 1-12, 2004.

Sheiman, S. L. and Pomerantz, J. "Tube Feeding in Dementia: A Controversial Practice." *Journal of Nutrition, Health & Aging* 2(3): 184-189, 1998.

Sink, K. M., et al. "Pharmacological Treatment of Neuropsychiatric Symptoms of Dementia: A Review of the Evidence." *Journal of the American Medical Association* 293(5): 596-608, 2005.

Sloane, P. D., et al. "The Public Health Impact of Alzheimer's Disease, 2000-2050: Potential Implication of Treatment Advances." *Annual Review of Public Health* 23: 213-231, 2002.

Stern, Y. "Lifestyle and Other Risk Factors: Cognitive Reserve." Presented at First International Conference on the Prevention of Dementia of the Alzheimer's Association. June 18-21, 2005.

VanScoy, H. "Viable Alzheimer's Treatments on the Horizon." January 7, 2005. http://health.myway.com/art/id/523301.html (accessed January 18, 2005).

Vedantam, S. "Study Looks Into Roots of Alzheimer's: Brain Area for Daydreaming Is Affected." *Washington Post.* August 24, 2005, p. A9.

Weiss, R. "A Tale of Politics: PET Scans' Change in Medicare Coverage." *Washington Post.* October 14, 2004, p. A1.

Wilcock, G., et al. "A Placebo-controlled, Double-blind Trial of the Selective Aß-42 Lowering Agent, Flurizan (MPC-7869, *(R)*-flurbiprofen) in Patients with Mild to Moderate Alzheimer's Disease." Presented at First International Conference on the Prevention of Dementia of the Alzheimer's Association. June 18-21, 2005.

Zlokovic, B. V. "Neurovascular Mechanisms of Alzheimer's Neurodegeneration." *Trends in Neurosciences* 28(4): 202-208, 2005.

Caregiving

Burdens & Benefits

Acton, G. and Kang, J. "Interventions to Reduce the Burden of Caregiving for an Adult with Dementia: A Meta-Analysis." *Research in Nursing Health* 24: 349-360, 2001.

AARP. *In the Middle: A Report on Multicultural Boomers Coping with Family and Aging Issues.* Washington, D.C.: AARP, 2001.

Bedard, M., et al. "Understanding Burden Differences Between Men and Women Caregivers: The Contribution of Care Recipient Problem Behaviors." *International Psychogeriatrics* 17: 99-118, 2005.

Bell, C. M., et al. "The Association between Caregiver Burden and Caregiver Health-Related Quality of Life in Alzheimer Disease." *Alzheimer Disease & Associated Disorders* 15(3): 129-136, 2001.

Black, W. and Almeida, O. "A Systematic Review of the Association Between the Behavioral and Psychological Symptoms of Dementia and Burden of Care." *International Psychogeriatrics* 16: 295-315, 2004.

Boerner, K., et al. "Positive Aspects of Caregiving and Adaptation to Bereavement." *Psychology and Aging* 19(4): 668-675, 2004.

Bourgeois, M. S., et al. "Interventions for Caregivers of Patients with Alzheimer's Disease: A Review and Analysis of Content, Process, and Outcomes." *International Journal of Aging and Human Development* 43(1): 35-92, 1996.

Brodaty, H., et al. "Meta-Analysis of Psychosocial Interventions for Caregivers of People with Dementia." *Journal of the American Geriatrics Society* 51(5): 657-664, 2003.

Carter, R. and Golant, S. K. *Helping Yourself Help Others: A Book for Caregivers.* New York: Times Books, 1996.

Caron, C. D. and Bowers, B. "Deciding Whether to Continue, Share, or Relinquish Caregiving: Caregiver Views." *Qualitative Health Research* 13(9): 1252-1271, 2003.

Chumbler, N., et al. "Gender, Kinship, and Caregiver Burden: The Case of Community-Dwelling Memory Impaired Seniors." *International Journal of Geriatric Psychiatry* 18(8): 722-732, 2003.

Ducharme, F., et al. "'Taking Care of Myself': Efficacy of an Intervention Programme for Caregivers of a Relative with Dementia Living in a Long-Term Care Setting." *Dementia* 4(1): 23-47, 2005.

Dunham, C. C. and Dietz, B. "'If I'm Not Allowed to Put My Family First': Challenges Experienced by Women Who Are Caregiving for Family Members with Dementia." *Journal of Women and Aging* 15(1): 55-69, 2003.

Emanuel, E., et al. "Understanding Economic and Other Burdens of Terminal Illness: The Experience of Patients and Their Caregivers." *Annals of Internal Medicine* 132(6): 451-459, March 21, 2000.

Fredman, L., et al. "Pragmatic and Internal Validity Issues in Sampling in Caregiver Studies: A Comparison of Population-Based, Registry-Based, and Ancillary Studies." *Journal of Aging and Health* 16(2): 175-203, 2004.

Gallicchio, L., et al. "Gender Differences in Burden and Depression Among Informal Caregiver of Demented Elders in the Community." *International Journal of Geriatric Psychiatry* 17(2): 154-163, 2002.

Gilley, D. W., et al. "Caregiver Psychological Adjustment and Institutionalization of Persons with Alzheimer's Disease." *Journal of Aging and Health* 17(2): 172-189, 2005.

Gilmour, H., et al. "Living Alone with Dementia: A Case Study Approach to Understanding Risk." *Dementia* 2(3): 403-420, 2003.

Gross, J. "Alzheimer's in the Living Room: How One Family Rallies to Cope." *New York Times.* September 16, 2004. Letters to the Editor, September 19, 2004, p. A1.

Gundersen, M. "Being a Burden: Reflections on Refusing Medical Care." *Hastings Center Report* 34(5): 37-43, September-October 2004.

Gwyther, L. "Family Issues in Dementia: Finding a New Normal." *Neurological Clinics* 18: 993-1010, 2000.

Haley, L., et al. "Well-Being, Appraisal, and Coping in African-American and Caucasian Dementia Caregivers: Findings from the REACH Study." *Aging & Mental Health* 8(4): 316-329, 2004.

Hellstrom, I., et al. "'We Do Things Together': A Case Study of 'Couplehood' in Dementia." *Dementia* 4(1): 7-22, 2005.

Heru, A. "Family Functioning in the Caregivers of Patients with Dementia." *International Journal of Geriatric Psychiatry* 19(6): 533-577, 2004.

Ho, A., et al. *A Look at Working-Age Caregivers' Roles, Health Concerns, and Need for Support.* Commonwealth Fund. 2005. http://www.cmwf.org/ (accessed August 25, 2005).

Janevic, M. and Connell, C. "Racial, Ethnic, and Cultural Differences in the Dementia Caregiving Experience: Recent Findings." *Geronotologist* 41(4): 334-347, 2001.

Karlawish, J. H. T., et al. "Why Would Caregivers Not Want to Treat Their Relative's Alzheimer's Disease?" *Journal of the American Geriatrics Society* 51(10): 1391-1397, 2003.

Kiecolt-Glaser, J., et al. "Chronic Stress Alters The Immune Response To Influenza Virus Vaccine In Older Adults." *Proceedings of the National Academy of Sciences of the United States of America* 93: 3043-3047, 1996.

Lawler, P. "The Caregiving Society." *New Atlantis* 8: 3-13, Spring 2005.

Ledoux, N. "Connecting with the Cognitively Impaired: Dementia and Alzheimer's Disease." *Caring* 22(8): 30-32; 33-35, 2003.

Levine, C. "One Loss May Hide Another." *Hastings Center Report* 34(6): 17-19, November-December 2004.

Mittelman, M. S., et al. "Sustained Benefit of Supportive Intervention for Depressive Symptoms in Caregivers of Patients with Alzheimer's Disease." *American Journal of Psychiatry* 161(5): 850-856, 2004.

Navaie-Waliser, M., et al. "When the Caregiver Needs Care: The Plight of Vulnerable Caregivers." *American Journal of Public Health* 92(3): 409-413, 2002.

Peacock, S. C. and Forbes, D. "Interventions for Caregivers of Persons with Dementia: A Systematic Review." *Canadian Journal of Nursing Research* 35(4): 88-107, 2003.

Perry, J. and O'Connor, D. "Preserving Personhood: (Re)Membering the Spouse with Dementia." *Family Relations* 51(1): 55-62, 2002.

Phillips, L. R., et al. "Abuse of Female Caregivers by Care Recipients: Another Form of Elder Abuse." *Journal of Elder Abuse & Neglect* 12(3-4): 123-143, 2000.

Phinney A. and Chesla, C. "The Lived Body in Dementia." *Journal of Aging Studies* 17: 283-299, 2003.

Raschick, M. and Ingersoll-Dayton, B. "The Costs and Rewards of Caregiving among Aging Spouses and Adult Children." *Family Relations* 53(3): 317-325, 2004.

Sands, L., et al. "What Explains Differences between Dementia Patients' and Their Caregivers' Ratings of Patients' Quality of Life?" *American Journal of Geriatric Psychiatry* 12: 272-280, 2004.

Savundranayagam, M., et al. "Investigating the Effects of Communication Problems on Caregiver Burden." *Journals of Gerontology Series B-Psychological Sciences and Social Sciences* 60: S48-S55, 2005.

Schulz, R. and Beach, S. "Caregiving as a Risk Factor for Mortality: The Caregiver Health Effects Study." *Journal of the American Medical Association* 282: 2215-2219, 1999.

Schulz, R. and Martire, L. "Family Caregiving of Persons with Dementia: Prevalence, Health Effects, and Support Strategies." *American Journal of Geriatric Psychiatry* 12: 240-249, 2004.

Snyder L. "Satisfactions and Challenges in Spiritual Faith and Practice for Persons With Dementia." *Dementia* 2(3): 299-313, 2003.

Szinovacz, M. "Caring for a Demented Relative at Home: Effects on Parent-Adolescent Relationships and Family Dynamics." *Journal of Aging Studies* 17: 445-472, 2003.

Ward, R., et al. "A Kiss Is Still a Kiss?: The Construction of Sexuality in Dementia Care." *Dementia* 4(1): 49-72, 2005.

By Family Members

Alzheimer's Association and National Alliance for Caregiving. *Families Care: Alzheimer's Caregiving in the United States 2004.* http://www.alz.org.Resources/factsheets/caregiverreport.pdf.

Acton, G. J. and Winter, M. "Interventions for Family Members Caring for an Elder with Dementia." *Annual Review of Nursing Research* 20: 149-179, 2002.

Annerstedt, L., et al. "Family Caregiving in Dementia—an Analysis of the Caregiver's Burden and the 'Breaking-Point' When Home Care Becomes Inadequate." *Scandinavian Journal of Public Health* 28(1): 23-31, 2000.

Barber, C. E. and Lyness, K. "Ethical Issues in Family Care of Older Persons with Dementia: Implications for Family Therapists." *Home Health Care Services Quarterly* 20(3): 1-26, 2001.

Brodaty, H. and Green, A. "Defining the Role of the Caregiver in Alzheimer's Disease Treatment." *Drugs & Aging* 19(12): 891-898, 2002.

Burgener, S. and Twigg, P. "Relationships among Caregiver Factors and Quality of Life in Care Recipients with Irreversible Dementia." *Alzheimer Disease & Associated Disorders* 16(2): 88-102, 2002.

"Caregiving: Strategies for Caring for Someone with Alzheimer's Disease. Learning How to Manage Alzheimer's-Related Behaviors Can Ease the Burden for Both the Person with Dementia and the Family." *Harvard Women's Health Watch* 11(4): 3-5, 2003.

Cloutterbuck, J. and Mahoney, D. "African American Dementia Caregivers: The Duality of Respect." *Dementia* 2(2): 221-243, 2003.

Coon, D. W., et al. "Well-Being, Appraisal, and Coping in Latina and Caucasian Female Dementia Caregivers: Findings from the Reach Study." *Aging & Mental Health* 8(4): 330-345, 2004.

Farran, C., et al. "Spirituality in Multicultural Caregivers of Persons with Dementia." *Dementia* 2: 353-377, 2003.

Gottlieb, B. H. and Wolfe, J. "Coping with Family Caregiving to Persons with Dementia: A Critical Review." *Aging & Mental Health* 6(4): 325-342, 2002.

Hagen, B. "Nursing Home Placement: Factors Affecting Caregivers' Decisions to Place Family Members with Dementia." *Journal of Gerontological Nursing* 27(2): 44-53, 2001.

Haight, B. K., et al. "Life Review: Treating the Dyadic Family Unit with Dementia." *Clinical Psychology & Psychotherapy* 10(3): 165-174, 2003.

Hepburn, K. W., et al. "The Savvy Caregiver Program: Developing and Testing a Transportable Dementia Family Caregiver Training Program." *Gerontologist* 43(6): 908-915, 2003.

Kneebone, I. and Martin, P. "Coping and Caregivers of People with Dementia." *British Journal of Health Psychology* 8: 1-17, 2003.

Levesque, L., et al. "Is There a Difference between Family Caregiving of Institutionalized Elders with or without Dementia?" *Western Journal of Nursing Research* 21(4): 472-497, 1999.

Levine, C., ed. *Always on Call: When Illness Turns Families into Caregivers.* Nashville, TN: Vanderbilt University Press, 2004.

Lo, B., et al. "Family Decision-making on Trial: Who Decides for Incompetent Patients?" *New England Journal of Medicine* 322: 1228-1232, 1990.

*Mace, N. and Rabins, P. *The 36-Hour Day: A Family Guide to Caring for Persons with Alzheimer Disease, Related Dementing Illnesses, and Memory Loss in Later Life.* New York: Warner Books, 1999.

Mausbach, B., et al. "Ethnicity and Time to Institutionalization of Dementia Patients: A Comparison of Latina and Caucasian Female Family Caregivers." *Journal of the American Geriatrics Society* 52: 1077-1084, 2004.

Navaie-Waliser, M., et al. "Informal Caregiving—Differential Experiences by Gender." *Medical Care* 40(12): 1249-1259, 2002.

Nelson, J. *Alzheimer's: Hard Questions for Families.* New York: Doubleday, 1996.

Nightingale, M. "Religion, Spirituality, and Ethnicity: What is Means for Caregivers of Persons with Alzheimer's Disease and Related Disorders." *Dementia* 2: 379-391, 2003.

Nolan, M., et al. "Working with Family Carers of People with Dementia: 'Negotiated' Coping as an Essential Outcome." *Dementia* 1(1): 75-93, 2002.

Schulz, R. *Handbook on Dementia Caregiving: Evidence-Based Interventions for Family Caregivers.* New York: Springer Publishing Co., 2000.

Shakespeare, C. and Clare, L. "Negotiating the Impact of Forgetting: Dimensions of Resistance in Task-Oriented Conversations between People with Early-Stage Dementia and Their Partners." *Dementia* 3(2): 211-232, 2004.

Winakur, J. "What Are We Going to Do With Dad?" *Washington Post.* August 7, 2005, p. B1.

By Institutions

Bailey, F., et al. "Improving Processes of Hospital Care During the Last Hours of Life." *Archives of Internal Medicine* 165(15): 1722-1727, August 8, 2005.

Carey, B. "In the Hospital, a Degrading Shift From Person to Patient." *New York Times.* August 16, 2005, p. A1.

Cohen, C. A., et al. "Dementia Caregiving: The Role of the Primary Care Physician." *Canadian Journal of Neurological Sciences* 28: S72-S76, 2001.

Connell, C. M., et al. "Attitudes toward the Diagnosis and Disclosure of Dementia among Family Caregivers and Primary Care Physicians." *Gerontologist* 44(4): 500-507, 2004.

Cummings, J. L., et al. "Guidelines for Managing Alzheimer's Disease: Part II. Treatment." *American Family Physician* 65(12): 2525-2534, 2002.

Dembner, A. "Ageism Said To Erode Care Given To Elders." *Boston Globe.* March 7, 2005 p. A1.

Fallis, D. "In Va.'s Assisted Living Homes, Violent Preyed on the Vulnerable." *Washington Post.* May 24, 2004, p. A1.

Hamilton, W. "The New Nursing Home, Emphasis on Home." *New York Times.* April 23, 2005, p. A1.

Kapp, M. "Legal Anxieties and End-of-Life Care in Nursing Homes." 19 *Issues in Law and Medicine* 111, Fall 2003.

Karp, N. and Wood, E. "Incapacitated and Alone: Health Care Decision-Making for the Unbefriended Elderly." American Bar Association Commission on Law and Aging, July 2003.

Leitsch, S. A., et al. "Medical and Social Adult Day Service Programs—A Comparison of Characteristics, Dementia Clients, and Their Family Caregivers." *Research on Aging* 23(4): 473-498, 2001.

Lieberman, M. A. and Fisher, L. "The Effects of Nursing Home Placement on Family Caregivers of Patients with Alzheimer's Disease." *Gerontologist* 41(6): 819-826, 2001.

Long, A. and Slevin, E. "Living with Dementia: Communicating with an Older Person and Her Family." *Nursing Ethics* 6(1): 23-36, 1999.

Petersen, A. "Negotiating the Terms Of Your Death: Medical Advances Give Patients More Control Over How and When They Die." *Wall Street Journal.* May 10, 2005, p. D1.

Said, C. "Physician's Personal Touch." *San Francisco Chronicle.* August 7, 2005, p. E1.

Schulz, R., et al. "Long-term Care Placement of Dementia Patients and Caregiver Health and Well-Being." *Journal of the American Medical Association* 292(8): 961-967, 2004.

Teno, J., et al. "Family Perspectives on End of Life Care." *Journal of the American Medical Association* 291(1): 88-93, January 7, 2004.

Tibaldi, V., et al. "A Randomized Controlled Trial of a Home Hospital Intervention for Frail Elderly Demented Patients: Behavioral Disturbances and Caregiver's Stress." *Archives of Gerontology and Geriatrics* 38: 431-436, 2004.

Wennberg, J., et al. "Use Of Medicare Claims Data To Monitor Provider-Specific Performance Among Patients With Severe Chronic Illness." *Health Affairs: The Policy Journal of the Health Sphere.* http://www.healthaffairs.org (accessed October 7, 2004).

Hospice

Fine, P. and Jennings, B. "Case Study: CPR in Hospice." *Hastings Center Report* 33(3): 9-10, May-June 2003.

Haley, W. E., et al. "Family Caregiving in Hospice: Effects on Psychological and Health Functioning among Spousal Caregivers of Hospice Patients with Lung Cancer or Dementia." *Hospice Journal* 15(4): 1-18, 2001.

Henig, R. "Will We Ever Arrive at the Good Death?" *New York Times.* August 7, 2005, p. 26.

Jennings, B., et al. *Access to Hospice Care: Expanding Boundaries, Overcoming Barriers.* Garrison, New York: Hastings Center, 2003.

Ryan, R. "Palliative Care and Terminal Illness." *National Catholic Bioethics Quarterly* 1(3): 313-320, Autumn 2001.

Caregiving Generally

Bornat, J., ed. *Reminiscence Reviewed: Evaluations, Achievements, Perspectives (Rethinking Old Age).* Bristol, PA: Open University Press, 1994.

Capossela, C., et al. *Share The Care: How to Organize a Group to Care for Someone Who Is Seriously Ill.* New York: Fireside, 2004.

Lawler, P. "Caregiving and the American Individual." Presented at the September 10, 2004 meeting of the President's Council on Bioethics, Washington, D.C., available online at http://www.bioethics.gov.

Lo, B. and Dornbrand, L. "Guiding the Hand That Feeds: Caring For the Demented Elderly." *New England Journal of Medicine* 311: 402-404, 1984.

*Lynn, J. and Harrold, J. *Handbook for Mortals: Guidance for People Facing Serious Illness.* New York: Oxford University Press, 1999.

*May, W. F. *The Patient's Ordeal.* Bloomington, IN: Indiana University Press, 1994.

Schulz, R. and Patterson, L. "Caregiving in Geriatric Psychiatry." *American Journal of Geriatric Psychiatry* 12(3): 234-237, 2004.

Dementia

Cayton, H. "Telling Stories: Choices and Challenges on the Journey of Dementia." *Dementia* 3: 9-17, 2004.

Farran C., et al. "Alzheimer's Disease Caregiving Information and Skills. Part II: Family Caregiver Issues and Concerns." *Research in Nursing and Health* 27: 40-51, 2004.

Forbat, L. "Relationship Difficulties in Dementia Care: A Discursive Analysis of Two Women's Accounts." *Dementia* 2(1): 67-84, 2003.

Hall, G. "Everyday Ethics: Issues in Caring For People with Dementing Illnesses." Presented at the June 24, 2004 meeting of the President's Council on Bioethics, Washington, D.C., available online at http://www.bioethics.gov.

Katsuno T. "Personal Spirituality of Persons with Early-Stage Dementia: Is It Related to Perceived Quality of Life?" *Dementia* 2: 315-335, 2003.

Ory, M., et al. "Prevalence and Impact of Caregiving: A Detailed Comparison Between Dementia and Non-Dementia Caregivers." *Gerontologist* 39(2): 177-185, 1999.

*Rabins, P., et al. *Practical Dementia Care.* 2nd ed. New York: Oxford University Press, forthcoming 2006 (1st ed. 1999).

Radin, L. and Radin, G., eds. *What If It's Not Alzheimer's? A Caregiver's Guide to Dementia.* Amherst, New York: Prometheus Books, 2003.

Rango, D. "The Nursing Home Resident with Dementia." *Annals of Internal Medicine* 102(6) 835-841, 1995.

Roeline, H., et al. "Discomfort in Nursing Home Patients With Severe Dementia in Whom Artificial Nutrition and Hydration Is Forgone." *Archives of Internal Medicine* 165(15): 1737-1742, August 8, 2005.

Sachs, G., et al, "Barriers to Excellent End-of-Life Care for Patients with Dementia." *Journal of the American Medical Association* 284(19): 2423, 2000.

Scarpinato, N., et al. "Kitty's Dilemma: Making Treatment Decisions When a Patient with Dementia Says She Wants to End Her Life." *American Journal of Nursing* 100(3): 49-51, March 2000.

Vernooij-Dassen, M. and Moniz-Cook, E. "Editorial: How Can the Quality of Home-Based Interventions Be Improved?" *Dementia* 4(2): 163-169, 2005.

End of Life

Albinsson, L. and Strang, P. "A Palliative Approach to Existential Issues and Death in End-Stage Dementia Care." *Journal of Palliative Care* 18(3): 168-174, 2002.

American Bar Association Commission on Law & Aging. *End of Life Care Legislation Summary*. Chicago, IL: ABA, June 2001.

American Bar Association Commission on Law & Aging. *End of Life Legal Trends*. Chicago, IL: ABA, April 2000.

Baird, R. and Rosenbaum, S., eds. *Caring for the Dying: Critical Issues at the Edge of Life*. Amherst, New York: Prometheus Books, 2003.

Blank, R., and Merrick, J., eds. *End-of-Life Decision Making: A Cross National Study*. Boston, MA: MIT Press, 2004.

Buchanan, A., et al. *Deciding For Others: The Ethics of Surrogate Decision Making*. Cambridge, U.K.: Cambridge University Press, 1990.

*Burt, R. *Taking Care of Strangers: The Rule of Law in Doctor-Patient Relations*. New York: Free Press, 1979.

Buzzee, S. "The Pain Relief Promotion Act: Congress's Misguided Intervention into End-of-Life Care." 70 *University of Cincinnati Law Review* 217, Fall 2001.

Caron, C. D., et al. "End-of-Life Decision Making in Dementia: The Perspective of Family Caregivers." *Dementia* 4(1): 113-136, 2005.

Hafemeister, T. "End-of-Life Decision Making, Therapeutic Jurisprudence, and Preventive Law: Hierarchial v. Consensus-Based Decision-Making Model." 41 *Arizona Law Review* 329, Summer 1999.

Kissine, D. "The Contribution of Demoralization to End of Life Decision-making." *Hastings Center Report* 34(4): 21-31, July-August 2004.

Kübler-Ross, E. *On Death and Dying.* New York: Macmillan Publishing Co., 1969.

Kunin, J. "Withholding Artificial Feeding from the Severely Demented: Merciful or Immoral? Contrasts between Secular and Jewish Perspectives." *Journal of Medical Ethics* 29(4): 208-212, 2003.

Lynn, J. "The End of Life." Testimony presented at the March 3, 2005 meeting of the President's Council on Bioethics, Washington, D.C., available at www.bioethics.gov.

Mendelson, D. and Jost, T. "A Comparative Study of the Law of Palliative Care and End-of-Life Treatment." 31 *Journal of Law, Medicine, and Ethics* 130, Spring 2003.

Miller, J. E. *When You Know You're Dying—Twelve Thoughts to Guide You Through the Days Ahead.* Fort Wayne, IN: Willowgreen Publishing, 1997.

Owen, J. E., et al. "End of Life Care and Reactions to Death in African-American and White Family Caregivers of Relatives with Alzheimer's Disease." *Omega-Journal of Death and Dying* 43(4): 349-361, 2001.

Quill, T. *Caring for Patients at the End of Life: Facing an Uncertain Future Together.* New York: Oxford University Press, 2001.

Sachs, G. "Sometimes Dying Still Stings." *Journal of the American Medical Association* 284(19): 2423, 2000.

Salmon, J. R., et al. "Transformative Aspects of Caregiving at Life's End." *Journal of Pain and Symptom Management* 29(2): 121-129, 2005.

Schulz, R., et al. "End-of-Life Care and the Effects of Bereavement on Family Caregivers of Persons with Dementia." *New England Journal of Medicine* 349(20): 1936-1942, 2003.

Financial Costs

Chiu, L., et al. "Cost Comparisons between Family-Based Care and Nursing Home Care for Dementia." *Journal of Advanced Nursing* 29(4): 1005-1012, 1999.

Langa, K., et al. "National Estimates of the Quantity and Cost of Informal Caregiving for the Elderly with Dementia." *Journal of Internal Medicine* 16: 770-778, 2001.

Seshamani, M., and Alastair, G. "Time to Death and Health Expenditure: An Improved Model for the Impact of Demographic Change on Healthcare Cost." *Age and Aging* 33: 556-561, 2004.

Living Arrangements

Gibson, M. *Assisted Living: Beyond 50.03: A Report to the Nation on Independent Living and Disability.* Washington, D.C.: AARP, May 2, 2005.

Graham, T. "Stay-At-Home Elders." *Washington Post.* August 2, 2005, p. F1.

Kalb, C., et al. "Aging: Small Is Beautiful." *Newsweek.* August 1, 2005, p. 46.

Pot, A. M., et al. "Institutionalization of Demented Elderly: The Role of Caregiver Characteristics." *International Journal of Geriatric Psychiatry* 16(3): 273-280, 2001.

Schafer, R. *Housing America's Seniors.* Cambridge, MA: Joint Center for Housing Studies of Harvard University, 2000.

Long-Term Care

Roper, A. W. *The Costs of Long-term Care: Public Perceptions Versus Reality.* Washington, D.C.: AARP, December 2001.

Spicker, S. F. and Ingman, S., eds. *Vitalizing Long-term Care.* New York: Springer Publishing Company, 1984.

U.S. Senate, Special Committee on Aging. *Long-term Care Report: Findings from Committee Hearings of the 107th Congress.* (S. Prt. 107-74), Washington, D.C.: U.S. Government Printing Office, 2002.

Death & Dying

Dignity

Caplan, A. "Dignity Is a Social Construct." December 24, 2003. http://bmj.bmjjournals.com (accessed January 5, 2004).

Kass, L. "A Commentary on Paul Ramsey: Averting One's Eyes, or Facing the Music?—On Dignity in Death." *Hastings Center Studies* 2(2): 67-80, May 1974.

Kass, L. *Life, Liberty and the Defense of Dignity: The Challenge for Bioethics.* San Francisco, CA: Encounter Books, 2002.

Kilner, J., Miller, A., Pellegrino, E., eds. *Dignity and Dying: A Christian Appraisal.* Grand Rapids, MI: Eerdmans Publishing Co., 1996.

Macklin, R. "Dignity Is A Useless Concept." (editorial) *BMJ* December 24, 2003. http://bmj.bmjjournals.com (accessed January 5, 2004).

McIntyre, M. "Dignity in Dementia: Person-Centered Care in Community." *Journal Of Aging Studies* 17: 473-484, 2003.

Mohler, R. "The Culture of Death and the Gospel of Life: An Evangelical Response to Evangelium Vitae." *Ethics & Medicine: An International Christian Perspective on Bioethics* 13(1): 2-4, 1997.

Sulmasy, D. "Death, Dignity, and the Theory of Value." *Ethical Perspectives* 9: 103-118, 2003.

Euthanasia & Assisted Suicide

Angelo, E. "Depression and Assisted Suicide in the Terminally Ill." *National Catholic Bioethics Quarterly* 1(3): 307-312, Autumn 2001.

Barton, M. "Oregon's Oxymoron: The Death with Dignity Act." *National Catholic Bioethics Quarterly* 4(4): 739-754, Winter 2004.

Carlson, E. *The Unfit: A History of a Bad Idea.* Cold Spring Harbor, N.Y.: Cold Spring Harbor Laboratory Press, 2001.

Doerflinger, R. "Assisted Suicide: Pro-choice or Anti-life?" *Hastings Center Report* 19(1): S16-19, 1989.

Dougherty, M. "Irrationality of the Irrationality Argument against Suicide." *National Catholic Bioethics Quarterly* 4(3): 489-493, Autumn 2004.

Evans, R. "How Then Should We Die?: California's 'Death with Dignity' Act." *Ethics & Medicine: An International Christian Perspective on Bioethics* 16(3): 79-86, 2000.

Fieger, G. and Pellegrino, E. "A Public Debate on Legalizing Physician-Assisted Suicide." Bannockburn, IL: Center for Bioethics and Human Dignity, 1995. (audio)

Fletcher, D. "Holy Dying, Assisted Dying?: An Anglican Perspective on Physician-Assisted Suicide." *Ethics & Medicine: An International Journal of Bioethics* 20(1): 35-42, Spring 2004.

Foley, K. and Hendin, H. "The Oregon Report: Don't Ask, Don't Tell." *Hastings Center Report* 29(3): 37-42, 1999.

Foley, K. and Hendin, H., eds. *The Case Against Assisted Suicide: For the Right to End-of-Life Care.* Baltimore, MD: Johns Hopkins University Press, 2004.

George, R. "Always to Care, Never to Kill." Interview by National Review Online. March 21, 2005. http://www.nationalreview.com (accessed March 24, 2005).

Gómez-Lobo, A. "On Euthanasia." in *Morality and the Human Goods: An Introduction to Natural Law Ethics.* Washington, D.C.: Georgetown University Press, 2002, pp. 98-111.

Gorsuch, N. "The Legalization of Assisted Suicide and the Law of Unintended Consequences: A Review of the Dutch and Oregon Experiments and Leading Utilitarian Arguments for Legal Change." *2004 Wisconsin Law Review 1347,* 2004.

Harrington, C. "Mental Competence and End-of-Life Decision Making: Death Row Volunteering and Euthanasia." 29 *Journal of Health Politics, Policy, and Law* 1109, December 2004.

Hendin, H., et al. "Physician-Assisted Suicide and Euthanasia in the Netherlands: Lessons from the Dutch." Presented at the March 3, 2005 Meeting of the President's Council on Bioethics. Washington, D.C., available online at http://www.bioethics.gov. Reprinted from the *Journal of the American Medical Association* 277(21): 1720-1722, 1997.

Hendin, H. *Suicide in America.* New York: W.W. Norton and Co., 1996.

Howsepian, A. "Some Reservations About Suicide." *Ethics & Medicine: An International Christian Perspective on Bioethics* 12(2): 34-40, 1996.

Jansen-van der Weide, M., et al. "Granted, Undecided, Withdrawn, and Refused Requests for Euthanasia and Physician-Assisted Suicide." *Archives of Internal Medicine* 165(15): 1698-1704, August 8, 2005.

Kaplan, K., et al. "Suicide, Physician-Assisted Suicide, and Euthanasia in Men versus Women Around the World: The Degree of Physician Control." *Ethics & Medicine: An International Journal of Bioethics* 18(1): 33-48, Spring 2002.

Kass, L. "Neither for Love nor Money: Why Doctors Must Not Kill." *The Public Interest* 94: 25-46, Winter 1989.

Kilner, J. and Mitchell, C. *Does God Need Our Help? Cloning, Assisted Suicide, & Other Challenges in Bioethics.* Wheaton, IL: Tyndale House Publishers, 2003.

Lawler, P. "Euthanasia." in *Postmodernism Rightly Understood: The Return to Realism in American Thought*. Lanham, MD: Rowman & Littlefield Publishers, 1999, pp. 141-146.

Lee, D. "Physician-Assisted Suicide: A Conservative Critique of Intervention." *Hastings Center Report* 33(1): 17-19, January-February 2003.

Lee, P. "Personhood, Dignity, Suicide, and Euthanasia." *National Catholic Bioethics Quarterly* 1(3): 329-343, Autumn 2001.

L'Heureux, J. "Victory in Maine on Physician-Assisted Suicide." *National Catholic Bioethics Quarterly* 1(3): 299-305, Autumn 2001.

Marker, R. "An Inside Look at the Right to Die Movement." *National Catholic Bioethics Quarterly* 1(3): 363-394, Autumn 2001.

Mathuan, D. "Did Paul Condone Suicide? Implications for Assisted Suicide and Assisted Euthanasia." *Ethics & Medicine: An International Christian Perspective on Bioethics* 12(3): 55-60, 1996.

Mayo, D. and Gunderson, M. "Vitalism Revitalized: Vulnerable Populations, Prejudice, and Physician-Assisted Suicide." *Hastings Center Report* 32(4): 14-21, July-August 2002.

McConchie, D. "Redefining the Active/Passive Euthanasia Debate— art I." *Ethics & Medicine: An International Christian Perspective on Bioethics* 15(3): 70-74, 1999.

McConchie, D. "Redefining the Active/Passive Euthanasia Debate—Part II." *Ethics & Medicine: An International Christian Perspective on Bioethics* 16(1): 6-11, 2000.

Meilaender, G. "Euthanasia and Christian Vision," in *The Limits of Love: Some Theological Explorations*. University Park, PA: Pennsylvania State University Press, 1987, pp. 79-99.

Myers, R. "Physician-Assisted Suicide: A Current Legal Perspective." *National Catholic Bioethics Quarterly* 1(3): 345-361, Autumn 2001.

New York State Task Force on Life and the Law. *When Death Is Sought: Assisted Suicide and Euthanasia in the Medical Context*. New York State Task Force on Life and the Law. May 1994.

Quill, T. "Opening the Black Box: Physicians' Inner Responses to Patients' Requests for Physician-Assisted Death." *Journal of Palliative Medicine* 7(3): 469-4711, June 2004.

Quill, T., et al. "Palliative Treatments of Last Resort: Choosing the Least Harmful Alternative." *Annals of Internal Medicine* 132(6): 488-493, March 21, 2000.

Quill, T. and Battin, P. *Physician-Assisted Dying: The Case for Palliative Care and Patient Choice.* Baltimore, MD: Johns Hopkins University Press, 2004.

Schneider, C., ed. *Law at the End of Life: The Supreme Court and Assisted Suicide.* Ann Arbor, MI: University of Michigan Press, 2004.

Schudt, K. "Choosing Oblivion: The Irrationality of Suicide." *National Catholic Bioethics Quarterly* 2(4): 609-614, Winter 2002.

Smith, W. *Forced Exit: The Slippery Slope from Assisted Suicide to Legalized Murder.* Dallas, TX: Spence Publishing Company, 2003.

Thomas, K. "Confronting End-of-Life Decisions: Should We Expand the Right To Die?" 44 *Federal Lawyer* 30, May 1997.

Valko, N. "Should Sedation be Terminal?" *National Catholic Bioethics Quarterly* 2(4): 601-608, Winter 2002.

Verhagen, E. and Sauer, P. "The Groningen Protocol—Euthanasia in Severely Ill Newborns." *New England Journal of Medicine* 352: 959-962, March 10, 2005.

Vermaat, J. "'Euthanasia' in the Third Reich: Lessons for Today?" *Ethics & Medicine: An International Journal of Bioethics* 18(1): 21-32, Spring 2002.

Wernow, J. "Confronting the Pine Box with the Ballot Box: A Critical Appraisal of Oregon's Attempt to 'Do' Medical Ethics by Public Ballot." *Ethics & Medicine: An International Christian Perspective on Bioethics* 13(3): 71-75, 1997.

Witteck, H. "Decision-Making at the End-of-Life and the Incompetent Patient: A Comparative Approach." 22 *Medicine and Law* 533, 2003.

Wolf, S. "Assessing Physician Compliance with the Rules for Euthanasia and Assisted Suicide." *Archives of Internal Medicine* 165(15): 1677-1679, August 8, 2005.

Wolfson, A. "Killing Off the Dying?" *The Public Interest* 131: 50-70, Spring 1998.

Medical Standards / Best Practices

Ahronheim, J., et al. "Treatment of the Dying in the Acute Care Hospital." *Internal Medicine* 156: 2094-2100, October 14, 1996.

Arras, J., ed. *Bringing the Hospital Home: Ethical and Social Implications of High-Tech Home Care.* Baltimore, MD: Johns Hopkins University Press, 1995.

Asch, D., et al. "The Sequence of Withdrawing Life-Sustaining Treatments from Patients." *American Journal of Medicine* 107: 153-156, August 1999.

Buntin-Mushock, M., et al. "Age-Dependent Opioid Escalation in Chronic Pain Patients." *Anesthesia & Analgesia* 100: 1740-1745, June 2005.

Carmel, S. "Life-Sustaining Treatments: What Doctors Do, What They Want for Themselves, and What Elderly Persons Want." *Social Science and Medicine* 49: 1401-1408, 1999.

Chevlen, E. and Smith, W. *Power Over Pain: How to Get the Pain Control You Need.* Steubenville, OH: International Task Force, 2002.

Health Care Provided to Non-Ambulatory Persons: Hearing Before the Senate Committee on Health, Education, Labor, and Pensions, 108th Congress. Statements of: Mr. Rud Turnbull, Co-Director, University of Kansas Beach Center on Disability; Dr. James L. Bernat, Professor of Medicine, Dartmouth Medical School; Dr. Deborah Warden, Director, Defense and Veterans Head Injury Program; and Dr. J. Donald Schumacher, President and CEO, National Hospice and Palliative Care Association. April 6, 2005.

New York State Task Force on Life and the Law. *The Determination of Death.* New York State Task Force on Life and the Law. January 1989.

Schwartz, J. "For the End of Life, Hospital Pairs Ethics and Medicine." *New York Times.* July 4, 2005, p. B1.

Wenger, N., et al. "Withholding Versus Withdrawing Life-Sustaining Treatment: Patient Factors and Documentation Associated with Dialysis Decisions." *Journal of American Geriatrics Society* 48: S75-S83, 2000.

Wennberg, J. "Variation in Use of Medicare Services Among Regions and Selected Academic Medical Centers: Is More Better?" Ducan W. Clark Lecture presented to the New York Academy of Medicine, January 24, 2005.

Williams, M. "End-of-Life Care and Organ Donation Decisions." 15 *Probate And Property* 58, September/October 2001.

Youngner, S., et al., eds. *The Definition of Death: Contemporary Controversies.* Baltimore, MD: Johns Hopkins University Press, 1999.

Nutrition & Hydration

Atkinson, A. "Artificial Nutrition and Hydration for Patients in Persistent Vegetative State: Continuing Reflections." *Ethics & Medicine: An International Christian Perspective on Bioethics* 16(3): 73-75, 2000.

Brown, S. "British Man Adds New Wrinkle in End-of-Life Debate." *Seattle Times.* May 31, 2005, http://www.seattletimes.nwsource.com (accessed May 31, 2005).

Cataldo, P. "Pope John Paul II on Nutrition and Hydration: A Change of Catholic Teaching?" *National Catholic Bioethics Quarterly* 4(3): 513-536, Autumn 2004.

Craig, G. "Palliative Care from the Perspective of a Consultant Geriatrician: The Dangers of Withholding Hydration." *Ethics & Medicine: An International Christian Perspective on Bioethics* 15(1): 15-19, 1999.

Craig, G. "Paradise Lost: The Devolution of Medical Practice." *Ethics & Medicine: An International Christian Perspective on Bioethics* 16(1): 1-3, 2000.

Kopaczynski, G. "Initial Reactions to the Pope's March 20, 2004, Allocution." *National Catholic Bioethics Quarterly* 4(3): 473-482, Autumn 2004.

Lynn, J., ed. *By No Extraordinary Means: The Choice to Forego Life-Sustaining Food and Water.* Bloomington & Indianapolis, IN: Indiana University Press, 1986.

Lynn, J. and Childress, J. "Must Patients Always be Given Food and Water?" *Hastings Center Report* 13(5): 17-21, October 1983.

Marker, R. "Case Study: Terri Schiavo and the Catholic Connection." *National Catholic Bioethics Quarterly* 4(3): 555-569, Autumn 2004.

Marker, R. "Mental Disability and Death by Dehydration." *National Catholic Bioethics Quarterly* 2(1): 125-136, Spring 2002.

Meilaender, G. "Withdrawing Food and Water," in *The Limits of Love: Some Theological Explorations.* University Park, PA: Pennsylvania State University Press, 1987, pp. 102-111.

Orr, R. "Clinical Ethics Case Consultation." *Ethics & Medicine: An International Journal of Bioethics* 18(1): 11-13, Spring 2002.

Quill, T. "Terri Schiavo—A Tragedy Compounded." *New England Journal of Medicine.* 352(16): 1630-1633, April 21, 2005.

Repenshek, M. and Sloser, J. "Medically Assisted Nutrition and Hydration." *Hastings Center Report* 34(6): 13-16, November-December 2004.

Shannon, T. and Walter, J. "Implications of the Papal Allocution on Feeding Tubes." *Hastings Center Report* 34(4): 18-20, July-August 2004.

Torchia, J. "Artificial Hydration and Nutrition for the PVS Patient." *National Catholic Bioethics Quarterly* 3(4): 719-730, Winter 2003.

Persistent Vegetative State

Hollins, S. "Something Worth Writing Home About: Clear and Convincing Evidence, Living Wills, and Cruzan v. Director Missouri Department of Health," 1991 Symposium: The Rehnquist Court. 22 *University of Toledo Law Review* 871, Spring 1991.

O'Brien, D., et al. "Utilitarian Pessimism, Human Dignity, and the Vegetative State: A Practical Analysis of the Papal Statement." *National Catholic Bioethics Quarterly* 4(3): 497-512, Autumn 2004.

Orr, R. and Meilaender, G. "Ethics & Life's Ending: An Exchange." *First Things* 145: 31-38, August/September 2004.

Pope John Paul II. "On Life-Sustaining Treatments and the Vegetative State: Scientific Advances and Ethical Dilemmas." *National Catholic Bioethics Quarterly* 4(3): 573-576, Autumn 2004.

Torchia, J. "Postmodernism and the Persistent Vegetative State." *National Catholic Bioethics Quarterly* 2(2): 257-275, Summer 2002.

World Federation of Catholic Medical Associations and the Pontifical Academy for Life. "Considerations on the Scientific and Ethical Problems Related to the Vegetative State." *National Catholic Bioethics Quarterly* 4(3): 579-581, Autumn 2004.

Quality of Life

Byock, I. *Dying Well: A Prospect for Growth at the End of Life.* New York: Riverhead Books, 1997.

Campbell, C. "A Relative Value?" *National Review* September 1, 2004. http://www.nationalreview.com (accessed September 1, 2004).

Nussbaum, M., et al. *The Quality of Life.* Oxford, U.K.: Clarendon Press, 1993.

Weyerer, S. and Schaufele, M. "The Assessment of Quality of Life in Dementia." *International Psychogeriatrics* 15(3): 213-218, 2003.

Trajectories

Brody, J. "Facing Up to the Inevitable, in Search of a Good Death." *New York Times*. December 30, 2003, p. F5.

Lynn, J. and Adamson, D. "Living Well at the End of Life: Adapting Health Care to Serious Chronic Illness in Old Age." Santa Monica, CA: RAND, 2003.

National Health Center for Health Statistics. "Home Health Care Patients: Data from the 2000 National Home and Hospice Care Survey." www.cdc.gov (accessed May 2, 2005).

Dementias other than Alzheimer's

Boccardi, M. et al. "Frontotemporal Dementia as a Neural System Disease." *Neurobiology of Aging* 26: 37-44, 2005.

Caselli, R. J. "Current Issues in the Diagnosis and Management of Dementia." *Seminars in Neurology* 23(3): 231-240, 2003.

Dawson, T. and Dawson, V. "Molecular Pathways of Neurodegeneration in Parkinson's Disease." *Science* 302(5646): 819-822, October 31, 2003.

DeKosky, S. and Marek, K. "Looking Backward to Move Forward: Early Detection of Neurodegenerative Disorders." *Science* 302(5646): 830-834, October 31, 2003.

Diehl, J., et al. "A Support Group for Caregivers of Patients with Frontotemporal Dementia." *Dementia* 2(2): 151-161, 2003.

Jeste, D., et al. "Consensus Statement on the Upcoming Crisis in Geriatric Mental Health: Research Agenda for the Next 2 Decades." *Archives of General Psychiatry* 56: 848-853, 1999.

Langa, K. M., et al. "Mixed Dementia: Emerging Concepts and Therapeutic Implications." *Journal of the American Medical Association* 292(23): 2901-2908, 2004.

Saint-Cyr, J., et al. "Neuropsychological Consequences of Chronic Bilateral Stimulation of the Subthalamic Nucleus in Parkinson's Disease." *Brain* 123: 2091-2108, 2000.

Demographics

American Society

Alzheimer's Community

Alzheimer's Association. "Statistics about Alzheimer's Disease." August 2005. http://www.alz.org/AboutAD/statistics.asp (accessed August 24, 2005).

Grant, W. "Year 2000 Prevalence of Alzheimer's Disease in the United States." *Archives of Neurology* 61: 802-803, 2004.

Hebert, L. E., et al. "Alzheimer Disease in the U.S. Population: Prevalence Estimates Using the 2000 Census." *Archives of Neurology* 60: 1119-1122, 2003.

Hebert, L. E., et al. "State-Specific Projections through 2025 of Alzheimer Disease Prevalence." *Neurology* 62(9): 1645, 2004.

Baby Boomers

Baek, E. and DeVaney, S. "Assessing the Baby Boomer's Financial Wellness." *Family and Consumer Sciences Research Journal* 32(4): 321-348, 2004.

Butrica, B. and Uccello, C. "How Will Boomers Fare at Retirement?" *AARP Public Policy Institute Issues Paper* 2004(05): 7-11, 2004.

Hodge, P. "Baby Boomer Public Policy: A New Vision" *Harvard Generations Policy Journal* 1: 7-21, Winter 2004.

International Longevity Center. *2004 Annual Report: Here Come the Baby Boomers*. New York: International Longevity Center, 2004.

Marsa, L. "Boomers Only—Employment of Baby Boomers Past Retirement Age." *Omni* October 1, 1992, http://www.findarticles.com (accessed May 2005).

Weiss, M. "Great Expectations—Baby Boomer Wealth Forecasts Wilt." *American Demographics* May 1, 2003, www.AdAge.com (accessed May 1, 2005).

Caregivers

Administration on Aging. "Family Caregiving." May 2003. http://www.aoa.gov/press/fact/alpha/fact_family_caregiver.asp (accessed May 2005).

Alzheimer's Association and National Alliance for Caregiving. *Families Care: Alzheimer's Caregiving in the United States 2004*. Washington, D.C.: Alzheimer's Association and the National Alliance for Caregiving, September 2004.

American Hospital Association. "TrendWatch." June 2001. http://www. hospitalconnect.com/ahapolicyforum/trendwatch/twjune2001.html (accessed August 22, 2005).

Feldman, P. "Labor Market Issues In Home Care" in Fox, D. and Raphael, C., eds. *Home-Based Care For a New Century*. Malden, MA: Blackwell Publishers, 1997.

Gibson, M., et al. *Across the States: Profiles of Long-term Care 2004*. Washington, D.C.: AARP, May 2, 2005.

Krisberg, K. "Public Health Work Force Not Prepared for Aging Population: Increasing Number of Seniors on Horizon." May 18, 2005. http://www.medscape.com (accessed May 18, 2005).

National Alliance for Caregiving. *Caregiving in the U.S.* Washington, D.C.: National Alliance for Caregiving and AARP, April 2004.

National Center for Assisted Living. *2001 Facts and Trends: The Assisted Living Sourcebook*. Washington, D.C.: National Center for Assisted Living, 2001.

National Council of State Boards of Nursing. *National Council Licensure Examination-Registered Nurse/Practical Nurse Examination Statistics: Statistics from Years 1995-2002*. 2002.

National Family Caregivers Association. "Caregiving Statistics." August 24, 2005. http://www.thefamilycaregiver.org/who/stats.cfm (accessed August 24, 2005).

National Family Caregivers Association. "Comparing Survey Stats and Understanding Why They Differ." 2000. http://www.thefamilycaregiver.org/ (accessed May 2005).

Public Policy Institute. *Fact Sheet Number 91: Family Caregiving and Long-Term Care*. Washington, D.C.: Public Policy Institute, November 2002.

Stone, R. "The Direct Care Worker: The Third Rail of Home Care Policy." *Annual Review of Public Health* 25: 521-537, 2004.

Stone, R. and Wiener, J. *Who Will Care For Us? Addressing the Long-Term Care Workforce Crisis*. Washington, D.C.: The Urban Institute and the American Association of Homes and Services for the Aging, 2001.

U.S. Department of Health and Human Services. *The Future Supply of Long-Term Care Workers in Relation to the Aging Baby Boom Generation*. Report to Congress. May 14, 2003, available at http://www.hss.gov (accessed April 2005).

Family Structure

Bureau of the Census, Economics and Statistics Administration, U.S. Department of Commerce. "United States: Selected Social Characteristics: 2003 American Community Survey Summary Tables." 2003. http://factfinder.census. gov (accessed May 2, 2005).

Gill, R. *Posterity Lost: Progress, Ideology, and the Decline of the American Family.* Lanham, MD: Rowman & Littlefield Publishers, 1997.

Liang, J., et al. "Health and Living Arrangements Among Older Americans." *Journal of Aging and Health* 17(3): 305-335, June 2005.

National Center for Health Statistics, U.S. Department of Health and Human Services. "Births, Marriages, Divorces, and Deaths: Provisional Data for October 2004." *National Vital Statistics Reports* 53(18), April 19, 2005.

Wellner, A. "Is 'Increasing Mobility' a Threat to U.S. Elder Care?" April 2005. http://www.prb.org (accessed April 30, 2005).

General

AARP, Public Policy Institute. *The State of 50+ America 2005*. Washington, D.C.: Public Policy Institute, 2005.

Administration on Aging. "Older Population by Age: 1900-2000." http://www.aoa.gov/prof/Statistics/online_stat_data/AgePop2050.asp (accessed April 30, 2005).

Administration on Aging. "A Profile of Older Americans: 2003." Washington, D.C.: U.S. Department of Health and Human Services, 2003.

Administration on Aging, U.S. Department of Health and Human Services. "A Statistical Profile of Older Americans Aged 65+." http://www.aoa.gov (accessed May 2005).

Binstock, R. "The Aging Society: An Introductory Overview." Testimony presented at the June 24, 2004 meeting of the President's Council on Bioethics, Washington, D.C., available online at http://www.bioethics.gov.

Bureau of the Census, Economics and Statistics Administration, U.S. Department of Commerce. "Facts for Features: Older Americans Month." Washington, D.C.: U.S. Department of Commerce, March 24, 2005.

Bureau of the Census, Economics and Statistics Administration, U.S. Department of Commerce. "United States: General Demographic Characteristics:

2003 American Community Survey Summary Tables." 2003. http://factfinder. census.gov (accessed May 2, 2005).

Bureau of the Census, Economics and Statistics Administration, U.S. Department of Commerce. "United States: Population and Housing Narrative Profile: 2003 American Community Survey Tables." 2003. http://factfinder.census.gov (accessed May 2, 2005).

Butler, R., ed. *Life in an Older America.* New York: Century Foundation Press, 1999.

Camarota, S. "Immigration in an Aging Society: Workers, Birth Rates, and Social Security." *Center for Immigration Studies,* April 2005.

Collins, G. "Rethinking Retirement in the Context of an Aging Workforce." *Journal of a Career Development* 30(2): 145-157, 2003.

Friedland, R. and Summer, L. "Demography Is Not Destiny, Revisited." Center on an Aging Society, Georgetown University, March 2005. Available online at http://ihcrp.georgetown.edu/agingsociety.

"Getting Older, Staying Healthier: The Demographics of Health Care." Testimony of James Lubitz, Acting Chief, Aging and Chronic Diseases, Statistics Branch, National Center for Health Statistics, Centers for Disease Control and Prevention, before the Joint Economic Committee, U.S. Senate, July 22, 2004.

Hogan, C., et al. *A Statistical Profile of Decedents in the Medicare Program.* Washington, D.C.: Medicare Payment Advisory Commission, 2000.

Hooyman, N. and Kiyak, H. *Social Gerontology.* Boston, MA: Allyn and Bacon, 1996.

Institute for Health and Aging, University of California-San Francisco. *Chronic Care in America: A Twenty-first Century Challenge.* Princeton, N.J.: Robert Wood Johnson Foundation, 1996.

International Longevity Center. *Annual Report 2003: Aging is a Woman's Issue.* New York: International Longevity Center, 2003.

Jitapunkul, S., et al. "Disability-free Life Expectancy of Elderly People in a Population Undergoing Demographic and Epidemiologic Transition." *Age and Aging* 32(4): 401-405, July 2003.

Johns Hopkins University Partnership for Solutions. "Chronic Conditions: Making the Case for Ongoing Care." September 2004 Update. http://www.rwjf. org (accessed August 24, 2005).

Kassner, E. and Bectel, R. *Midlife and Older Americans with Disabilities: Who Gets Help? A Chartbook.* Washington, D.C.: AARP Public Policy Institute, 1998.

Knickman, J. "The 2030 problem: Caring for Aging Baby Boomers." *Health Services Research* 37(4): 849-884, August 2002.

Korczyk, S. *Back to Which Future: The U.S. Aging Crisis Revisited,* Washington, D.C.: Public Policy Institute, December 2002.

Living Stronger, Earning Longer: Redefining Retirement in the 21ˢᵗ Century Work Place. Hearing Before the Senate Special Committee on Aging, 108th Congress. Statements of Senator Herb Kohl, Ranking Member, and Senator Gordon Smith, Chairman. April 27, 2005.

Manton, K. and Gu, X. L. "Changes in the Prevalence of Chronic Disability in the United States Black and Nonblack Population Above Age 65 from 1982 to 1999." *Proceedings of the National Academy of Sciences of the United States of America* 98: 6354-6359, 2001.

Moody, H. *Aging: Concepts and Controversies.* 4th ed. Thousand Oaks, CA: Sage Publications, Inc., 2002.

National Aging Information Center, Administration on Aging. *Aging In The Twenty-first Century.* Washington, D.C.: Government Printing Office, 1996.

Novelli, W. "2011 in America: A Blueprint for Change." *Harvard Generations Policy Journal* 1: 23-33, Winter 2004.

Older Americans 2004: Key Indicators of Well-Being. Federal Interagency Forum on Aging-Related Statistics. Available online at http://www.agingstats. gov.

Poterba, J. "Demographic Structure and Asset Returns." *The Review of Economics and Statistics* 83(4): 565-584, November 1, 2001.

Rix, S. *Aging and Work—A View from the United States.* Washington, D.C.: Public Policy Institute, 2004.

Social Security Administration. "Income of the Population 55 and Older." March 2005. SSA Publication No. 13-11871. http://www.ssa.gov/policy/docs/statcomps/income_pop55 (accessed May 2, 2005).

U. S. Census Bureau. *Estimates of the Resident Population by Selected Age Groups for the United States and States and for Puerto Rico: July 1, 2004.* U.S. Census Bureau, 2005. Available online at http://www.census.gov.

U.S. Census Bureau. *State Interim Population Projections by Age and Sex: 2004–2030,* Table 3, "Ranking of States by Projected Percent of Population Age 65 and

Over: 2000, 2010, and 2030." U.S. Census Bureau, 2005. Available online at http://www.census.gov.

U.S. Census Bureau. *U.S. Interim Projections by Age, Sex, Race, and Hispanic Origin*, Table 2a, "Projected Population of the United States, by Age and Sex: 2000 to 2050." U.S. Census Bureau, 2004. Available online at http://www.census.gov.

Vallin, J. "The Demographic 'Givens': Changes in the Generational Structures of Human Populations." Presentation to the X Plenary Session of the Pontifical Academy of Social Sciences. Rome, April 28, 2004.

Winn, F. "Structural Impediments to the Efficient Use of Older Workers in the United States." *Experimental Aging Research* 25(4): 451-459, October 1999.

Global

Callahan, D., ed. *A World Growing Old*. Washington, D.C.: Georgetown University Press, 1995.

Hewitt, P. "The Geopolitics of Global Aging." *Harvard Generations Policy Journal* 1: 103-113, Winter 2004.

International Longevity Center. *Annual Report 2002: The ILC Explores the Impact of the World's Decreasing Birth Rates, Increasing Longevity, and Population Aging*. New York: International Longevity Center, 2002.

Longman, P. *The Empty Cradle: How Falling Birthrates Threaten World Prosperity and What to Do About It*. New York: Basic Books, 2004.

McKinsey Global Institute. *The Coming Demographic Deficit: How Aging Populations Will Reduce Global Savings*. Washington, D.C.: McKinsey Global Institute, 2004.

United Nations Division for Social Policy and Development. "The Aging of the World's Population." January 15, 2003. http://www.un.org (accessed May 2, 2005).

Wattenberg, B. *Fewer: How the New Demography of Depopulation Will Shape Our Future*. Chicago, IL: Ivan R. Dee Publisher, 2004.

Whiteford, P. "Anticipating Population Ageing—Challenges And Responses." May 2, 2005. http://www.oecd.org (accessed May 2, 2005).

Economic Matters

Collins, S., et al. "Will You Still Need Me? The Health and Financial Security of Older Americans." *Commonwealth Fund.* http://www.cmwf.org (accessed June 2005).

Lee, R. and Edwards, R. "The Fiscal Impact of Population Aging in the US: Assessing the Uncertainties." Prepared for the National Bureau of Economic Research's Tax Policy and Economy Meeting, October 30, 2001. http://repositories.cdlib.org (accessed May 2, 2005).

Lindquist, L. and Golub, R. "Cruise Ship Care: A Proposed Alternative to Assisted Living Facilities." *Journal of the American Geriatrics Society* 52(11): 1951-1954, November 2004.

Rivlin, A. and Sawhill, I., eds. *Restoring Fiscal Sanity 2005*. Washington, D.C.: Brookings Institution Press, 2005.

Robertson, T. "More Retirees Pay the Bills with Reverse Mortgages." *Boston Globe.* April 25, 2005, p. A1.

Ethical Reflections

Autonomy & Its Limits

Bellard, L. "Restraining the Paternalism of Attorneys and Families in End-of-Life Decision-Making while Recognizing that Patients Want More than Just Autonomy." 14 *Georgetown Journal of Legal Ethics* 803, Spring 2001.

*Burt, R. *Death Is That Man Taking Names: Intersections of American Medicine, Law, and Culture.* Berkeley, CA: University of California Press, 2002.

Channick, S. "The Myth of Autonomy at the End-of-Life: Questioning the Paradigm of Rights." 44 *Villanova Law Review* 577, 1999.

Davis, J. "The Concept of Precedent Autonomy." *Bioethics* 16: 114-133, 2002.

Dresser, R. "Autonomy Revisited: The Limits of Anticipatory Choices." in Binstock, R., et al., eds. *Dementia and Aging: Ethics, Values, and Policy Choices.* Baltimore, MD: Johns Hopkins University Press, 1992.

Dresser, R. and Robertson, J. "Quality of Life and Non-Treatment Decisions for Incompetent Patients: A Critique of the Orthodox Approach." *Law, Medicine & Health Care* 17(3): 234-244, Fall 1989.

Dworkin, R. *Life's Dominion: An Argument About Abortion, Euthanasia, and Individual Freedom.* New York: Vintage Books, 1994.

Dworkin, R. *Limits: The Role of the Law in Bioethical Decision Making.* Bloomington, IN: Indiana University Press, 1996.

Francis, L. "Decision Making at the End of Life: Patients with Alzheimer's or Other Dementias." 35 *Georgia Law Review* 539, Winter 2001.

Gready, R., et al. "Actual and Perceived Stability of Preferences for Life-Sustaining Treatment." *Journal of Clinical Ethics* 11(4): 334-346, Winter 2000.

Hyun, I. "Waiver of Informed Consent, Cultural Sensitivity, and the Problems of Unjust Families and Traditions." *Hastings Center Report* 32(5): 14-22, September-October 2002.

Meier, D. and Morrison, R. "Autonomy Reconsidered." *New England Journal of Medicine* 346(14): 1087-1089, April 4, 2002.

Peters, Jr., P. "The Illusion of Autonomy at the End of Life: Unconsented Life Support and the Wrongful Life Analogy." 45 *UCLA Law Review* 673, February 1998.

Price, M. "Mercy and Autonomy: The Failure of Battin's Justification for Euthanasia." *National Catholic Bioethics Quarterly* 4(3): 483-487, Autumn 2004.

Roser, T. "Are Patients Suffering from Dementia Ready to Make End-of-Life Decisions?" Presented at the Ethics and Aging Conference of the Center for Clinical Bioethics, Georgetown University. June 17-19, 2004.

Schneider, C. *The Practice of Autonomy: Patients, Doctors, and Medical Decisions.* New York: Oxford University Press, 1998.

Soto de Mayor, S. "Autonomy, Euthanasia, and the Holy Spirit." *Ethics & Medicine: An International Christian Perspective on Bioethics* 16(3): 75-79, 2000.

Meaning of Aging

*Butler, R. and Kiikuni, K., eds. *Who Is Responsible for My Old Age?* New York: Springer Publishing Company, 1993.

Callahan, D. *The Troubled Dream of Life: In Search of a Peaceful Death.* Washington, D.C.: Georgetown University Press, 2000.

Cole, T. "After the Life Cycle: The Moral Challenge of Later Life." Presented at the December 2, 2004 meeting of the President's Council on Bioethics. Washington, D.C., available online at http://www.bioethics.gov.

Cole, T. *The Journey of Life: A Cultural History of Aging in America*, Cambridge, U.K: Cambridge University Press, 1992.

Cole, T. and Winkler, M., eds. *The Oxford Book of Aging*. Oxford, U.K.: Oxford University Press, 1994.

*Cole, T., ed. *What Does It Mean to Grow Old? Reflections from the Humanities*. Durham, N.C.: Duke University Press, 1986.

Hollinger, D. "Theological Foundations for Death and Dying Issues." *Ethics & Medicine: An International Christian Perspective on Bioethics* 12(3): 60-65, 1996.

Jecker, N., ed. *Aging & Ethics: Philosophical Problems in Gerontology*. Totowa, New Jersey: Humana Press, 1992.

Kass, L. "The Case for Mortality." *The American Scholar* 52(2): 173-191, 1983.

Maxwell, F. *The Measure of My Days*. New York: Penguin, 1968.

*May, W. F. "The Virtues and Vices of the Elderly" in Cole, T., et al., eds. *What Does It Mean to Grow Old? Reflections from the Humanities*. Durham, N.C.: Duke University Press, 1986. pp. 41-61.

McFadden, S., and Atchley, R., eds. *Aging and the Meaning of Time: A Multidisciplinary Exploration*. New York: Springer Publishing, 2001.

*Meilaender, G. "I Want To Burden My Loved Ones" in *Things That Count: Essays Moral and Theological*. Wilmington, DE: ISI Books, 2000. pp. 79-84. (Originally published in *First Things*, October 1991); "Addendum to 'I Want To Burden My Loved Ones.'" Presented at the September 9, 2004 meeting of the President's Council on Bioethics. Washington, D.C., available at online at http://www.bioethics.gov.

Moody, H. *Ethics in an Aging Society*. Baltimore, MD: Johns Hopkins University Press, 1992.

Nuland, S. *How We Die: Reflections on Life's Final Chapter*. New York: Alfred A. Knopf, 1994.

*Pipher, M. *Another Country: Navigating the Emotional Territory of Our Elders*. New York: Riverhead Books, 1999.

Walker, M. *Mother Time: Women, Aging, and Ethics*. Lanham, MD: Rowman & Littlefield Publishers, 1999.

Medical Ethics

Arras, J. "The Severely Demented, Minimally Functional Patient: An Ethical Analysis." *Journal of the American Geriatric Society* 36(10): 938-944, October 1988.

Cameron, N. *The New Medicine: Life and Death After Hippocrates.* Chicago, IL: Bioethics Press, 2001.

Cohen, C. *Casebook on the Termination of Life-Sustaining Treatment and the Care of the Dying.* Bloomington, IN: Indiana University Press, July 1, 1988.

Dresser, R. "Schiavo's Legacy: The Need for an Objective Standard." *Hastings Center Report* 35(3): 20-22, March-April 2005.

Dresser, R. "Treatment Decisions for Dementia Patients: The Search for Normative Boundaries," Presented at the December 2, 2004 meeting of the President's Council on Bioethics. Washington, D.C., available online at http://www.bioethics.gov.

Field, M. and Cassel, C., eds, Institute of Medicine. *Approaching Death: Improving Care at the End of Life.* Washington, D.C.: National Academy Press, 1997.

Firlik, A. "Margo's Logo." *Journal of the American Medical Association* 265: 201, 1991.

Hanson, M. and Callahan, D., eds. *The Goals of Medicine: The Forgotten Issue in Health Care Reform.* Washington, D.C.: Georgetown University Press, 1999.

Hardwig, J. *Is There a Duty to Die? And Other Essays in Medical Ethics.* New York: Routledge, 2000.

Hastings Center. *Guidelines on the Termination of Life-Sustaining Treatment and the Care of the Dying.* Bloomington, IN: Indiana University Press, 1987.

Hippocrates. *The Theory and Practice of Medicine.* New York: Philosophical Library, 1964.

Hollinger, D. "Curing, Caring, and Beyond: Reflections for a Clinical Ethic." *Ethics & Medicine: An International Journal of Bioethics* 19(1): 45-53, Spring 2003.

Kaplan, K. and Schwartz, M. "Watching over Patient Life and Death: Kevorkian, Hippocrates and Maimonides." *Ethics & Medicine: An International Christian Perspective on Bioethics* 14(2): 49-53, 1998.

Kass, L. "Ethical Dilemmas in the Care of the Ill I: What is the Physician's Service?" *Journal of the American Medical Association* 244(16): 1811-1816, October 17, 1980.

Kass, L. "Ethical Dilemmas in the Care of the Ill II: What is the Patient's Good?" *Journal of the American Medical Association* 244(17): 1946-1949, October 24/31, 1980.

Kelly, D. *Contemporary Catholic Health Care Ethics.* Washington, D.C.: Georgetown University Press, 2004.

Kelly, G. *Medico-Moral Problems.* St. Louis, MO: The Catholic Hospital Association of the United States and Canada, 1958.

Keoian, J. "'Double Effect' and Palliative Care: A Legal and Ethical Outline." *Ethics & Medicine: An International Christian Perspective on Bioethics* 15(2): 53-54, 1999.

Kilner, J. *Who Lives? Who Dies? Ethical Criteria in Patient Selection.* New Haven, CT: Yale University Press, 1990.

Lo, B. "Ethical Decisions in Clinical Medicine" in Fauci, A., et al., eds. *Harrison's Principles of Internal Medicine.* 14th ed. New York: McGraw Hill, 1998.

Lo, B. *Resolving Ethical Dilemmas: A Guide for Clinicians.* Baltimore, MD: Williams & Wilkins, 1995.

Macklin, R. *Against Relativism.* Oxford, U.K.: Oxford University Press, 1999.

Markova, S. "Opinions and Attitudes of Medical Students Towards Basic Principles of the Hippocratic Oath." *Ethics & Medicine: An International Christian Perspective on Bioethics* 15(3): 66-69, 1999.

May, W. E. *Catholic Bioethics and the Gift of Human Life.* Huntington, IN: Our Sunday Visitor, 2000.

May, W. F. *The Physician's Covenant: Images of the Healer in Medical Ethics.* Louisville, KY: Westminster John Knox Press, 2000.

McHugh, P. "Annihilating Terri Schiavo." *Commentary* 119(6): 27-32, June 2005.

McKenny, G. *To Relieve the Human Condition: Bioethics, Technology, and the Body.* Albany, N.Y.: State University of New York Press, 1997.

Meilaender, G. "Living Life's End." *First Things* 153: 17-21, May 2005.

Monagle, J. and Thomasma, D., eds. *Health Care Ethics: Critical Issues for the 21ˢᵗ Century*. Gaithersburg, MD: Aspen Publishers, 1998.

Osler, W. *The Principles and Practice of Medicine*. 3ʳᵈ ed. New York: D. Appleton, 1898.

Pellegrino, E. "Ethics and Aging: The Physician Patient Relationship." Presented at the Ethics and Aging Conference of the Georgetown University Center for Clinical Bioethics. June 17-19, 2004.

Pellegrino, E. and Thomasma, D. *Virtues in Medical Practice*. New York: Oxford University Press, 1993.

Pence, G. *Classic Cases in Medical Ethics*. New York: McGraw-Hill, 1990.

Pence, G., ed. *Classic Works in Medical Ethics*. Boston: McGraw-Hill, 1998.

The President's Commission For The Study of Ethical Problems In Medicine and Biomedical and Behavioral Research. *Deciding to Forgo Life-Sustaining Treatment*. Washington, D.C.: U.S. Government Printing Office, 1983.

Quill, T. "Principle of Double Effect and End-of-Life Pain Management: Additional Myths and a Limited Role." *Journal of Palliative Medicine* 1(4): 333-336, Winter 1998.

Quill, T. *Death and Dignity: Making Choices and Taking Charge*. New York: W.W. Norton & Co., 1993.

Quill T., et al. "Palliative Options of Last Resort: A Comparison of Voluntarily Stopping Eating and Drinking, Terminal Sedation, Physician-assisted Suicide, and Voluntary Active Euthanasia." *Journal of the American Medical Association* 278: 2099-2104, 1997.

Rae, S., et al. *Bioethics: A Christian Approach in a Pluralistic Age*. Grand Rapids, MI: William B. Eerdmans Publishing Company, 1999.

Ramsey, P. *Ethics at the Edges of Life: Medical and Legal Intersections*. New Haven, CT: Yale University Press, 1978.

*Ramsey, P. *The Patient as Person*. New Haven, CT: Yale University Press, 1970.

Siberski, J. "Decisional Capacity in the Elderly: Dementia, Executive Function, and Assessment." Presented at the Ethics and Aging Conference of the Georgetown University Center for Clinical Bioethics. June 17-19, 2004.

Intergenerational Readings

Abramson, A. and Silverstein, M. *Images of Aging in America 2004: A Summary of Selected Findings.* Washington, D.C.: AARP, November 2004.

*Daniels, N. *Am I My Parent's Keeper?: An Essay on Justice Between the Young and the Old.* Oxford, U.K.: Oxford University Press, 1988.

Davis, D. "What Does Society Owe the Elderly?" Presented at the Ethics and Aging Conference of the Georgetown University Center for Clinical Bioethics. June 17-19, 2004.

Donati, P. "Social Policy, the Family, and Intergenerational Solidarity." Presentation to the X Plenary Session of the Pontifical Academy of Social Sciences. Rome, April 30, 2004.

Etzioni, A. "End Game: What the Elderly Have Earned." *American Scholar Journal.* Spring 2005. pp. 32- 40.

Fukuyama, F. *Economic, Political and Cultural Consequences of Changes in Generational Relations.* Presentation to the X Plenary Session of the Pontifical Academy of Social Sciences. Rome, April 29, 2004.

Glendon, M. "Discovering Our Dependence." *First Things* 146: 11-13, October 2004.

Lewin, T. "Financially-Set Grandparents Help Keep Families Afloat, Too." *New York Times.* July 14, 2005, p. A1.

Neale, A. "Intergenerational Equity and Age-Based Rationing." Presented at the Ethics and Aging Conference of the Center for Clinical Bioethics, Georgetown University. June 17-19, 2004.

Tietmeyer, H. "Intergenerational Solidarity and the Crisis of the Welfare State: Pensions, Social Security, and Health Care." Presentation to the X Plenary Session of the Pontifical Academy of Social Sciences. Rome, April 30, 2004.

Longevity

Conboy, I. "Notch-Mediated Restoration of Regenerative Potential to Aged Muscle." *Science* 302(5650): 1575-1577, November 28, 2003.

Couzin, J. "Is Long Life in the Blood?" *Science* 302(5644): 1373-1375, October 17, 2003.

Dominus, S. "Life in the Age of Old, Old Age." *New York Times.* February 22, 2004, sec. 6, p. 26.

Doyle, J. "The Burden of Immortality: Slowing the Aging Process Gives Birth to Ethical, Sociological Questions." *San Francisco Chronicle*. April 25, 2004, p. E1.

Finch, C. and Crimmins, E. "Inflammatory Exposure and Historical Change in Human Life-Spans." *Science* 305(5691): 1736-1739, September 17, 2004.

Hall, S. *Merchants of Immortality: Chasing the Dream of Human Life Extension*. Boston, MA: Houghton Mifflin Company, 2003.

Hekimi, S. and Guarente, L. "Genetics and the Specificity of the Aging Process." *Science* 299(5611): 1351-1354, February 28, 2003.

Kipling, D., et al. "What Can Progeroid Syndromes Tell Us About Human Aging?" *Science* 305(5689): 1426-1431, September 3, 2004.

LaFee, S. "So, You Want to Live to be 125?" *Copley News Service*. December 12, 2004, http://www.copleynews.com (accessed December 13, 2004).

Longo, V. and Finch, C. "Evolutionary Medicine: From Dwarf Model Systems to Healthy Centenarians?" *Science* 299(5611): 1342-1346, February 28, 2003.

Mueller, L. "A Demographic View of Limits on Life-Span." *Science* 301(5637): 1185, August 29, 2003.

Olshansky, S. and Carnes, B. *The Quest for Immortality: Science at the Frontiers of Aging*. New York: W.W. Norton & Company, 2001.

Redfearn, S. "Joy…Or Pain? To Some Extent, How You Feel for the Rest of Your Life Is Under Your Control. Here's What Science Shows Can Boost Your Chances of Living Healthier, Happier and Longer." *Washington Post*. August 2, 2005, p. F1.

Tatar, M., et al. "The Endocrine Regulation of Aging by Insulin-like Signals." *Science* 299(5611): 1345-1351, February 28, 2003.

Scott, J. "Life at the Top in America Isn't Just Better, It's Longer." *New York Times*. May 16, 2005, p. A1.

Woods, M. "Walking Towards a Better Memory." *Toledo Blade*. August 3, 2005, p. D1.

Literary Sources

Albee, E. *Three Tall Women: A Play in Two Acts*. New York: Dutton, 1995.

Bernlef, J. *Out of Mind*. Translation by Adrienne Dixon. London, U.K.: Faber, 1989.

Cicero. *On Old Age*. The Harvard Classics. http://www.bartleby.com/9/2/1.html (accessed August 24, 2005).

Delinksy, B. *Shades of Grace*. New York: Harper & Collins, 1996.

Dische, I. *Strange Traffic: Stories*. New York: Metropolitan Books, 1995.

Ignatieff, M. *Scar Tissue*. New York: Farrar, Strauss & Giroux, 1994.

Lewis, C. S. *A Grief Observed*. New York: Bantam Books, 1980.

President's Council on Bioethics. *Being Human: Readings from the President's Council on Bioethics*. Washington, D.C.: The President's Council on Bioethics, 2003.

Shakespeare. *King Lear* in Harbage, A., ed., *William Shakespeare: The Complete Works*. New York: Penguin Books, Inc. 1969.

Siddons, A. *Fault Lines*. New York: Harper & Collins, 1995.

Xenophon. *Apology of Socrates*. Translated by H. G. Dakyns. Project Gutenberg e-text #1171. January 1988.

Miscellaneous

Alzheimer's Association. *Ethical Issues in Alzheimer's Disease*. Chicago, IL: Alzheimer's Disease and Related Disorders Association, Inc., 2001.

Callahan, D., et al., eds. *A World Growing Old: The Coming Health Care Challenges*. Washington, D.C.: Georgetown University Press, 1997.

Chong, L., et al. "Deconstructing Aging." *Science* 305(5689): 1419-1419, September 3, 2004.

Federal Health Programs and Those Who Cannot Care for Themselves: What Are Their Rights, and Our Responsibilities? Hearing Before the Senate Subcommittee on Criminal Justice, Drug Policy, and Human Resources, 108th Congress. Statements of the Honorable Dave Weldon, MD, Member of the U.S. House of Representatives; Mr. Donald A. Young, MD, Deputy Assistant Secretary for Planning and Evaluation, Department of Health and Human Services; Ms. Diane Coleman, J.D., President, Not Dead Yet; Mr. Bob Sedlmeyer; Ms. Kate Adamson; and Mr. Robert Destro, Professor, Columbus School of Law, Catholic University of America. April 19, 2005.

Fukuyama, F. *Our Posthuman Future: Consequences of the Biotechnology Revolution.* New York: Farrar, Straus, and Giroux, 2002.

Helmuth, L. "The Wisdom of the Wizened." *Science* 299(5611): 1300-1302, February 28, 2003.

Huget, J. "Blogging Through the Ages." *Washington Post.* July 25, 2005, p. F01.

Martin, G., et al. "Research on Aging: The End of the Beginning." *Science* 299(5611): 1339-1341, February 28, 2003.

Public Policy

Andrews, E. "Greenspan Urges Congress To Rein In Federal Benefits." *New York Times.* April 22, 2005, sec. C, p. 2.

Binstock, R., et al., eds. *Dementia and Aging: Ethics, Values, and Policy Choices.* Baltimore, MD: Johns Hopkins University Press, 1992.

Bonnie, R. and Wallace, R., eds. National Research Council of the National Academies. *Elder Mistreatment: Abuse, Neglect, and Exploitation in an Aging America.* Washington, D.C.: National Academy Press, 2002.

Burt, R. "The Aging Society: Policy Implications." Presented at the September 10, 2004 meeting of the President's Council on Bioethics. Washington, D.C., available online at http://www.bioethics.gov.

Callahan, C. and Mays, J. "Estimating the Number of Individuals in the U.S. Without Health Insurance." Report by Actuarial Research Corporation for U.S. Department of Health and Human Services. http://aspe.hhs.gov (accessed April 8, 2005).

Callahan, D. "Medical Technology, Innovation, and the Nature of Medical Progress." Presented at the March 3, 2005 meeting of the President's Council on Bioethics. Washington, D.C., available at online at http://www.bioethics.gov.

Callahan, D. *Setting Limits: Medical Goals in an Aging Society.* Washington, D.C.: Georgetown University Press, 2000.

Carson, B. "Diagnosing the Crisis in Health Care" in *The Big Picture: Getting Perspective on What's Really Important in Life.* Grand Rapids, MI: Zondervan, 1999, pp. 218-257.

Chopko, M. "Responsible Public Policy at the End-of-Life." 75 *University of Detroit Mercy Law Review* 557, Spring 1998.

Friedland, R. "Policy Options for Caregivers." Presented at the September 8, 2005 meeting of the President's Council on Bioethics. Washington, D.C., available online at http://www.bioethics.gov.

Friedland, R. and Feder, J. "The Value of Social Security and Medicare to Families." *Generations*, Spring 2005.

Fumento, M. *Bioevolution: How Biotechnology Is Changing Our World*. San Francisco, CA: Encounter Books, 2003.

Glendon, M. "Challenges Posed by the Changing Age Structure and Dependency Ratio in the United States." Presented at the September 10, 2004 meeting of the President's Council on Bioethics, Washington, D.C., available online at http://www.bioethics.gov.

Gross, J. "The Middle Class Struggles in the Medicaid Maze." *New York Times*. July 9, 2005, sec. B, p. 1.

Hendricks J. "Public Policies and Old Age Identity." *Journal of Aging Studies* 18: 245-260, 2004.

Hilfiker, D. "Allowing the Debilitated to Die, Facing our Ethical Choices." *New England Journal of Medicine* 308(12): 716-719, 1983.

International Longevity Center. *Redesigning Healthcare for an Older America: Seven Guiding Principles*. New York: International Longevity Center, 2004.

Johnson, S. "End-of-Life Decision Making: What We Don't Know, We Make Up; What We Do Know, We Ignore." 31 *Indiana Law Review* 13, 1998.

Kuttner, R. "A New Model for Elder Care." *Boston Globe*. May 11, 2005, p. A17.

Lubitz, J. and Prihoda, R. "Use and Cost of Medicare Services in the Last Two Years of Life." *Health Care Financing Review* 5: 117-131, 1984.

Lynn, J. *Sick to Death: And Not Going to Take It Anymore!* Los Angeles, CA: University of California Press, 2004.

Organization for Economic Cooperation & Development. "Ensuring Quality Long-term Care for Older People." March 16, 2005. http://www.oecd.org (accessed May 2, 2005).

Sternberg, S. "A Bitter Pill for Older Patients: Excluded from Drug Trials, the Elderly Face Unknown Risks." *USA Today*. May 5, 2005, p. 1D.

Steuerle, C. E. and Van de Water, P., "Long-Run Budget Projections and Their Implications for Funding Elderly Entitlements" in Altman, S. and

Shactman, D., eds., *Policies for an Aging Society*. Baltimore, MD: Johns Hopkins University Press, 2002.

Temkin-Greener, H., et al. "The Use and Cost of Health Services Prior to Death: A Comparison of the Medicare-only and the Medicare-Medicaid Elderly Populations." *Milbank Quarterly* 70(4): 679-701, 1992.

Thomas, R. "Eldercare: The Challenge of the Twenty-First Century." *Harvard Generations Policy Journal*, 2004, http://www.genpolicy.com (accessed May, 2004).

Ubel, P. *Pricing Life: Why It's Time for Health Care Rationing*. Cambridge, MA: MIT Press, 2000.

U.S. Congress, Office of Technology Assessment. *Life-Sustaining Technologies and the Elderly, OTA-BA-306*. Washington, D.C.: U.S. Government Printing Office, July 1987.

Sources of Information and Support

Institutional

Government

Administration on Aging
Washington, D.C. 20201
(202) 619-0724
http://www.aoa.dhhs.gov
State and Area Agencies on Aging Locator: http://www.aoa.gov/eldfam/How_To_Find/Agencies/Agencies.asp
Elders & Families Website: http://www.aoa.gov/eldfam/eldfam.asp

Agency for Healthcare Research and Quality
Office of Communications
540 Gaither Rd., Ste. 2000
Rockville, Maryland 20850
(301) 427-1364
http://www.ahrq.gov
AHRQ supports research on health care outcomes; quality; cost, use, and access.

Alzheimer's Disease Education and Referral Center
P.O. Box 8250 Silver Spring, Maryland 20907-8250
1-800-438-4380
http://www.alzheimers.org
Created by Congress to "compile, archive, and disseminate information concerning Alzheimer's disease" for health professionals and the public.

Centers for Medicare and Medicaid Services
7500 Security Boulevard
Baltimore, Maryland 21244-1850
1-800-MEDICARE
(410)-786-3000
Main Website: http://www.cms.hhs.gov
Medicare Website: http://www.medicare.gov
Medicaid Consumer Information Website: http://www.cms.hhs.gov/medicaid/consumer.asp

Department of Health and Human Services
200 Independence Ave., S.W. Washington, D.C. 20201
1-877-696-6775   (202)-619-0257
Main Website: http://www.hhs.gov/
National Strategy for Suicide Prevention- Suicide Among the Elderly Website: http://www.mentalhealth.samhsa.gov/suicideprevention/elderly.asp

Department of Veterans Affairs
810 Vermont Ave., N.W. Washington, D.C. 20420
1-800-827-1000
Main Website: http://www.va.gov/
National Cemetery Administration Website: http://www.cem.va.gov

Eldercare Locator, U.S. Administration on Aging
1-800-677-1116
http://www.eldercare.gov/
The Eldercare Locator connects older Americans and their caregivers with sources of information on senior services. The service links those who need assistance with state and local area agencies on aging and community-based organizations that serve older adults and their caregivers.

MedLinePlus Health Information
U.S. National Library of Medicine
8600 Rockville Pike
Bethesda, Maryland 20894
(888) FIND-NLM (888) 346-3656
http://www.nlm.nih.gov/medlineplus

National Institutes of Health
National Institutes of Health
9000 Rockville Pike Bethesda, Maryland 20892
(301) 496-4000
Main Website: http://www.nih.gov
NIH Senior Health Website: http://nihseniorhealth.gov/listoftopics.html
> Includes: **The National Center for Complimentary and**
> **Alternative Medicine**
> 1-888-644-6226 http://nccam.nih.gov/
> *and*

The National Institute of Neurological Disorders and Stroke
(800) 352-9424 http://www.ninds.nih.gov/

National Institute on Aging
Building 31, Rm. 5C27
31 Center Drive, MSC 2292 Bethesda, Maryland 20892
http://www.nia.nih.gov/
NIA leads the federal effort on aging research and its site includes written materials and other educational resources.

National Library of Medicine
8600 Rockville Pike
Bethesda, Maryland 20894
(888) FIND-NLM
(301) 594-5983
http://www.nlm.nih.gov/

Senate Special Committee on Aging
G31 Dirksen Senate Office Building
Washington, D.C. 20510
(202) 224-5364
http://www.senate.gov/~aging

Senior Community Service Employment Program, Department of Labor
Employment and Training Agency of the U.S. Department of Labor
Frances Perkins Building
200 Constitution Ave., N.W.
Washington, D.C. 20210
1-877-US-2JOBS
http://www.doleta.gov/seniors/

Senior Corps
1201 New York Ave., N.W.
Washington, D.C. 20525
(202) 606-5000
(202) 565-2799
http://www.seniorcorps.org/
Network of local volunteer opportunities for persons 55 and older organized by the federal government.

Social Security Administration
Office of Public Inquiries
Windsor Park Building
6401 Security Blvd.
Baltimore, Maryland 21235
1-800-772-1213
http://www.ssa.gov

White House Conference on Aging
4350 East-West Highway, Ste. 300
Bethesda, Maryland 20814
(301) 443-9462
http://www.whcoa.gov/

Private

AARP
601 E St., N.W.
Washington, D.C. 20049
1-888-OUR-AARP
http://www.aarp.org
AARP is a nonprofit, membership organization for people age 50 and over that provides health information, advocates in the public policy arena, and supplies information on aging resources.

Aging with Dignity
P.O. Box 1661
Tallahassee, Florida 32302
1-888-5-WISHES
http://www.agingwithdignity.org
Provides the Five Wishes Living Will.

Alliance for Aging Research
2021 K St., N.W., Ste. 305
Washington, D.C. 20006
(202) 293-2856
http://www.agingresearch.org/
Promotes medical and behavioral research into the aging process and works toward improving baby boomer health by "developing, implementing and advocating programs in research, professional and consumer health education and public policy."

Alliance for Retired Americans
888 16th St., N.W.
Washington, D.C. 20006
(202) 974-8222
http://www.retiredamericans.org/

Alzheimer's Association
225 N. Michigan Ave., Fl. 17
Chicago, Illinois 60601-7633
1-800-272-3900 312-335-8700
http://www.alz.org/

American Academy of Hospice and Palliative Medicine
4700 W. Lake Ave.
Glenview, Illinois 60025
(847) 375-4712
http://www.aahpm.org/

American Academy of Pain Medicine
4700 W. Lake
Glenview, IL 60025
(847) 375-4731
http://www.painmed.org/

American Association for Geriatric Psychiatry
7910 Woodmont Ave., Ste. 1050
Bethesda, Maryland 20814-3004
(301) 654-7850
Main Website: http://www.aagponline.org/
Geriatric Mental Health Foundation (GMHF) Website: http://www.gmhf online.org/gmhf/
A national association representing and serving members of the field of geriatric psychiatry. The Foundation website includes mental health information for older adults and their families, including finding a geriatric psychiatrist.

American Association of Homes and Services for the Aging
2519 Connecticut Ave., N.W.
 Washington, D.C. 20008-1520 (202) 783-2242
http://www.aahsa.org/
The AAHSA represents over 5,600 not-for-profit nursing homes, retirement communities, assisted living facilities, and home and community-based service providers. The site includes consumer information and member information.

American Association of Suicidology
5221 Wisconsin Ave., N.W.
 Washington, D.C. 20015
(202) 237-2280
http://www.suicidology.org
National 24-Hour Suicide Prevention Lifeline: 1-800-273-TALK
Also provides referrals for mental health professionals, substance abuse assistance, housing, etc.

American Bar Association Commission on Law and Aging
740 15th St., N.W.
Washington, D.C. 20005-1022
(202) 662-8690
http://www.abanet.org/aging/

American Chronic Pain Association
P.O. Box 850
Rocklin, California 95677
1-800-533-3231
http://www.theacpa.org/
This organization coordinates local groups that provide support for those suffering from chronic pain. The site also provides educational materials.

American Federation for Aging Research
70 West 40th St., 11th Floor
New York, New York 10018
(888) 582-2327 (212) 703-9977
http://www.afar.org/

American Geriatrics Society (AGS)
The Empire State Building
350 Fifth Ave., Ste. 801
New York, New York 10118
1-800-563-4916 (212) 755-6810
Main Web Site: http://www.americangeriatrics.org
Foundation for Health in Aging Website: http://www.healthinaging.org/

American Health Assistance Foundation
22512 Gateway Center Dr.
Clarksburg, Maryland 20871
1-800-437-2423 (301) 948-3244
http://www.ahaf.org
A nonprofit funding research on age-related and degenerative diseases, educating the public, and providing emergency financial assistance to Alzheimer's disease patients and their caregivers.

American Hospice Foundation
2120 L St., N.W., Ste. 200
Washington, D.C. 20037
(202) 223-0204
http://www.americanhospice.org
"Provides a searchable database of hospices, teaches courses and workshops on end of life issues for consumers, providers, and hospices, and researches consumer needs."

American Physical Therapy Association
Section on Geriatrics
1111 North Fairfax St.
Alexandria, Virginia 22314
1-800-999-2782 ext.3238
http://www.geratricspt.org

American Society on Aging
833 Market St., Ste. 511
San Francisco, California 94103
(800) 537-9728 (415) 974-9600
Main Website: http://www.asaging.org/
Lifetime Education and Renewal Network Website: http://www.asaging.org/learn/index.html
An association for professionals in the aging field offering educational programming, publications and training.

Americans for Better Care of the Dying
P.O. Box 5578
Washington, D.C. 20016
http://www.abcd-caring.org/
Advocating for "public policy reforms such as improved pain management, better financial reimbursement systems, enhanced continuity of care, and support for family caregivers."

Assisted Living Federation of America
11200 Waples Mill Rd, Ste. 150
Fairfax, Virginia 22030
(703) 691-8100
http://www.alfa.org/
The site provides consumer information on assisted living, including lists of residences.

Association for Death Education and Counseling
60 Revere Drive, Ste. 500
Northbrook, Illinois 60062
(847) 509-0403
http://www.adec.org

Center for Advanced Illness Coordinated Care
113 Holland Avenue, 11T
Albany, New York 12208
(518) 626-6125
http://www.coordinatedcare.net/
A non-profit educational organization that provides training and consultation in the AICC Program, a 6-visit intervention of structured conversations and specialized care coordination for patients with advanced illness and their families.

Center for Home Care Policy and Research
Visiting Nurse Service of New York
107 East 70th St.
New York, New York 10021
(212) 609-1531
http://www.vnsny.org/research/

Center on an Aging Society
Health Policy Institute
Georgetown University
2233 Wisconsin Avenue, NW, Suite 525
Washington, D.C. 20007
(202) 687-9840
http://www.aging-society.org

Center to Advance Palliative Care
1255 Fifth Ave., Ste. C-2
New York, New York 10029
(212) 201-2670
http://www.capc.org/
Supported by the Robert Wood Johnson Foundation and the Mount Sinai School of Medicine (NY), "CAPC provides health care professionals with the tools, training, and technical assistance necessary to start and sustain palliative care programs in hospitals and other health care settings."

Children of Aging Parents
P.O. Box 167
Richmond, Virginia 18954
1-800-227-7294
http://www.caps4caregivers.org/
A nonprofit offering assistance to caregivers of the elderly or chronically ill by providing information, referrals and support on caregiving, including respite care, and housing.

City of Hope Pain/Palliative Care Resource Center
1500 East Duarte Rd.
Duarte, California 91010
(626) 359-8111 ext. 63829
http://www.cityofhope.org/prc
A clearinghouse collecting and "disseminating information and resources to assist others in improving the quality of pain management and end of life care (such as) pain assessment tools, patient education materials, quality assurance materials, end of life resources, research instruments." An index of documents is available for downloading from their website.

Family Caregiver Alliance
180 Montgomery St., Ste. 1100
San Francisco, California 94104
(800) 445-8106
(415) 434-3388
http://www.caregiver.org/
Support group for caregivers of those suffering from Alzheimer's and other brain disorders.

Fisher Center for Alzheimer's Research Foundation
One Intrepid Square
West 46th Street & 12th Ave.
New York, New York 10036
1-800-ALZINFO
http://www.alzinfo.org/

Funeral Consumers Alliance
33 Patchen Rd.
South Burlington, Vermont 05403
1-800-765-0107
http://www.funerals.org/
A nonprofit organization that provides educational materials on funeral choices, refers individuals to appropriate societies and agencies supplying local services, and serves as a consumer advocate for reforms on the national, state, and local levels.

Generations United
1333 H St., N.W., Ste. 500 W
Washington, D.C. 20005
(202) 289-3979
http://www.gu.org
A membership organization promoting intergenerational strategies, programs, and public policies. It also provides training for practitioners who work with grandparents caring for grandchildren.

Gerontological Society of America
1030 15th St., N.W., Ste. 250
Washington, D.C. 20005
Main Telephone: (202) 842-1275
National Academy on an Aging Society: (202) 408-3375
Main Website: http://www.geron.org/
National Academy on an Aging Society Web Site: http://www.agingsociety.org/

Global Action on Aging
P.O. Box 20022
New York, New York 10025
(212) 557-3163
http://www.globalaging.org/
A non-profit organization with special consultative status with the United Nations Economic and Social Council. It carries out research on emerging topics and publishes the results on its website.

Grantmakers In Aging
7333 Paragon Rd., Ste. 220
Dayton, Ohio 45459-4157
(937) 435-3156

http://www.giaging.org/
A professional organization for grantmakers working for older adults.

Gray Panthers
733 15th St., N.W., Ste. 437
Washington, D.C. 20005
1-800-280-5362
(202) 737-6637
http://www.graypanthers.org
Think tank concerned with forced retirement, government programs, health insurance, and nursing home abuse.

HelpAge International
P.O. Box 32832
London N1 9ZN, United Kingdom
011-44-20-7278-7778
http://www.helpage.org/
Focuses on the health status and other needs of older adults in developing countries.

Hospice and Palliative Nurses Association
One Penn Center West, Ste. 229
Pittsburgh, Pennsylvania 15276
(412) 787-9301
http://www.hpna.org

Hospice Association of America
228 Seventh Street, S.E.
Washington, D.C. 20003
(202) 546-4759
http://www.nahc.org/haa/
A national organization representing more than 2,800 hospices and thousands of caregivers and volunteers who serve terminally ill patients and their families. Its website provides basic consumer information about hospice care and the hospice industry.

Hospice Education Institute
3 Unity Square
P.O. Box 98
Machiasport, Maine 04655-0098
1-800-331-1620 (207) 255-8800
http://www.hospiceworld.org
An independent, not-for-profit organization, serving members of the public and health care professionals with information and education about caring for the dying and bereaved. It provides information about good hospice and palliative care, information and referrals to hospices and palliative care organizations in the U.S., and help discussing issues related to caring for the dying and bereaved.

Hospice Foundation of America
1621 Connecticut Ave., N.W., Ste. 300
Washington, D.C. 20009
1-800-854-3402
http://www.hospicefoundation.org
With programs for heath care professionals, and individuals "who are coping with issues of caregiving, hospice selection, terminal illness, and grief."

Institute for the Study of Aging
1414 Ave. of the Americas, Ste. 1502
New York, New York 10019
(212) 935-2402
http://www.aging-institute.org/
ww.hospicecare.com

Intergenerational Innovations
3200 N.E. 125th St., Ste. 1
Seattle, Washington 98125
(206) 525-8181
http://www.intergenerate.org
A nonprofit organization that develops and implements programs and activities connecting youth and the elderly in volunteer service to each other.

International Longevity Center
60 E. 86th St.
New York, New York 10028
(212) 288-1468
http://www.ilcusa.org/

International Psychogeriatric Association
550 Frontage Rd., Ste. 3759
Northfield, Illinois 60093
United States
(847) 501-3310
http://www.ipa-online.org

John Douglas French Alzheimer's Foundation
11620 Wilshire Blvd., Suite 270
Los Angeles, California 90025
(310) 445-4656
http://www.jdfaf.org/

Kaiser Family Foundation
2400 Sand Hill Rd.
Menlo Park, California 94025
(650) 854-9400
Main Website: http://www.kff.org/
State Health Facts Website: http://www.statehealthfacts.kff.org/

Conducts policy research on health and health policy issues. The website also provides resources on the health benefits available in each state.

Kennedy Institute of Ethics at Georgetown University
Georgetown University
Washington, D.C. 20057
(202) 687-8099
http://kennedyinstitute.georgetown.edu/

Little Brothers-Friends of the Elderly
954 W. Washington Blvd., 5th Fl.
Chicago, Illinois 60607-2224
(312) 829-3055
http://www.littlebrothers.org
A national, non-profit, volunteer-based organization "committed to relieving isolation and loneliness among the elderly."

Meals On Wheels Association of America
203 S. Union St.
Alexandria, Virginia 22314
(703) 548-5558
http://www.mealsonwheels.org/
Includes a list of local chapters of the volunteer program that provides meals to the homebound.

Medicare Rights Center
1460 Broadway, 17th Floor
New York, New York 10036
(212) 869-3850
http://www.medicarerights.org
An independent source of health care information and assistance for people with Medicare, "MRC provides telephone hotline services, teaches people with Medicare and those who counsel them, and brings the consumer voice to the national policy debate."

Michigan Center on the Demography of Aging
P.O. Box 1248
Ann Arbor Michigan 48106-1248
(734) 647-5000
http://www.icpsr.umich.edu/NACDA/
Hosts the National Archive of Computerized Data on Aging.

National Academy of Elder Law Attorneys, Inc.
1604 North Country Club Rd.
Tucson, Arizona 85716
(520) 881-4005
http://www.naela.org/
Provides a database of elder law attorneys practicing in the U.S.

National Alliance for Caregiving
4720 Montgomery Lane, 5th Floor
Bethesda, Maryland 20814
(301) 718-8444
http://www.cargiving.org
A non-profit coalition of national organizations working on family caregiving
issues.

National Asian Pacific Center on Aging
1511 Third Ave., Ste. 914
Seattle, Washington 98101
(206) 624-1221
http://www.napca.org

National Association of Area Agencies on Aging
1730 Rhode Island Ave, N.W., Ste. 1200
Washington, D.C. 20036
(202) 872-0888
http://www.n4a.org

National Association of Professional Geriatric Care Managers
1604 N. Country Club Rd.
Tucson, Arizona 85716
(520) 881-8008
http://www.caremanager.org/
A non-profit association of professional practitioners "working towards the
highest quality of care for the elderly and their families." They provide a
pamphlet detailing what to look for when hiring a care manager.

National Caucus and Center on Black Aged
1220 L St., N.W., Ste. 800
Washington, D.C. 20005
(202) 637-8400
http://www.ncba-aged.org

National Center on Women & Aging
The Heller School for Social Policy and Management
Brandeis University
Waltham, MA 02454-9110
1-800-929-1995 (781) 736-3866
http://heller.brandeis.edu/national/

National Chronic Pain Outreach Association
P.O. Box 274
Millboro, Virginia 24460
(540) 862-9437
http://www.chronicpain.org/

A non-profit organization seeking "to lessen the suffering of people with chronic pain by educating pain sufferers, health care professionals, and the public about chronic pain and its management through written materials and support groups."

National Council on the Aging
300 D St., S.W., Ste. 801
Washington, D.C. 20024
(202) 479-1200
Main Site: http://www.ncoa.org
BenefitsCheckUp Site: http://www.benefitscheckup.org
A national network of organizations including senior centers, adult day service centers, local agencies on aging, faith congregations, senior housing facilities, employment services, and other consumer organizations that hosts a website detailing government benefit programs.

National Family Caregivers Association
10400 Connecticut Ave., Ste. 500
Kensington, Maryland 20895-3944
1-800-896-3650 (301) 942-6430
http://www.thefamilycaregiver.org/

National Gerontological Nursing Association
7794 Grow Dr.
Pensacola, Florida 32514
1-800-723-0560
(850) 473-1174
http://www.ngna.org/

National Hispanic Council on Aging
1341 Connecticut Ave., 4th Fl.
Washington, D.C. 20036
(202) 429-0787
http://www.nhcoa.org

National Hospice & Palliative Care Organization
1700 Diagonal Rd., Ste. 625
Alexandria, Virginia 22314
1-800-658-8898
(703) 837-1500
Main Web Site: http://www.nhpco.org/
Caring Connections Website: http://www.caringinfo.org/
Includes resources on advance directives, grief loss, caregiving, financial issues, hospice and palliative care. The site provides free, state-specific advance directive documents and instructions.

National Indian Council on Aging
10501 Montgomery Blvd., N.E., Ste. 210
Albuquerque, New Mexico 87111-3846
(505) 292-2001
http://www.nicoa.org

National Network of Estate Planning Attorneys
10831 Old Mill Rd., Ste. 400
Omaha, Nebraska 68154
1-800-638-8681
http://the.nnepa.com/public/

National Pain Education Council
1010 Washington Blvd., 7th Fl.
Stamford, Connecticut 06901
(888) 536-7545
http://www.npecweb.org/

National Pain Foundation
300 E. Hampden Ave., Ste. 100
Englewood, Colorado 80113
http://www.painconnection.org/

National Policy & Resource Center on Nutrition & Aging
Florida International University, OE 200
Miami, Florida 33199
(305) 348-1517
http://www.fiu.edu/~nutreldr

National Resource Center on Native American Aging
P.O. Box 9037
Grand Forks, North Dakota 58202-9037
(701) 777-3848
http://www.med.und.nodak.edu/depts/rural/nrcnaa/index.html

National Resource Center on Supportive Housing and Home Modification
Andrus Gerontology Center, University of Southern California
3715 McClintock Avenue
Los Angeles, California 90089
(213) 740-1364
http://www.homemods.org/

National Self-Help Clearinghouse
Graduate School and University Center of the City University of New York
365 5th Ave., Ste. 3300
New York, New York 10016
(212) 817-1822
http://www.selfhelpweb.org/

A not-for-profit organization providing support for self-help groups and referral services for individuals.

National Senior Citizens Law Center
1101 14th St., N.W., Ste. 400
Washington, D.C. 20005
(202) 289-6976
http://www.nsclc.org

Older Women's League
1750 New York Ave., N.W., Ste. 350
Washington, D.C. 20006
1-800-825-3695
(202) 783-6686
http://www.owl-national.org

Palliative Care Policy Center
RAND Health
1200 South Hayes St., Ste. 6402
Arlington, Virginia 22202-5050
(703) 413-1100 ext. 5457
http://www.medicaring.org/
Providing support to "hospitals, nursing homes, health systems, hospices, and other organizations that serve individuals nearing the end of life," in part by providing a database of information designed to "help improve the experience of dying patients and their families."

POLST
"Physician Orders for Life-Sustaining Treatment"
Center for Ethics in Health Care
Oregon Health & Science University
3181 S.W. Sam Jackson Park Rd.
Mailcode: UHN-86
Portland, Oregon 97239-3098
Phone: (503) 494-3965
http://www.polst.org
See Chapter 2 of our report for more information on this document, designed to help health care professionals honor the end-of-life treatment desires of patients.

Rainbow Bridge
P.O. Box 12675
Denver, Colorado 80212-0675
(303) 623-1176
http://www.rainbowb.org/
Rainbow Bridge is a non-profit dedicated to improving the lives of elders in nursing homes through intergenerational relationships with children. Over 13,000 children have participated since 1994.

Retirement and Intergenerational Studies Laboratory
The Strom Thurmond Institute of Government & Public Affairs
Clemson University
Silas Pearman Boulevard
Clemson, South Carolina 29634
(864) 656-4700
http://www.strom.clemson.edu/teams/risl/index.html
The Retirement and Intergenerational Studies Laboratory provides resources and assistance to community organization seeking to add intergenerational programs to their activities.

Rural Assistance Center
P.O. Box 9037
Grand Forks, North Dakota 58202
1-800-270-1898
http://www.raconline.org
RAC helps rural communities and other rural stakeholders access the full range of available programs, funding, and research that can enable them to provide quality health and human services to rural residents. It offers customized assistance, searchable databases, and research publications.

SeniorNet
1171 Homestead Rd., Ste. 280
Santa Clara, California 95050
(408) 615-0699
http://www.seniornet.org
A non-profit providing older adults education for and access to computer technologies. The organization supports over 240 Learning Centers throughout the U.S., publishes a quarterly newsletter and a variety of instructional materials, offers discounts on computer-related and other products and services, holds regional conferences, and operates numerous online discussion boards.

Share the Care
P.O. Box 957
Murray Hill Station
New York, New York 10156
http://www.sharethecare.org
A non-profit organization dedicated to educating the public, health professionals and clergy about group caregiving as an option for meeting the needs of the seriously ill or dying, those in rehabilitiation, the elderly in need of assistance and their caregivers. Provides a blueprint for how to take a group of friends, relatives, neighbors, coworkers, and acquaintances and turn them into a "caregiver family."

Temple University Center for Intergenerational Learning
1601 North Broad St., Room 206
Philadelphia, Pennsylvania 19122
(215) 204-6970
http://www.temple.edu/cil/
A national resource for intergenerational educational programming.

University of California-Irvine Institute for Brain Aging and Dementia
23461 El Toro Rd., Ste. 150
Laguna Woods, California 92653
(949) 768-3635
http://www.alz.uci.edu/

University of North Texas Media Library
Film and Video Collection on Aging
P.O. Box 305190
Denton, Texas 76203
(940) 565-2484
http://www.library.unt.edu/media/fvca.htm
Their collection is home to over 700 audio-visual titles concerned with different aspects of aging and long-term care available for rent by educational institutions.

U.S. Living Will Registry
523 Westfield Ave., P.O. Box 2789
Westfield, New Jersey 07091-2789
1-800-LIV-WILL
http://www.uslivingwillregistry.com/
A privately held organization that electronically stores advance directives, organ donor information and emergency contact information, and makes them available to health care providers across the country 24 hours a day through an automated system. Registration is free when through a member health care provider or community partner.

Volunteer Services of America
1660 Duke St.
Alexandria, Virginia 22314
(800) 899-0089
(703) 341-5000
http://www.voa.org
Volunteers of America is a national, nonprofit, spiritually based organization providing local human service programs and opportunities for individual and community involvement. It provides educational information and assisted living resources.

Well Spouse Association
63 West Main St., Ste. H
Freehold, New Jersey 07728
1-800-838-0879
http://www.wellspouse.org/

Women's Institute for a Secure Retirement
1725 K St., N.W., Ste. 201
Washington, D.C. 20006
(202) 393-5452

http://www.wiser.heinz.org/
WISER is a non-profit organization that provides women with the skills and information they need to improve their economic circumstances and plan for a financially sound retirement. It operates through workshops, seminars, newsletters, reports, fact sheets, consumer guides and its website.

World Health Network
American Academy of Anti-Aging Medicine
1510 W. Montana St.
Chicago, Illinois 60614
(773) 528-1000
http://www.worldhealth.net/
A non-profit organization with a membership of 11,500 physicians and scientists from 65 countries dedicated to the advancement of therapeutics related to the science of longevity medicine. A⁴M educates physicians, scientists, and members of the public on anti-aging issues.

Web-Based Resources

Ageing and Life Course Programme (World Health Organization)
http://www.who.int/hpr/ageing/index.htm
The WHO Ageing and Life Course website highlights global issues in aging, including elder abuse, health care access and quality, and age-friendly standards.

AgeVenture News Service
http://www.demko.com/
AgeVenture seeks to communicate scientific advances in aging research by reporting peer-reviewed findings, researching retirement lifestyle trends, and publishing self-help resources.

Alzheimer Research Forum
http://www.alzforum.org/
The Alzheimer Research Forum was founded in 1996 to create an online scientific community dedicated to developing treatments and preventions for Alzheimer's disease. Access to the web site is free and available to the public.

Alzheimer's Solutions
http://www.caregiving-solutions.com/
Hosted by the son of an Alzheimer's patient, this site provides general information about the disease.

American Self-Help Group Clearinghouse
http://www.mentalhelp.net/selfhelp/selfhelp.php?id=858
The Self-Help Sourcebook Online is a searchable database that includes information on over 1,000 national, international and demonstration model self-help support groups, ideas for starting groups, and opportunities to link with others to develop new national or international self-help groups.

Beyond Indigo
http://www.beyondindigo.com/
Beyond Indigo provides grief support services and related information.

Beyond the Veil
http://www.beyondtheveil.net
Provides resources on dying, caregiving, spirituality, funerals, advance directives, and organ donation.

CareGuide@Home
http://www.eldercare.com/
Run by a care management company offering products and services for sale, the website also provides free information on caregiving and aging.

Death and Dying
http://www.online96.com/seniors/dying.html
Provides links to resources on aging, death, dying, hospice, funerals, grief, and more.

Dying Well
http://www.dyingwell.org/
Dr. Ira Byock, long-time palliative care physician and advocate for improved end-of-life care, and a past president of the American Academy of Hospice and Palliative Medicine, provides written resources and referrals to organizations, web sites and books to "empower persons with life threatening illness and their families to live fully".

ElderCare Online
http://www.ec-online.net/
ElderCare Online provides knowledge, tools and community to help caregivers improve the quality of life for both themselves and their aging loved ones.

ElderNet
http://www.eldernet.com
A seniors' guide to health, housing, legal, financial, retirement, lifestyles, news and entertainment information on the web.

End of Life/ Palliative Education Resource Center
http://www.eperc.mcw.edu/index.htm
EPERC shares educational resource material among health professional educators involved in palliative care education.

Ethical Wills
http://www.ethicalwill.com/
Dr. Barry K. Baines, a family physician and medical director of a home-based hospice program in Minnesota, hosts this site, which provides resources to help people "write and preserve their legacy of values at any stage of life."

Ethnic Elders Care

http://www.ethnicelderscare.net/

Ethnic Elders Care seeks "to increase public awareness of dementia among ethnic elders and to optimize the quality of life of family caregivers and ethnic elders with Alzheimer's disease and related disorders."

Finding Our Way: Living with Dying in America

http://www.findingourway.net

Archives for a 15-week articles series that ran in 160 newspapers in 2001.

Friendly4Seniors

http://www.friendly4seniors.com

With a database of over 2,000 senior-related listings.

Geriatric Web

http://geriatricweb.sc.edu/

GeriatricWeb is a web-based geriatric digital library intended to be used in the education of health care professionals and in the clinical care of the older patient.

GeroNurse Online

http://www.geronurseonline.org/

GeroNurseOnline is a comprehensive website providing current best practice information on care of older adults. It is hosted by the American Nurses Association.

GriefNet, Inc.

http://www.griefnet.org/

An internet community of persons dealing with grief, death, and major loss, the site hosts numerous email support groups and two web sites offering "an integrated approach to on-line grief support."

GrowthHouse.org

http://www.growthhouse.org

Growth House, Inc., provides links to resources for life-threatening illness and end-of-life care. Includes a search engine that gives access to a comprehensive collection of reviewed resources for end-of-life care.

HealthFinder

http://www.healthfinder.gov

A guide to government agencies, publications, databases, non-profit organizations, and support groups compiled by the U.S. Department of Health and Human Services.

Health and Age

http://www.healthandage.com/

Written and edited by medical professionals this site presents health information that "empowers people of all ages to identify, understand, prevent, treat, and communicate effectively with their health professionals" about their medical conditions. It is funded by Health Education Foundation (WHEF), an independent, non-profit organization.

Health and Retirement Study
http://hrsonline.isr.umich.edu/
The University of Michigan Health and Retirement Study (HRS) surveys more than 22,000 Americans over the age of 50 every two years. Supported by the National Institute on Aging, the study paints an emerging portrait of an aging America's physical and mental health, insurance coverage, financial status, family support systems, labor market status, and retirement planning. HRS data products are available without cost *to researchers and analysts.*

Hospice Net
http://www.hospicenet.org
Hospice Net is an independent, nonprofit organization that publishes information on dealing with life-threatening illnesses for patients and caregivers. Topics include bereavement, pain management, hospice care, talking to children, and caregiving. The site also includes tips on finding and choosing a hospice. (See also, http://www.hospiceweb.com.)

Infoaging.org
http://www.infoaging.org
Launched by the American Federation for Aging Research and supported by a grant from Pfizer Inc., the site contains the latest research-based information on a wide range of age-related diseases, conditions, issues, features, and news.

Intergenerational Initiative
http://www.siu.edu/offices/iii/
Hosted by Southern Illinois University, this website hosts several publications and a retiree volunteer program.

MealCall.org
http://www.mealcall.org/
MealCall helps seniors and family members connect with local *Meals-on-Wheels* and other similar programs. MealCall also helps find volunteers for *Meals-on-Wheels* delivery.

MedWeb
http://www.medweb.emory.edu/medweb/
Maintained by the staff of the Robert W. Woodruff Health Sciences Center Library of Emory University, MedWeb is a catalog of biomedical and health related web sites with a primarily for the academic and research community.

Merck Manual of Geriatrics
http://www.merck.com/mrkshared/mmg/home.jsp
An online, interdisciplinary manual regarding geriatric care for clinicians and residents.

MyZiva.net (Nursing Home Guide)
http://www.myziva.net/
MyZiva.Net is an independent, free nursing home resource for prospective residents, caregivers and healthcare professionals that helps with finding and comparing nursing homes.

National Public Radio: The End of Life
http://www.npr.org/programs/death/
Includes transcripts of roundtable discussions and conferences, readings, and a bibliography.

Nolo.com Encyclopedia: Health Care & Elder Care
http://www.nolo.com/encyclopedia/ret_ency.html
Includes articles on health and financial issues such as Medicare, long-term care, and estate planning.

On Our Own Terms: Moyers on Dying
http://www.pbs.org/wnet/onourownterms/
This website, based on a PBS special, includes resources on care, and links to final days sites, and therapy sites.

Our Senior Years
http://www.ourseniotyears.com

Pain.com
http://www.pain.com/
Sponsored by a private foundation, this site is an educational resource on pain and pain management for health care professionals and consumers.

Painlaw.org
http://www.painlaw.org/
A public resource of general information on the legal aspects of pain management and end-of-life care hosted by the Bazelon Center for Mental Health Law, a national legal advocacy group for people with mental disabilities.

Palliative Drugs
http://www.palliativedrugs.org/
This site provides independent information for health professionals about the use of drugs in palliative care.

Secrets of Aging
http://www.secretsofaging.org/
Produced by the Boston Museum of Science, this website provides public access to the latest scientific research on aging.

SeniorJournal.com
http://www.seniorjournal.com
This site provides daily news and information for baby boomers.

Senior Corner
http://seniors.tcnet.org/
Includes articles on health, caregiving, and senior needs and local and national resources for seniors.

Senior Women Web
http://www.seniorwomen.com/
This website attempts to address women's interests and concerns, especially the issues of community and connectivity.

WebMD
Main Website: http://my.webmd.com/
RxList Website: http://www.rxlist.com/
Provides generalized health information.

WidowNet
http://www.widownet.org/
Hosted by a widower, this site provides online resources and discussion opportunities.

WiredSeniors.com
http://www.wiredseniors.com
Includes SeniorsSearch.com, a search engine geared to individuals over 50.

ISBN 0-16-072915-7

9 780160 729157

90000